P9-AGA-599

Applied Psychology for Criminal Justice Professionals

Applied Psychology for Criminal Justice Professionals

Virginia L. Revere, Ph.D.

Illustrated by **Rick Staub**

Nelson-Hall Law Enforcement Series
George W. O'Connor, *Consulting Editor*
Superintendent of Public Safety, Troy, New York

Nelson-Hall/*Chicago*

364.019
R452a

LIBRARY OF CONGRESS CATALOGING IN PUBLICATION DATA

Revere, Virginia L.
Applied psychology for criminal justice professionals.

(Nelson-Hall law enforcement series)
Includes index.
1. Criminal justice, Administration of—
Psychological aspects. I. Title. II. Series.
HV6789.R42 364'.01'9 81-16923
ISBN 0-911012-98-2 AACR2

Copyright © 1982 by Virginia L. Revere

All rights reserved. No part of this book may be reproduced in any form without permission in writing from the publisher, except by a reviewer who wishes to quote brief passages in connection with a review written for broadcast or for inclusion in a magazine or newspaper. For information address Nelson-Hall Inc., Publishers, 111 North Canal Street, Chicago, Illinois 60606.

Manufactured in the United States of America

10 9 8 7 6 5 4 3 2 1
The paper in this book is pH neutral (acid free).

5/82

To the memory of my mother, Essie H. Lehr, who never lost her sense of childlike wonder and delight in the world; and of my father, Joseph Lehr, whose interest in others, stories and poems, set the example for my wanting to become a psychologist and write about it.

Contents

Acknowledgments

My first acknowledgment must be to the many clients and students who have shared their experiences with me. I would also like to thank Charles Edelstein, Esq., and Robert Revere, Ph.D., for their insights about the criminal justice system and their numerous suggestions. Typing and editorial help were provided most competently and helpfully by Kathy Stuter, Cecilia Sefler, and Violet McLitus. Kate Hickey provided a final and enlightened editorial revision.

I would like to thank my husband and my younger children, Lisa, Andy, and Robbie, for helping the family team to function throughout the writing of this book.

Finally, I would like to thank those who were most instrumental in providing the background for my understanding of psychology—Bert Karon, Morton Lieberman, Lester Luborsky, Bernice Neugarten, and Sheldon Tobin.

For even where one may not be able to avoid harming or hurting, forcing or demeaning another whenever one must coerce him, one should try even in doing so, not to violate his essence, for such violence can only evoke counter-violence . . . .

—Erik H. Erikson, *Gandhi's Truth*

CHAPTER 1

Introduction

Over the past twenty-five years, I have observed thousands of persons as I have performed my roles of therapist, diagnostician, teacher, and research psychologist. It is difficult to translate into words the sense of wonder that their lives have conveyed to me. Behavior that may have seemed bad, crazy, or simply stupid took its place along with so-called enlightened behavior as part of a complex and impressive attempt to cope with the world.

The appreciation of individuals as they attempt to cope with their worlds has an added bonus. As one learns to understand a person's world, one also learns how to deal with that person in an effective and humane way.

It is this understanding, an understanding that makes one capable of doing a better job, which I hope you will begin to acquire through reading this book. I have attempted to present the basics of psychological understanding in nontechnical language. As a clinical psychologist, I experienced the vital significance psychological understanding could have in people's lives. As a teacher, I knew that many students became bored with a subject presented academically. I found that my students could share my excitement if I gave them a chance to see psychology as part of real life, rather than as a series of difficult concepts. By seeing psychological concepts as they operate from day to day, students could use the psychological experience they have all had as human beings to become more effective in their interpersonal dealings.

The aim of this book is to help you use your own experience as a basis for understanding, predicting, and influencing the behavior of others. I hope it will also convey to you the same feelings of excitement, difficulty, frustration, and hope—but never boredom—that the practice of psychology has brought to me.

Part 1 introduces relevant principles of psychology. Such principles as the self-concept and the self-fulfilling prophecy will be useful throughout the book, giving you ways to understand and predict how people may behave in a variety of situations. Chapter 3 suggests ways in which you can get help from psychologists in understanding, predicting, and influencing behavior, and how psychologists can help in criminal justice settings. Other chapters deal with special problems of those in the criminal justice field—the use of authority, interviewing, and traffic work; and with such topics as reward and punishment, perception, social class, and mental illness, all of which are of particular concern to criminal justice practitioners.

Part 2 deals with an area that consumes a large proportion of criminal justice time and effort—that of criminals without victims. A general discussion of nonvictim crime is followed by chapters on suicide and drug dependence.

Part 3 covers sex crimes and white-collar crime, and Part 4 deals with an area of immediate concern to law enforcement officers, and of less direct but equal importance to others concerned with understanding a large segment of crime—that of family and youth-related disturbances. In this section, family and neighborhood crises, child abuse and neglect, and youthful offenders are discussed.

The final part deals with how psychological and social changes affect society, how these may lead to demonstrations and riots, and how to understand these changes.

A concluding chapter summarizes the book and offers suggestions for the most effective use of the material. Because of the practical urgency of the problems of suicide and family and neighborhood crises, appendixes on ways to deal with potential suicides and family crises are included.

Throughout the book, you will notice that psychological concepts and criminal justice problems are intermingled, so that you, as practitioners or future practitioners in the field of criminal justice, may know immediately how the material is applicable to the work that you are or will be engaged in.

I hope that you will find the application of psychology to criminal justice important, exciting, and useful.

Part One

General Principles

CHAPTER 2

Understanding and Effectiveness: Three Steps to Interpersonal Competence

Interpersonal competence requires three steps: an open mind; a desire to observe, understand and work with others; and a knowledge of basic psychology.

1. An open mind is achieved by being willing to look at people and situations in novel ways, putting together new and old information. You will learn to "educate" your intuition. An example of educated intuition is the observation that what you had expected may not be correct. A person looking like a bum may turn out to be educated, sensitive, and an excellent source of street information.
2. A desire to observe, understand, and work with others enables you to make use of information acquired in Step 1. For example, observing that a fellow worker is irritable in the morning tells you you should discuss problems with him at

other times. Seeing that a group of teenagers has changed a pattern of corner-lounging may clue you in to new influences in a neighborhood. Understanding that crowds will seek an outlet and will disperse if there is a way out may be essential for keeping a demonstration orderly. Wanting to work with others will give you the motivation to try to observe and understand and to use the information you acquire to become more competent. Knowing that a colleague is having marital problems would help you to refrain from taking his irritability personally. Being persistent in trying is also essential. Knowing that if one thing doesn't work, another will, is especially important for correctional personnel.

3. Learning the following principles will give you a good start in understanding basic psychology.
   a Each of us has an image of himself called a self-image or *self-concept*. This image can, and does, direct our behavior.
   b The ideas we have about what will happen to us can cause certain things to happen. This phenomenon is called the *self-fulfilling prophecy*.
   c Communication is largely *nonverbal*. Understanding others requires observing their behavior as well as their words.
   d Behavior is *motivated*; it is rarely accidental. Whatever we do is done for a reason.
   e Behavior is often *unconsciously* motivated. While almost everything we do is done for a reason, we sometimes are not aware of the reason.
   f Everything we do is done to *maximize pleasure* and *minimize pain*.
   g We learn by *association, reinforcement,* and *imitation*.

Discussion of the Principles

Self-Concept

Each person has an image of himself or herself, called a *self-concept,* that directs his or her behavior. When we must decide something, whether trivial or important, we rely on this image for decision-making. For example, I might be undecided about whether to enroll in an evening course. If my self-concept is one of a person who finds study satisfying, I will enroll in the course. If my self-concept is that I do not like study, I will not enroll in the course.

The self-concept comes from two major areas of experience: (1) what we have been able to do and how we feel about what we have done and (2) how others see us. For example, those who are successful in sports see themselves as "good at sports, likely to succeed." Those who have been unsuccessful see themselves as "not much good at athletic activities, likely to fail." This notion, which stays with us, determines whether someone will choose a sports activity.

On the other hand some people may have been not very good at sports, though others saw them as better than they were. They were encouraged by being told they were doing very well. They therefore kept trying, seeing themselves as people who were doing well. They therefore became better through practice and continued to enjoy sports because of the reactions of others.

Our self-concept is composed of both general attitudes about ourselves and how we fit in, and specific attitudes. These attitudes come from particular experiences. For example, some see themselves as generally "successful" or not. In addition they may feel that, despite their general success, they are poor at mechanical activities, or artistic endeavors. Or they may feel that they are generally failures, but, despite this, good at carpentry, or music, or intellectual pursuits.

The reactions of others are particularly important in defining these general attitudes that become part of the self-concept. Think of your own experiences. Were you the apple of your mother's eye? Or were your folks negative about you, always criticizing you no matter how well you did? What about teachers? Did most of them call on you for special tasks, praise your work? Or were you the one who was always in trouble? What about your classmates? Did they ignore you? Taunt you? Look up to you? Take you for granted? All such experiences leave a lasting impression and determine one's general attitudes.

In terms of skills, or particular areas of the self-concept, the reaction of others is most important if our abilities and interests in a skill area fall in the middle range (see Figure 2.1). This means that the reactions of others will either encourage us in a skill so that we will eventually succeed, or discourage us, in which case we may give up altogether. If we are superior at some things, what others say will probably not prevent our succeeding. If we are very poor at something, no amount of encouragement will make much difference. The development of middle-range interests and skills is most dependent on the reactions of others.

Figure 2.1
Encouragement or discouragement

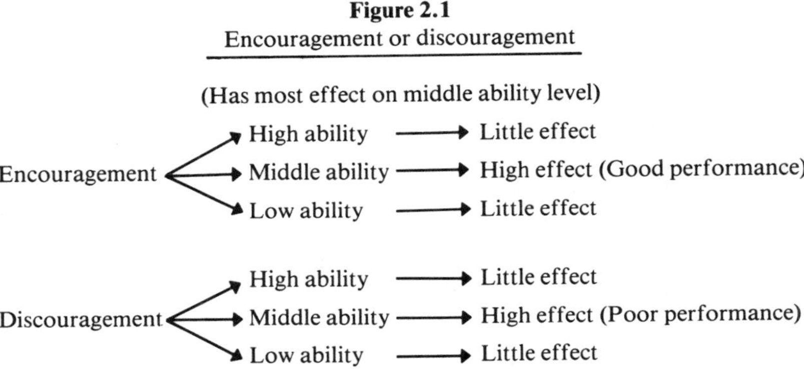

These general and specific areas of the self-concept make a difference, not only in decision-making, but also in how well a person does in the world. Those with very positive general attitudes will generally be successful, continue to do well, and receive positive reactions from others. Those with negative attitudes toward themselves will expect others to be negative and will induce negative reactions. This cycle becomes part of the self-fulfilling prophecy discussed in the next section. It is therefore essential that we develop and help others to develop positive self-concepts.

Why is self-concept an important principle for criminal justice professionals?

Crimes are usually committed by persons with negative self-concepts. Youthful offenders often have such negative self-concepts that they do not even *try* to get jobs or enter noncriminal careers. Many other offenders can be similarly described—for example, the gambler who sees himself as unable to be successful will not try to succeed in a job. Understanding someone's self-concept is therefore a way of predicting how he will behave.

Since changing a person's self-concept will also change his behavior, self-concept theory provides an approach to change. To help people change their self-concept, you must first encourage them to talk about how they feel about themselves now. The second step is to convince them that their negative feelings can be changed. You can often accomplish this by showing them the positive, productive things they have done or can do. My experience in working with people has convinced me that everyone has some talents and abilities. A self-concept of failure may be altered by pointing out special abilities.

Self-concept discussions take place most easily in individual therapy or in therapy groups, where group members can discuss their problems with the aid of a mental health specialist. Such work can also be done in sensitivity groups, which might be led by criminal justice professionals with appropriate special training.

Another approach to changing self-concept is through groups like Synanon (a group for drug addicts), in which persons' negative behaviors are attacked. These attacks can lead to an improved self-concept by inducing the individual to change his behavior. When behavior changes, the reactions of others change, and the person changes his or her self-concept. (See discussion of Synanon in Chapter 12.)

Self-Fulfilling Prophecy

Self-concept theory is closely related to the second principle, that of the self-fulfilling prophecy. The self-fulfilling prophecy concept was developed by sociologist Robert Merton. It states that what you *think* is going to happen to you frequently does happen. For example, if you get up in the morning feeling that life is wonderful, you will smile at everyone; they will smile back at you; you will be friendly and cooperative; they will be friendly and cooperative in return—and your notion that life is wonderful will be confirmed.

Self-fulfilling prophecies can also be negative, however. If you get up in the morning feeling that everything is going to be awful, you may scream at your kids, argue with your colleagues, and generally have a terrible day—confirming your original prediction.

Self-fulfilling prophecies tend to maintain or perpetuate your current self-concept. If you are a failure at mechanical things, you don't try very hard, and you continue to fail.

Most criminals believe that they will continue to get into trouble, and this belief becomes a self-fulfilling prophecy. If they could understand this, they would have some freedom to change their lives.

Such changes can take place in individual therapy or in the kind of groups described in the discussion of the self-concept. Such groups have been successful in helping youthful offenders and many other groups of criminals.

Nonverbal Communication

Communication is largely nonverbal, and it is extremely important for criminal justice professionals to be aware of such messages. In dealing with suspects or clients, in performing service functions, in answering complaints, and even in dealing with colleagues, employees, and bosses, it is important to know what people really feel. Often we cannot find out unless we look for nonverbal clues.

Eyes, mouth, lines in the face, and posture all tell us what people are feeling. Experienced officers frequently can tell whether a person is telling the truth by the set of his mouth, his willingness to look at his questioner, the "openness" of his demeanor. If a person moves toward you, he is more likely to be willing to talk than if he turns his body slightly away.

Motivated Behavior

Almost everything we do is motivated; we have reasons for our actions. Frequently the reasons are clear. We go to see a western because we enjoy westerns. We play tennis because it gives us a good feeling. We hunt or fish because we enjoy it.

However, the reasons for some of our other actions are less transparent. Why are some of us always late? Not because our cars go more slowly than others' or because we cannot walk fast. The reasons can be understood by attending to the consequences of our actions. Does our being late make someone else uncomfortable? Many times we do not want to admit that we are angry, but we manage to do small things that irritate others. If your spouse or girlfriend or boyfriend does a number of little irritating things, it may be easy to see that he or she does these things when angry. Often the anger is indirect. I may be angry at my boss and take it out on my husband. That is called *displacement,* and much anger is like that. Other motives are similarly indirect.

It is important for criminal justice professionals to recognize that behavior is motivated because, in understanding criminals, they must know why they commit criminal acts. Do juveniles "corner-lounge" for no reason? Or do they have a reason, and can they change their behavior if their motivation changes? Does a probationer break probation because he is angry at an overprotective mother? Or is it because he wants to be popular with his friends? Does a group of inmates start a riot because they are being put down by a particularly nasty guard, or because they cannot watch the end of their favorite TV show?

People need also to be aware of their own motives. This awareness then makes it possible for them to choose whether to continue the behavior or change it. For example, if street kids know that they want to be respected, they may choose more acceptable ways of earning respect than street crime. If they do not know this, they will be stuck with thinking that committing crimes, not wanting respect, is their bag.

Unconscious Motivation

Much behavior is *unconsciously* motivated, including much of the behavior described above. This means that we are not directly aware of it. Some things we do without awareness are done out of habit—"I always do it that way" or "I just never think about it." Often well-learned skills are like that. Try to describe to someone how to walk, to drive a car, or to bat a ball. These are well-learned skills. Unless you think about it, you do not know what you are doing, and why, in these rather complicated behaviors.

Unconscious motivation also occurs when we do not wish to

admit our less-than-noble motives. Doing favors for friends because we want them to do something for us is an example. Being sick or late to avoid work or to make someone else uncomfortable is another example.

Maximization of Pleasure

Everything we do is done to maximize pleasure and/or minimize pain. This principle seems to be simple common sense until we consider the numerous examples of people who appear voluntarily to be behaving in ways that cause more pain than pleasure. Some people confine themselves to a small room and never enjoy the company of others. Some people gamble, become drug addicts, or engage in criminal acts for which they are repeatedly caught. How can we say that these people are maximizing pleasure?

We can understand only if we see that their behavior appears to them to be *less* painful than other behaviors. People who gamble, for example, may do so to save themselves from facing their inability to form meaningful interpersonal relationships. An example from experimental psychology is even clearer: Cats who were blasted with air while eating stopped eating. This was not because they did not *want* to eat, but because they found not eating less painful than blasts of air.

Association, Reinforcement, Imitation

We learn by association, reinforcement, and imitation. We perceive many things as "going together," as associated. The expression "two plus two" is associated with "four": we have heard them together so often that we automatically repeat them. Similarly, school and being bored often "go together."

Reinforcement means reward. We learn to repeat behaviors when we are rewarded for them. The reward may be of various types. Some activities are intrinsically rewarding; we do them because we enjoy them. Other activities provide extrinsic rewards; at least part of the reason we work is to get a paycheck.

The concept of reinforcement is important for criminal justice professionals because criminals are usually reinforced for their criminal behavior. The reinforcements come in the form of excitement, material gains, not getting caught. In order for criminals to stop committing crimes, at least some of these reinforcements must be eliminated. In addition, other, noncriminal behaviors must be rewarded. Reinforcement is the basis of the success of such preventive police programs as the Police Athletic League. Here young people are rewarded for activities engaged in *with* rather than *against* the police.

Imitation is another important concept. Through imitation, children become like their parents. We often hear parents say, "Don't do what I *do*; do what I *say*." This is exactly what does *not* happen. Parents who are angry and violent will raise children who are angry and violent. Parents who are well adjusted will similarly help their children become well adjusted.

Police, probation, and correctional officers can serve as models for the youth in their area, both in preventive programs such as the Police Athletic League and in the way they deal with offenders, complainants, and clients. These possibilities are especially important in community relations.

Predicting and Influencing Behavior

The principles just outlined have many applications, six of which are especially important in predicting and influencing behavior:

1. To be able to control our behavior, we must be aware of our motives.
2. To find out why a person does something, we must look at the consequences of his actions.
3. To predict what a person is going to do, we must find out what he has done in the past.
4. To change a person's behavior, we must act differently from the way he expects us to act.
5. To engage in rational behavior, we must feel competent.
6. To predict behavior, we must know that behavior changes in different situations.

1. *To be able to control our behavior, we must be aware of our motives.* If I am unaware of why I always turn in my reports late, I cannot decide whether or not to continue the behavior. If I know it's a way of getting even, I might be able to think of less destructive

ways to get even, or ways to be less defeated so that I don't have to get even. Or I could decide that I want to continue the behavior.

Awareness is especially important in relation to anger. Many crimes committed by mentally ill persons are carried out because the person has no awareness or control over his feelings. If a person knows he is angry and that it is reasonable to be angry, he can control expression of the anger. He can express anger in ways that are not harmful. He doesn't have to allow it to build up to a point at which it is uncontrollable.

Further, it is important for people to know *why* they are committing crimes before they decide whether crime is the best way to accomplish their goals. For example, a boy who is stealing things in order to prove his manhood could find other satisfactions—if he realized what he was doing and had some help in finding a better way to be manly.

2. *To find out why a person does something, we must look at the consequences of his actions.* While this does not apply in a truly accidental occurrence—such as getting to work late because of a freak storm—it will be true of acts that are repeated more than two or three times. If "somehow or other" your relief officer or your probationer is always late, he probably is being late purposefully (even if he isn't consciously aware of the fact). Part of his purpose can be understood by looking at what his behavior does to you. It is a good bet that he is angry—you are a handy target. Once he becomes aware of his anger, his purpose is no longer unconscious, as it was before. He then can decide whether he wants to continue or to behave in a more cooperative fashion.

Another example would be a criminal who constantly gets caught. He must "want to get caught." Does his getting caught embarrass his family (as is sometimes the case with juvenile offenders)? This may well be the reason. If a person says, "I'm really concerned that this is going to bother my wife," you will know that part of his goal is to bother his wife. He is not aware of this, however, and can continue the behavior without feeling guilty about trying to "get" her.

3. *To predict what a person is going to do, we must find out what he has done in the past.* People's behavior tends to be consistent. They repeatedly use the same means of solving their problems and finding pleasure.

4. *To change a person's behavior, we must act differently from the way he expects us to act.* For example, calm, reassuring behavior is the best way to deal with a screaming man. If you come to an accident scene and find a woman crying loudly, you would not start to cry yourself. Similarly, if you come upon a group of kids who curse you, you can surprise them by your calmness.

Do not match aggressive behavior with further aggressive behavior. Matching aggression with strength, not hostility, is more likely to change behavior. It not only surprises the person, but provides nothing to feed the flames of his anger. If your response to an angry person is calm and respectful—"Let's go talk about it over at the station; I can't understand what's wrong until you calm down"—you can help change behavior.

5. *To engage in rational behavior, we must feel competent.* Seeing oneself as competent enables one to understand and deal with persons and situations. For example, a crowd throwing rocks can cause a person who feels incompetent to become irrational. A person with a feeling of competence will analyze the situation—see whether certain people can be isolated from the crowd to stop the rock throwing, find out what's causing it—and disperse the crowd without violence.

6. *To predict behavior, we must know that behavior changes in different situations.* While behavior is generally consistent, it does change according to the situation. A person's behavior in a mob is very different from his behavior alone. It is different when he is with his family, or with a bunch of pals going fishing. Sometimes one can manipulate behavior by changing the situation. Rumors during demonstrations are an example. Officers may not be aware of the importance of making sure that rumors are dealt with promptly. Otherwise crowds may turn violent on the basis of an untruth.

A Model for Decision-Making

These principles and applications make possible a model for decision-making (see Figure 2.2). In order to make decisions that are psychologically and professionally sound, the following steps should be taken:

1. Define the problem.

2. Ask yourself: How would I feel in this situation?
3. Ask yourself: What are the realities of the situation?
4. Ask yourself: What are my professional responsibilities? My human responsibilities?

Figure 2.2
The decision-making process

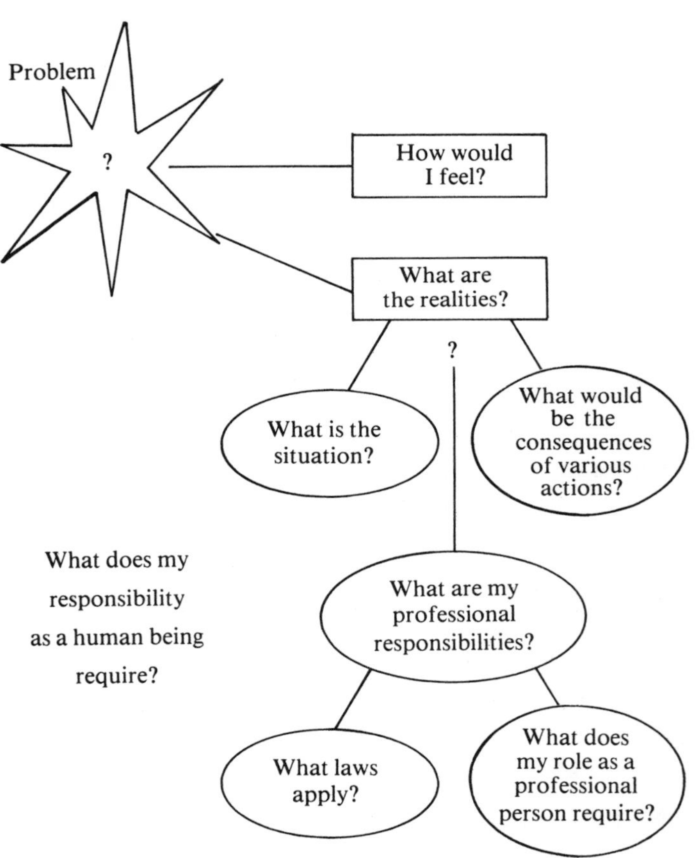

Examples of the use of this model will be found in the Appendixes.

Summary

This chapter has discussed three steps to interpersonal competence: keeping an open mind, observing others' behavior, knowing basic psychology.

Having an open mind and observing others enable us to learn. Understanding basic psychology provides us with a means of structuring our observations.

The self-concept organizes a person's experiences and determines much of his behavior. The self-fulfilling prophecy is the mechanism by which he frequently brings about events that reinforce the self-concept. Communication is frequently nonverbal, and body cues must be understood. We must also understand that behavior is almost always motivated, sometimes indirectly, since we often hide the reasons we do something from ourselves. When we are unaware of these reasons, our motivation is called unconscious. Making the unconscious conscious gives us the ability to change behavior. In understanding our motivations, we must realize that everything we do is done to maximize pleasure and minimize pain. Sometimes people appear to be seeking pain. When this happens, it is because they feel that the pain is less disturbing than the consequences of seeking pleasure.

The ability to predict and control behavior comes from understanding and applying these principles: that we must become aware of our motivations if we want to change our behavior, that we can understand the motivation of others by looking at the consequences of their actions, that a person's future behavior is best predicted by looking at his past behavior. Further, since people continue habitual behavior when others act in reciprocal ways, the best way to change other people's behavior is to react in ways they do not expect.

Behavior will be more rational if a person feels competent, but it will change in different situations.

In order to make valid psychological decisions, it is also important to think about a situation psychologically. To do so, it is important first to define the problem, then to ask yourself how you would feel in a similar situation. You must also be aware of situational and professional realities. What is really happening? What are your professional and human responsibilities?

Discussion Questions

1. Can you think of some personal achievements that you accomplished because of your self-concept? Can you think of problems that arose from your self-concept?
2. A homework assignment: Pretend to feel very good, and smile at everyone on a day when you do not feel good. See what happens. Report your experiences to your class.
3. Have each individual strike a posture suggesting a particular emotion—anger, sadness, happiness. Can the others correctly interpret the emotion?
4. Think of a decision you recently made. Did your self-concept influence the decision? In what way?

Suggested Reading

Brim, O. G., Jr. *Constancy and Change in Human Development*. Cambridge, Mass.: Harvard University Press, 1980.

Freud, Sigmund. *Question of Lay Analysis*. Edited and translated by James S. Strachey. New York: Norton, 1969.

Glaros, A. *Study Guide for Maladaptive Behavior*. Glenview, Ill.: Scott, Foresman and Co., 1980.

Hall, E. T., *The Silent Language*. Westport, Conn.: Greenwood Press, 1980.

Lange, A. J., and Jakubowski, P. *Responsible Assertive Behavior*. Champaign, Ill.: Research Press, 1977.

Lecky, P. *Self-Consistency: A Theory of Personality*. 2d ed. Hamden, Ct.: Shoe String Press, 1973.

Mann, J. *Learning to Be: The Education of Human Potential*. Glencoe, Ill.: Free Press of Glencoe, 1972.

Mehrabian, A. *Nonverbal Communication*. New York: Aldine-Atherton, 1972.

Schmidt, J. *Help Yourself: A Guide to Self-Change*. Champaign, Ill.: Research Press, 1977.

CHAPTER 3

Predicting and Influencing Behavior: The Uses of Psychologists

Even if you understand the principles outlined in Chapter 2, sometimes you may need to use the skills of the psychologist.

Mental Health Professionals

First of all, who is a psychologist? How does he or she differ from a social worker, a psychiatrist, or another mental health professional? Figure 3.1 indicates the training and areas of competence of psychologists, social workers, psychiatrists, other mental health professionals, and psychoanalysts.

In making referrals, consider first the degree to which the training of the professional is related to the problem. Social workers have training that is directed almost totally toward helping people. Their services are least expensive. Psychologists specializing in

Figure 3.1
Comparison of mental health professionals

	Training	Can effectively deal with	Does not deal with
Psychologist (clinical)	Usually Ph.D. (Doctor of Philosophy) with graduate training in psychology and internship in a clinic; training in research and applications.	Emotional problems; prediction through psychological evaluation.	Medical problems
Psychologist (counseling)	Usually has a degree in education or counseling.	Less serious emotional problems.	Serious emotional difficulties; medical problems
Social worker	Master of Social Work (M.S.W.) or Master of Social Service (M.S.S.); two years of graduate training; applied rather than research oriented.	Emotional difficulties; trained to be especially aware of the social causes and settings of behavior.	Medical problems
Other mental health professionals	Frequently has a bachelor's degree which may or may not be related to the task; often works in community mental health clinics, drug and alcohol abuse clinics.	Special problems; under supervision can work with interpersonal problems.	
Psychiatrist	M.D. degree; graduate training in medicine; internship in medicine. Board-certified psychiatrists have additional training working with mental patients.	Problems involving medical difficulties, neurological damage; psychiatrists also deal with nonmedical problems.	Psychological evaluation
Psychoanalyst	Usually M.D., sometimes Ph.D. training as above plus additional intensive training in treatment of	Emotional and interpersonal problems.	Personality disorders

areas such as clinical or counseling psychology are also appropriate for most of your purposes. Psychiatrists are trained primarily for medical work. If they also have training in the area of psychological problems, they can be helpful in dealing with the emotional and interpersonal problems of individuals. Psychoanalysts are usually psychiatrists who have additional training in Freudian methods. Community agencies employ people who are not trained in any of these specialties. Some are very good, some quite inadequate. They have had to depend on the quality of supervision on the job, or their own talents, for development of skills.

In any mental health profession, the personal qualities of the individual are important. If an individual is sensitive to his own inner dynamics and those of others, if he or she is caring and warm, the person will be able to provide some help. If these qualities are absent, help will be limited or the results may even be negative.[1]

In seeking help for clients, the most appropriate agency to contact may well be a social work agency. Family service agencies exist in most communities, and one of their primary functions is the referral of individuals to other appropriate agencies. The family service agency may be the best choice unless an individual's problem is specific to another agency—a drug addict, for example, needs drug rehabilitation. Community mental health clinics can also offer direct help or referral services.

Psychologists are helpful in resolving emotional and interpersonal difficulties. They are uniquely helpful if prediction is desirable. Will a person be able to return to the community after a suicide attempt? Is a juvenile offender ready to seek or hold a job? What kind of help is best for an addict? Names of psychologists in private practice can be found in the telephone book or in a National Register of Health Service Providers in Psychology (available through the American Psychological Association, 1200 17th St. N.W., Washington, D.C.). An American Psychological Association directory of psychologists is available at some libraries. Psychologists working on teams may be contacted through community mental health agencies.

Psychiatrists should be contacted if physical or neurological conditions seem important. Psychiatrists or medical doctors should be contacted immediately in the case of a drug emergency or physical trauma. A local hospital emergency room is usually the best route. Psychiatrists also treat emotional difficulties in ways similar to those of social workers or psychologists. If they are not board certified, however, they may have little training in understanding emotional processes, since any medical doctor may call himself a psychiatrist without special training.

Functions of the Psychologist

Psychologists have training in a wide variety of specialties. The list includes experimental psychology, industrial psychology, social psychology, school psychology, counseling psychology. We will be discussing yet another area of psychology—clinical psychology—through examining three of the clinical psychologist's functions: prediction of behavior through testing, helping people change through counseling or psychotherapy, and consulting.

Predicting Behavior through Testing

The clinical psychologist's training in psychological testing is important since he is the only mental health professional trained in this area. Psychological tests are of two types—so-called *objective tests* and *projective tests.* Later we will also discuss a psychophysiological test—the polygraph or lie detector.

Objective Psychological Tests. You may already be familiar with some intelligence tests such as personality tests that ask you to describe yourself or your behavior. A typical question on a personality test might be: "When someone pushes ahead of you on a line, do you (*a*) get mad and push back, (*b*) get mad and say nothing, (*c*) find it perfectly all right?" Such tests, if carefully developed, can yield predictive information about a person's behavior.

Other types of objective tests measure interests, aptitudes, and achievements. For example, if you are not sure what you would like to do with your life, it is a good idea to take a vocational preference test, such as the Kuder Vocational Preference Record or the Strong Vocational Interest Blank.[2] If your interests are similar to those of individuals who are successful in a job or job area, you will be advised to think seriously of pursuing a similar occupation. Your interests might be similar to those of successful accountants. If so, it is likely that you, too, would be a successful accountant.

You might then want to know whether you have the ability or skills to become an accountant, and you could take a mathematics aptitude test or a mathematics achievement test. The aptitude test would tell you how easy or difficult it would be for you to learn mathematical skills; the achievement test would tell you how many of these necessary skills you already have.

Since much delinquency and crime are related to unsuitable employment or unemployment, it is important for criminal justice practitioners in rehabilitative areas to refer clients for such testing. State vocational rehabilitation offices sometimes provide substantial help for individual clients.

Projective Tests. Another type of personality test is the projective test. An example of this is the Ink-Blot or Rorschach Test. Look at Figure 3.2. What do you see? It is not a clear picture; so what each person sees reflects his own life and perceptions.

Figure 3.2

Another example of a projective test is the Thematic Apperception Test (TAT). It shows pictures of people in typical and important life situations—such as a person alone, a person with an older man, and so on, and asks the subject to tell a story about each one.

Figure 3.3
Psychological tests

Projective	**Objective**
Personality tests	Intelligence (IQ) tests Wechsler Adult Intelligence Scale (WAIS) Stanford-Binet (S-B)
Tests that ask how you look at the world and others	Personality tests that ask you to describe yourself
Rorschach (ink-blot) Thematic Apperception Test (TAT)	Interest tests Aptitude tests Achievement tests
Drawing tests House-tree-person (HTP) Draw-a-person (DAP)	

Then the story each person invents about the situation gives a good picture of the way he would behave in a similar situation.

For example, suppose you are worried about an elderly man who has been booked on suspicion of rape. How could you find out whether he probably committed the rape or would be likely to commit one in the future?

A trained clinical psychologist interprets the stories he tells in response to the TAT. Suppose he tells a story like the following:

> Here is a lonely man. He wants to be close to someone. He grabs the girl on the corner. Then he runs home. He feels better.

You have a likely suspect.

The story need not be that obvious.

> Here is a man who is looking into the bakery. He feels hungry. He figures if he can wait till no one is looking, he will be able to pick up something and no one will be the wiser.

This story would make him equally suspect. A different kind of story would be:

> Here is a man feeling very lonely and sorry for himself. He looks out the window for quite a long time. There is a bakery there, but nothing for him. There are children outside, but he does not know them. He sits there till it is time to go to bed.

This man is not a likely suspect. However, it is important to note that the final interpretation is made on the basis of a variety of indicators—besides the strength of motivation, the psychologist will look at his controls, other motivations, and so forth. For example, an individual might meet needs for pleasure by *actions*—stealing, fighting, or killing. If you found these ideas in a subject, it would be important to know whether the individual felt that such actions would have negative consequences. For example, if an individual believes that stealing leads to jail, he has a reason not to steal. If he believes that there are no consequences, he has less reason to check himself. In short, the psychologist looks for both tendencies to action and tendencies to block action.

Psychophysiological Tests—Magic or Mismanagement? Psychophysiological tests promise to tell whether suspects are telling the truth, by the use of physical measurements. What could be more simple and significant? Consulting a graph to tell whether or not a person is lying seems so much easier than trying to sort through a person's story. Many such devices have been tried, including an audiograph test, which derives conclusions about an individual's veracity from voice changes. Since voices can be recorded and analyzed, it is easy to get data for this test. The classic psychophysiological test is the polygraph, or lie detector. Since we have most information on its use, it is worth reviewing in more detail.

First, what is the polygraph and how does it work?

The polygraph or lie detector test is a recording of a person's automatic functioning—that is, the way some of his internal organs operate. This is not as complex as it sounds. If a person blushes, we deduce that he is embarrassed about something. Or if he turns "red in the face" and his jaws are clenched, we diagnose anger.

Both of these physical reactions are effects of a change in heartbeat and blood vessel size. When a person is upset, his heart usually beats faster. His surface blood vessels enlarge (dilate). When that happens, he turns red.

As we all know, such responses are not under conscious control. The polygraph uses this fact to find out whether someone becomes upset when asked certain questions. "Upset" is defined differently by different polygraph machines, but most of them record changes in pulse and blood pressure. They sometimes measure changes in perspiration (another indicator of stress) and muscular changes. The polygraph, meaning "many graphs," therefore charts or graphs changes in internal functioning.

Whether or not the polygraph works depends on a number of factors. The first is the expertise or skill of the operator. An expert will not simply "read" a test. He will interpret it.

To interpret a lie detector test, the operator must discover how an examinee normally functions. For example, some people are embarrassed by questions about their sex lives. If a person like this happened to be a suspect in a sex crime case, he might react to any and all questions involving sex in a "guilty" or anxious manner. His heart rate and perspiration level would change. But his reaction might have nothing to do with a crime.

Therefore, the expert polygraph operator will ask neutral questions to obtain a "base line" of non-crime-related functioning. He will then ask questions that encourage a person to lie. In a burglary case, a suspect might be asked if ever he had stolen anything. In a sex case, a suspect might be asked whether he ever had thought of forcing a woman to have intercourse with him. These questions give an indication of a "control" level of functioning, the way a person normally acts when he lies. If he reacts more strongly to these questions than to questions concerning the crime, he is likely to be innocent. If the opposite is true, he is likely to be guilty.

It is also useful for the polygraph operator to include questions of detail that would be unknown to anyone except the criminal. For example, if a warehouse in which a murder took place contained boxes filled with Schlitz beer, a reaction to a mention of Schlitz beer would be more diagnostic than a reaction to details of the murder, which might have been reported in the newspaper. Some people react strongly to such words as *blood, murder,* or *stealing*. An innocent person who feels guilty about his own anger might react strongly to the *idea* of a murder, even though he had nothing to do with it.

The polygraph operator must have the skill to get a good profile of a person's level of guilt as well as the situations that provoke guilt. He needs to ensure that he does not interpret overreactions to emotion-laden subjects as evidence of guilt.

It is also important for the operator to know when a person simply underreacts. Some sociopaths (see Chapter 9 on mental illness) do not react to questions about crimes because they have no feelings of guilt. Therefore, they would come out looking "clean." In addition, certain people can train themselves not to react. This training is being used to help patients control diseases such as high blood pressure through a procedure called biofeedback; it can also be used by criminals who have learned how useful lack of response can be.

Because of all these difficulties, many people feel that the polygraph has been overused. Information obtained by the polygraph usually is not admissible in court, so its main function is in pretrial investigation. Some criminal justice practitioners feel that good investigative work eliminates most of the need for any type of confession—whether it be involuntary, as with the polygraph, or voluntary.

How to Use the Psychologist's Services for Testing. While most people in the criminal justice community do not have enough background in psychology to interpret psychological tests, they should know how to make use of the psychologist who administers these tests.

You should follow four steps in making a referral to a psychologist.

1. Define the problem with which you want help. Is it a matter of probation? Detective work? Parole? Community relations? Handling juveniles?

2. Think through your questions with regard to this problem. Do you want to know whether parole would lead to another crime? Be as specific as possible about your questions. Sometimes you have a vague feeling about a person; something seems wrong. Let the psychologist know this. Do you feel that a certain area seems troublesome? For example, does a youth get into trouble whenever he is with his father? Or perhaps you have a vague feeling that he has more sexual problems than he has discussed.

3. Insist that the psychologist address the problem. Perhaps he or she cannot give you the answer you wish. But then make sure you are informed that the question cannot be answered. Psychologists can get bogged down in jargon. Hearing that a person has an

"inferiority complex" or a "weak ego" or "loose associations" may not be very meaningful to you. Specific questions prevent meaningless generalities.

I once tested a young woman who had murdered her four children. The mental hospital wanted to know whether she could be released or whether she was likely to murder again. It appeared that she would, but only if she were in a similar situation. The hospital could then decide on the conditions under which she could be safely released.

4. Ask the psychologist the best way of helping an individual. After all, the objective is preventing future crime. You may find that you cannot implement the psychologist's suggestions. Let her or him know your alternatives and ask which would be most helpful.

To summarize, let the psychologist know the problems, the background, and the possibilities for action on your part.

What the Psychologist Can Tell You. The psychologist can provide a great deal of useful information about a person's abilities, interests, achievements, and intellectual potential. He or she does so by comparing the information from tests with the answers of many, many other people on these same tests. Test performance can also be compared to other factors. Using some tests, it is possible to make predictions about what people can comfortably accomplish. The intelligence test is a good example. Though it does not give the whole picture of a person's functioning, it suggests that, unless a person's score is at least average, he should not plan to go to college. If he is low average, he can still make it if he is well motivated. You can already see how the psychologist must put together several aspects of a person's functioning—in this case, intelligence and motivation—before making a prediction about future behavior.

In making predictions about what a person will do in any given situation, the psychologist looks at a number of factors:

1. What are the person's needs and desires?
2. What methods does he have for meeting these needs and desires?
3. What controls does he have for limiting his actions?
4. Does he see other people as helpful (and in what ways?) or destructive (and in what ways)?
5. Does he see himself in positive or negative terms?

6. What are his major preoccupations?

Let us take an example to see how this works.

A young schizophrenic woman whom the writer tested could be described as follows:

1. Her major needs were to minimize pain rather than to maximize pleasure. She felt the need to escape from the danger of her, and others', destructive urges.
2. Her methods for meeting these needs were to pretend that her real life did not exist, to develop her own world, and to think about problems in symbolic, abstract terms.
3. Her controls were not adequate. She tried to control herself and others by not allowing herself to be effective.
4. She saw others as extremely destructive.
5. She saw herself as destructive—in negative terms, in other words.
6. Her major preoccupations were saving herself from the dangers of others and herself.

A psychologist *can* predict what a person will do under specific circumstances: This person would steal, but only if he could do so without violence. This person will hold a job if someone is there to help him get up on time in the morning. This person will commit suicide if a loved one leaves and there is no one to take her place. This person will stay off drugs if he can have immediate rewards of another kind. The psychologist *cannot,* however, predict the circumstances of the individual's future life.

The Helping Processes

The helping processes used by psychologists and others can be divided into three categories: (1) classical, individual helping processes—psychotherapy and psychoanalysis, (2) behavior modification techniques, which are based on learning theory, and (3) group methods.

Classical Techniques. In psychotherapy and psychoanalysis, the classical therapies, a person talks about the ways the problems of his past are interfering with solving the problems of the present.

Behavior Modification. Behavior modification uses principles of reward and punishment, but primarily reward, in order to induce people to change their behavior. For example, a child might get a reward every time he uses courteous language. Or he might receive a shock every time he reaches for a forbidden object, but receive a reward if he waits for a signal before getting it. Images are sometimes used. An alcoholic might be asked to picture himself in a grave every time he looks at liquor. Or he might be given Antabuse (a drug that causes vomiting if the patient also drinks alcohol) so that he will associate being sick with drinking liquor; or he might be given a token every time he resists drinking. Token economies are used in behavior modification programs in mental hospitals (the patients are "paid" in objects or privileges for appropriate behavior). Alcoholics Anonymous also makes use of token rewards.

Group Methods. Another promising method is for groups of people to get together to help each other and support changes in group members. Prominent groups include Synanon (for drug addicts), Gamblers Anonymous, Parents Anonymous (for persons who abuse or are afraid they will abuse their children), Alcoholics Anonymous, and Recovery, Inc. (for persons with emotional problems).

Another type of group is the sensitivity or human potential group, in which normal people meet to try better ways of dealing with people and problems. Similar groups help people relax and draw on their strengths. Still other groups give people a chance to express emotions that have been bottled up; they include groups such as Gestalt and Primal Scream groups.

Some groups combine several techniques. A very promising method seems to be helping people relive emotions that they have forced out of awareness. Reliving and dealing with these emotions can give them a chance to proceed with their lives realistically instead of spending their time "covering up." A good example would be a delinquent whose primary feelings are sadness and abandonment but who covers up those feelings by anger. His anger is expressed in antisocial acting out. The youth gets punished. He then gets angrier. If, instead, he had been forced to face his sadness, he would not need to repeat his criminal actions.

Consulting

Psychologists and other mental health personnel frequently serve as consultants. Some police forces have gone further and have put mental health professionals on their permanent staffs.

What additional functions does a house psychologist have? Most criminal justice functions require expertise in human relations. The psychologist is trained in such human relations work. He can serve as an advisor to train criminal justice personnel to deal with human relations situations effectively. To do this he must have a sound understanding of clinical psychology as well as the particular problems of the setting.

For example, the psychologist can help police deal with human relations situations, not by lecturing, but by allowing staff to experience difficult situations and to experiment with alternative reactions. Such experimentation is usually done in group training sessions, and it has been proven effective in preventing injury and death in family crises.

An allied function is in intergroup relations, helping police and other criminal justice professionals develop more favorable views of the people they work with and vice versa. This kind of group training involves people with whom police must work but with whom police are sometimes in conflict, such as blacks, students, Mexican-Americans. The groups act out situations that cause conflict and practice acting out each other's roles. The policemen may take the roles of the blacks, the blacks of the policemen. It is possible for groups that have been in conflict for years to learn to work together.

Why is this so? Years ago it was discovered that when people who dislike each other in advance—about whom they are prejudiced—are put in a situation in which they work together, attitudes change. Group training sessions do something similar; they give antagonists a chance to get to know each other better and work out their problems.

Another contribution of the psychologist can be to provide a listening ear for members of the force. The psychologist can help both with personal problems and with problems connected with criminal justice work. If police and others are to withstand the enormous burdens their jobs place upon them, it is important to be able to turn to someone.

When problems are related directly to the job, group sessions similar to the training sessions mentioned can help individuals see that they are not alone in their problems. The group can help them to manage their problems more effectively as well as to get rid of strong feelings—often anger and frustration—by providing the same kind of sounding board that the psychologist provides in individual conferences.

Psychologists can have still other functions in relation to police departments. Through their research, they can help a force pinpoint major problems and discern the most effective techniques for solving them. They can analyze the positive or negative effects of changes in the structure of the force and the effect of different management procedures on performance. Endless problems and procedures need to be evaluated by a progressive, questioning police force.

Psychologists can also help discover what types of individuals should be recruited for the criminal justice positions, including police academies, and what types eliminated; they can show how evaluation can help the subjects as well as the organization they serve.

Further areas in which psychologists can help are dealing with citizen complaint groups and with the disillusionment that young officers may feel after leaving the police academy, or burnout in other areas.

Summary

Of all mental health professionals, the clinical psychologist is particularly trained to help in prediction, as well as in psychotherapy and consulting. Clinical psychologists can predict how a person will function in a variety of situations through both objective and projective testing. Objective testing is more frequently used to evaluate abilities—intelligence, skills, vocational aptitudes—whereas projective tests can be used to predict behavior based on personality characteristics. Psychologists interpreting these tests can achieve a high degree of accuracy in predicting behavior in particular situations. They *cannot*, however, predict the situations an individual may encounter.

Psychologists and other mental health practitioners can help people change in many ways. Techniques include: (1) behavior modification, (2) methods that involve the release of emotions, and (3) sensitivity groups, which help normal people function more effectively.

Given the variety of functions of the psychologist, would it be useful to include a psychologist on the police force? Functions the psychologist could perform when available to the police in this way include consulting on crime problems and police-community relations and providing direct counseling services to the police.

Discussion Questions

1. How can psychology be used for prediction? What principles apply? What limitations are there in predicting?
2. What are some of the methods used by psychologists for helping others? How do they compare to methods used by people to help their friends?
3. Discuss pros and cons of the polygraph. Would you want to use it? Under what circumstances?

Suggested Reading

Brodsky, Stanley L. *Psychologists in the Criminal Justice System.* Urbana: University of Illinois Press, 1973.

Clark, Robert S. *Police and the Community: An Analytic Perspective.* New York: Franklin Watts, 1980.

Coffey, Alan; Edelfonso, E.; and Hartinger, W. *Police-Community Relations.* Englewood Cliffs, N.J.: Prentice-Hall, 1971.

Dudycha, G. J. *Psychology for Law Enforcement Officers.* Springfield, Ill.: Charles C. Thomas, 1976.

Lykken, D. T. "The Right Way to Use a Lie Detector." *Psychology Today* 8 (1975):56–60.

Mann, P. A. *Psychological Consultation with a Police Department.* Springfield, Ill.: Charles C. Thomas, 1973.

Platt, J. J., and Wicks, R. J. *The Psychological Consultant.* New York: Grune and Stratton, 1979.

Reid, J. E., and Inbau, F. E. *Truth and Deception: The Polygraph ("Lie Detector") Technique.* Baltimore: Williams and Wilkins, 1966.

Reiser, M. *The Police Department Psychologist.* Springfield, Ill.: Charles C. Thomas, 1972.

CHAPTER 4

How to Be an Authority, Work under Authority, and Survive

Problems related to authority are central to careers in criminal justice. The police world, with all its symbols—the badge, the gun, the squad car—is one of authority. Once a police officer dons his uniform, he becomes something quite different from the person he is without it, someone who may wield great power over others. As a result, policemen everywhere are looked upon with some combination of fear and respect. For others in the criminal justice system, authority is similarly central. For example, probation officers may encounter widely varied reactions from their probationers because of their authority.

Major Pitfalls in Handling Authority

There are three major pitfalls in handling authority: (1) difficulties in handling the reactions to authority, which may range from insults to reverence; (2) abusing power by enjoying it too much; and (3) difficulties in using authority effectively because one is afraid of it. These pitfalls confront all those working in criminal justice; however, we shall discuss them in relation to police officers, since they are on the front lines of these problems.

Difficulties in Handling Reactions to Authority

Problems in handling others' reactions to authority may be alleviated by an understanding of when and why positive or negative reactions will occur.

Situations in which authorities will be treated respectfully include those in which an officer is helping others. Since officers spend a majority of their time in service functions, this means that they will be treated respectfully for many of their working hours. At such times citizens are glad to see an officer. A sick person may need to be taken to the hospital. Someone has had an accident. A store owner wants drunks off the street. A homeowner is worried about prowlers. In all these situations, the officer will be treated with courtesy.

Situations in which an officer is likely to be treated discourteously include those in which he performs law enforcement functions, such as apprehending felons, stopping motorists, dealing with juveniles, and intervening in family and neighborhood disturbances, demonstrations, and riots. In order to be able to predict accurately how a citizen will react in one of these situations, however, it is important to look at social-class, individual, and situational differences.

For example, an officer who stops a middle-class motorist, or knocks on the door of a middle-class home, is likely to be treated courteously, since middle-class persons have been taught to respect authority. They tend to see an officer as helpful rather than threatening. They believe that they will be treated well if they cooperate.

Individual differences also occur because people see situations differently and react to the threat of punishment differently. Some of the factors involved include the following.

1. Does the person regard the situation as one in which restriction or punishment is just—and justified? Or does he see it as one in which his rights are being violated?

The reaction depends on the offender's view of the situation. If he has been driving seventy miles per hour in a fifty-mile-per-hour zone, he may feel that he would be lucky *not* to get a ticket. His arguments, if any, against a citation would probably be routine. If, however, he has been driving fifty-five miles per hour, he might argue strongly against being ticketed.

2. Does the person perceive the situation as one that can be manipulated, or does he feel that the actions of the officer are inevitable?

If a juvenile feels he can outrun an officer, he will do so. If a motorist feels he can bribe an officer, he may slip a $10 bill into his palm and get angry if the officer refuses it. If he feels he is "special" in some way, he may think he can get exceptional treatment, and he will be angry when he doesn't. In such cases, special *courtesy* may counteract the individual's disappointment.

3. Does the offender feel that the punishment will put him in an intolerable position?

If a motorist is speeding to a hospital with a sick child, his reaction to being stopped is bound to be emotional. In another case, suppose that the person stopped is on the "point system" in a state where a driver's license is revoked after several citations. This person feels he would lose his job if he were to lose his license. The officer could expect the offender to give him a difficult time in trying to prevent a citation.

A much more serious situation is that in which an offender knows he will receive a maximum punishment; for example, he might be an escaped "lifer" or a "pusher" who expects to receive a life sentence. Such a person might reason that shooting an officer would not put him in further jeopardy—and try it.

Dealing with such extremes of reaction is a difficult problem for any officer. Most of us are treated in a variety of ways—sometimes well, sometimes badly, often with indifference. When we walk down a street, we do *not* expect people either to beg us for a word or to glare at us. We assume that most people won't notice us, or they will treat us reciprocally—if I shove someone, he'll shove back; if I hold the door for someone, I may get a nod of thanks. Unless we see someone we know, we do not expect responses from others.

How does it feel, then, suddenly to become the object of opposite and extreme reactions? Most of us respond strongly; we either feel very good if people are admiring or get angry if they are insulting.

Professionalism is the answer to handling such reactions. Officers with a professional attitude realize that all those positive and negative reactions are meant for the badge—not for them as individuals.

Enjoying Power Too Much

Loving power and then abusing it is a problem of some people whom we have all met and wish we hadn't. These abusers of authority—the bully in the schoolyard, the teacher who raps the knuckles of a child who whispers, the parent who beats a child, the clerk in the unemployment office who shoves clients to the rear while he has coffee, the officer who curses kids—cause a great deal of harm.

We all face such abusers of power. We all wish we didn't have to. Such people fill us with helpless rage. We feel we would like to attack them, to give them some of their own medicine. But, since they are backed up by force—either their own or that of an institution they represent (a school, an agency of the government)—we usually accept their treatment without protest.

Being Afraid of Using Authority

Some officers may fear using their authority or seeing others use it. This problem may occur more frequently in such persons as probation officers, who feel they must be "nice" to their clients in order to establish a relationship with them. Such behavior is usually ineffective. Clients perceive the officers as frightened and weak. Fear of using authority comes from a failure to understand the positive aspects of its proper use.

Appropriate Use of Authority

Psychologists distinguish between two types of authority: *authoritarianism* and *authoritative behavior.* Authoritarianism is authority abused. Authoritative behavior is authority wisely used.

The previous examples of individuals who enjoy power too much illustrate the authoritarian use of power.

Authority can be essential to a society's well-being. The function of authority is to stop the bully in the schoolyard, to ensure that order is maintained in a classroom, that lines of communication are kept open, and that someone takes responsibility for the well-being of a group and those affected by group behavior. It is to ensure that children are not allowed to endanger themselves or others. It is to enable the clerk in the unemployment office to help people conduct their business in a fair and orderly fashion.

A common denominator in these examples is that authority involves the power and responsibility to ensure the safety and well-being of the individuals involved, as well as those they may contact. If all people used power in this way, there would still be disputes, but they would be less likely to involve violence (see Figure 4.1).

If, on the other hand, people use authority to try to dominate others rather than ensure their rights and help them respect the rights of others, a constant spiral of ever-increasing violence will result.

If a person in authority can be calm and firm, it will be easier to follow some specific rules:

1. Tell people why they must do something.

"Traffic can't get through unless we keep this alley clear."

"The teachers here can't go home until you kids leave."

"If you guys don't shut up for a minute, we won't ever get this argument settled."

"There've been some problems this evening, so I have to check out everyone new in the neighborhood."

2. Do be courteous:

"Excuse me, sir, but I'd appreciate it if you could get this car out of the way."

"Hi, kids; how are things going? We've got a problem here. Have to ask you to leave."

"I'd like to be able to hear what you have to say. Could you come out in the car a minute?"

"Excuse me; I'm Sgt. Brown. I'd like a few minutes of your time. I've had a complaint about . . ."

Figure 4.1
Appropriate use of authority

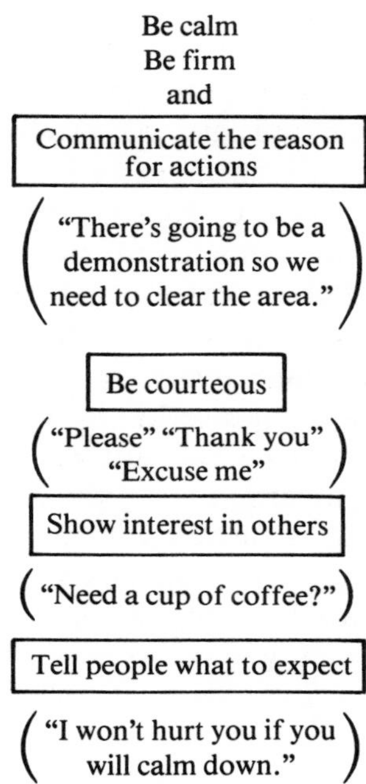

Be calm
Be firm
and
Communicate the reason for actions
"There's going to be a demonstration so we need to clear the area."
Be courteous
"Please" "Thank you" "Excuse me"
Show interest in others
"Need a cup of coffee?"
Tell people what to expect
"I won't hurt you if you will calm down."

Courtesy may or may not be expressed in "please," "thank you," and "pardon me." Courtesy can mean inquiring after someone's health, or giving a "How ya doin'?" greeting. Courtesy can mean waiting a few minutes after ringing the bell instead of pounding on the door. Courtesy can mean a friendly smile, or an expression of concern. Courtesy can mean really listening to what someone has to say.

Courtesy can also mean not hurling insults back at someone. The officer who listens quietly and goes about his business is acting professionally and effectively.

Training officers have found that when officers are taught to respond to neighborhood and domestic quarrels in these ways, many fewer police injuries occur. The officers complete their work more quickly and efficiently. They are safer. Among complaints, lack of courtesy ranks high.[1]

Courtesy also works with juveniles, traffic violators, and persons committing more serious crimes.

Why is this true?

Teddy Roosevelt said a long time ago (in regard to international relations), "Speak softly and carry a big stick." If an officer knows he has the authority of the entire police force behind him, he does not need to speak loudly. He does not need to threaten people physically. He does not need to use his gun. He may need to overpower someone; but he remembers that he has the entire police force and, ultimately, the force of the U.S. government backing him up. From this perspective, it would seem demeaning for an officer to trade insults with powerless individuals.

The officer who is self-confident can act courteously and effectively—even if it means pinning someone down or searching him. The way a search is carried out may be calming or it may make the suspect more violent and harder to handle. "OK, just settle down, and this will be over in a minute. I won't hurt you any more than I have to; but if you keep struggling, you're going to get hurt." People will calm down more quickly with this kind of firm, courteous treatment.

Of course, in some circumstances officers cannot be careful of someone's physical integrity. However, that is different from kicking someone after he is already subdued. An officer may be scared himself and feel like kicking an offender who has given him a lot of trouble. But he will be causing a lot more trouble, for both himself and others, if he hurts people when it isn't necessary. The officer's professionalism and self-respect must dominate this kind of situation. Otherwise, not only will the suspect get even if he can, but so will his friends. A cycle of violence will have been initiated.

Telling people what to expect is another way of using authority well because it invites their cooperation. Good doctors and nurses tell a patient what is going to happen. Good police officers do, too:

"If you come along quietly, I won't have to use these cuffs."

"If you continue to hold onto that gun, I'll have to arrest you."

"If you leave now, I won't have to arrest you."

In these situations, an officer exerts his authority, but he also allows people some control over what happens to them. They have a choice. They are therefore less likely to resist his authority.

Development of Feelings about Authority

Submitting to authority is a part of growing up. Parents use their authority in good or bad ways from the time a child is born. Later, a child's teachers continue to exercise authority over him. Sometimes it is good, sometimes bad.

Parents instill attitudes toward authority in their children by their example—some parents are authoritarian; others are authoritative. Some use authority well, some badly.

Parents who use authority well respect their children, including their abilities and limitations. They show respect for limitations by not sending a young child to play on a busy street where he may be hit by a car. Similarly, they show respect for strengths by not preventing him from playing freely in playgrounds or yards. Parents who use authority well allow their children freedom to use time as they wish as long as they don't interfere with others. They provide a child-world in which their children will not get into trouble when they are active. They set limits and they set them firmly and calmly. Children are allowed to have feelings, to express them, but not always to act upon them. For example, a child will be allowed to say, "I hate my baby brother," but not to beat his baby brother. A child may say "I hate you" to his parents, and the parents will respect his feeling—but they will still insist on his going to bed at the designated hour (see Figure 4.2).

Harsh and punishing parents use authority badly. The smallest thing provokes punishment, sometimes brutal beatings. These parents do not respect their children's rights to privacy or the freedom to do things that the children want to do. "Do it because I say so," is their watchword. They demand blind obedience from a child, and as a result the child becomes angry. These parents practice authoritarianism.

Scientists have studied many authoritarian persons who tend to be unconcerned about the rights of others and who bully people into doing what they wish. These people have four major characteristics: (1) they tend to believe that harsh punishment is good; (2) they cannot accept their own feelings or the feelings of others; (3) they look at things in terms of all good or all bad; and (4) they are prejudiced. Such authoritarian persons have no place in a criminal justice system because they do not know how to use authority appropriately.

Persons whose parents treated them respectfully usually are tolerant and respectful toward authority. They have grown up to believe that authorities have their welfare at heart.

Persons whose parents treated them harshly have a different attitude toward authority. This attitude has two aspects: feelings toward those above them and feelings toward those below them. Those who have had good experiences with authority treat those below and above in the same impartial way.

Figure 4.2
Basis for feelings about authority

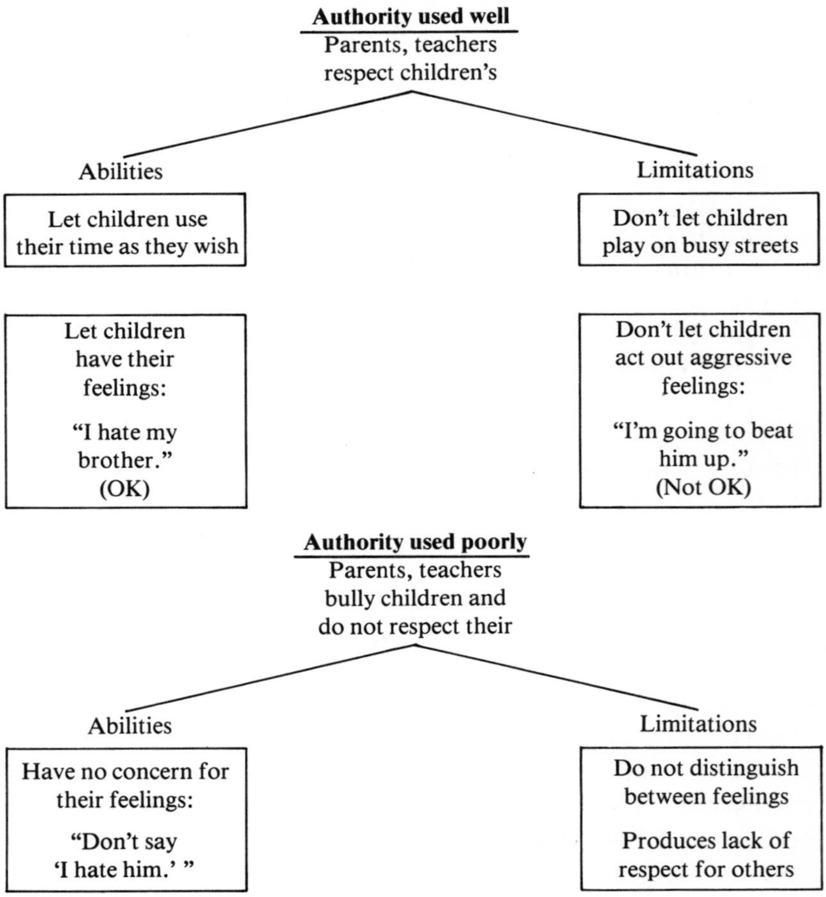

Authority used well
Parents, teachers
respect children's

Abilities

Let children use their time as they wish

Let children have their feelings:

"I hate my brother." (OK)

Limitations

Don't let children play on busy streets

Don't let children act out aggressive feelings:

"I'm going to beat him up." (Not OK)

Authority used poorly
Parents, teachers
bully children and
do not respect their

Abilities

Have no concern for their feelings:

"Don't say 'I hate him.' "

Limitations

Do not distinguish between feelings

Produces lack of respect for others

Those with bad experiences, however, treat their superiors with great courtesy and respect. But because they tend to resent and fear their superiors, they turn their anger toward those below them. This is the mechanism of *displacement*. Therefore, they treat anyone in an inferior position very badly, causing the misuse of authority discussed earlier.

Models of Authority in Police Commands

Unfortunately, many police commands are built on a military model of obedience and authoritarianism. This structure tends to lead to situations that make everyone angry rather than to those that promote peace and cooperation.

For example, a police chief who carefully works out a plan for dealing with demonstrations can be ruined by a militaristic command situation. This can happen when his superior has no understanding of demonstrations or a local situation, but nevertheless demands total and blind obedience.

More effective police systems provide for a different kind of command situation—one that allows individuals to talk things out, to have feelings, to be respected. In short, such systems allow for communication. They are promoted by persons who are sufficiently secure to listen to opinions that may differ from their own.

When these more effective police systems come about, they do so from increased professionalization of their members. They come as a result of actions from persons like yourselves who are seeking to understand better how to deal with the complex task of promoting and preserving the peace.

Summary

Being a law enforcement officer, or another member of the criminal justice system, means being an authority. Pitfalls in using authority include: (1) reactions to the feelings of both respect and anger that authority provokes, (2) enjoying power too much, and (3) being afraid to use authority.

Feelings about authority come from feelings and attitudes developed in childhood. Some of these attitudes are called *authoritarian* because they involve a bullying use of power. Authority that is both firm and respectful of others is *authoritative.*

Unfortunately, much of the authority in the police structure is authoritarian rather than authoritative; thus it leads to resentment on the part of police officers and citizens.

While it might appear that authority is incompatible with concern for others, it *is* possible to be both firm and understanding. This combination of traits in police officers and other criminal justice professionals will lead to more efficiency in the criminal justice system and improved community relations.

Discussion Questions

1. Role-play an arrest situation. Do it first with empathy and then without empathy. Have the arresting officer and the suspect change roles each time. Discuss the feelings evoked in each case. How can empathy and firmness be combined?
2. How difficult is it to be concerned about people who have broken the law? Think of times when you have broken the law. Discuss your feelings and those of others.

Suggested Reading

Bittner, Egan. *The Functions of the Police in Modern Society.* New York: Jason Aaronson, 1975.

Bordua, David J. *The Police: Six Sociological Essays.* New York: John Wiley, 1967.

Coffey, Alan; Edelfonso, Edward; and Hartinger, Walter. *Human Relations: Law Enforcement in a Changing Community.* Englewood Cliffs, N.J.: Prentice-Hall, 1971.

Cohn, A. W., and Viano, E. E., eds. *Police Community Relations: Images, Roles, Realities.* Philadelphia: J. B. Lippincott, 1976.

Kroes, W. H. *Society's Victim—The Policeman: An Analysis of Job Stress in Policing.* Springfield, Ill.: C. C. Thomas, 1977.

Lundman, R. J., ed. *Police Behavior, A Sociological Perspective.* New York: Oxford University Press, 1980.

Milgram, S. *Obedience to Authority.* New York: Harper, 1975.

Sowle, C. R., ed. *Police Power and Individual Freedom.* Springfield, Ill.: C. C. Thomas, 1962.

Spring Hill Center. *Police—Minority Community Relation: The Control and Structuring of Police Discretion.* Hoel, D., and Ziegenhagen, J., eds. Wayzata, Minn.: Spring Hill, 1978.

Sterling, Jane W. *Changes in Role Concepts of Police Officers.* Gaithersburg, Md.: International Association of Chiefs of Police, 1972.

CHAPTER 5

Special Problems in Criminal Justice: Interviewing and Traffic Work

Interviewing and traffic work are two activities that demand a great deal of time from criminal justice personnel. Both frequently seem tedious and repetitive. However, positive attitudes and special techniques can facilitate work in these areas, making them more efficient and productive.

Interviewing

Interviewing poses a special problem for persons in the criminal justice structure. Good interviewing requires a special interest in, and concern for, the person interviewed. But since criminal justice professionals are in an adversary position in relation to most of their clients, it would seem difficult for them to follow this basic rule.[1] The interviewer must therefore resolve the conflict between being interested, honest, and concerned and his role as a criminal justice representative, authority figure, and possible punishing agent. He can do so by realizing and communicating to the suspect that he usually can be helpful and collaborative if both parties are honest. His caring can be communicated by such statements as, "I don't approve of what you did, but I do see how you were led to do it."

The job is made easier by the fact that many offenders are desperate for someone to care about them. They probably won't show this on the surface: the juvenile who talks tough is frequently covering up his need for help. By showing interest in him as a person, you may gain his willingness to cooperate. Telling him that he cannot be forced to talk is also important. A suspect has a choice, and the chance that he will talk to you is better if you acknowledge that. A suspect knows he is in a bad position. He must realize that the officer will be more helpful if he cooperates.

Twelve Steps to Effective Interviewing

Effective interviewing skills can be applied to a variety of functions: interrogating suspects; presentence investigations, counseling probationers, prisoners, and parolees; and gathering information related to patrolling—for example, gathering information about current or potential disturbances (see Figure 5.1).

Figure 5.1

Twelve steps to effective interviewing

1. Give the interviewee some control over his situation.
2. Be honest.
3. Show interest.
4. Use nonverbal as well as verbal communication.
5. Show empathy.
6. Communicate understanding.
7. Handle silence by attempting to formulate what is on the interviewee's mind.
8. Express acceptance of the interviewee's feelings.
9. Ask open-ended questions.
10. Clearly communicate alternatives throughout the interview.
11. Communicate what you know about a situation.
12. Use appropriate timing.

1. *Give the interviewee some control over his situation.* Not only should an officer follow the requirements of the *Miranda* decision by informing a suspect of his rights, but he also should provide the suspect with whatever more specific information he has available: when the suspect can be assigned an attorney, how long he will be detained, and so on.

The suspect will be most likely to cooperate if he feels that the officer has been sufficiently interested to provide such information.

2. *Be honest.* Suspects, witnesses, and all other interviewees will appreciate honesty. Do not make promises or pretend you are doing one thing when you are really doing something else. By being dishonest, an interviewer can provoke a number of negative consequences. If the suspect is lied to, he will eventually find out and become angry, just as you would in a similar situation. And an angry suspect, witness, criminal, probationer—or citizen—can cause trouble for criminal justice professionals.

Those involved in criminal justice must stand for, and serve as examples of, the principles of fairness embodied in the law. Basic honesty is one of these principles. Otherwise, professionals will be serving as models of the very kind of behavior they are trying to prevent and punish. Citizens then become cynical, asking themselves why they should obey the law if officers are dishonest.

It is also difficult to follow through on a lie. Lies can make an officer uncomfortable about himself and others. On the other hand, honesty about a situation gives both interviewer and interviewee a chance to move forward. If an interviewee feels he is being given "straight" information, he is much more likely to level with the interviewer.

3. *Show interest.* Interviewers who seem bored and unconcerned get poor results; so give your full attention to the person you are interviewing.

4. *Use nonverbal as well as verbal communication.* Nonverbal communication may be more effective than words during an interview. Saying, "I would like to hear your side of the story," can be followed by listening attentively, looking directly at the person with whom you are speaking, and leaning forward as you speak.

5. *Show empathy.* An apt definition of *empathy* is "walking in another person's moccasins." It involves understanding another

person's situation by seeing it "through his eyes." But how can an officer be empathic with child abusers? Criminals? Drug pushers? Loud, provocative juveniles?

In working with criminals on a psychological level, I have found it possible to understand a person's *motives* even though his crime may be horrible.

For example, a patient of mine called his father into the bedroom and hit him over the head with a hammer. In talking with this patient, I found that his mother was in a state of unbearable tension because the father was constantly in the process of building each house that the family lived in, producing chaotic living conditions. When a house was finished, the family would move to an unfinished one. After many years, the son took matters into his own hands: he murdered his father.

Clearly, this was not sufficient reason for the man to kill his father, but following the situation through the patient's eyes enabled me to understand why he had committed his crime. In the hospital the patient made an outstanding adjustment, and after his release he was able to hold responsible work positions.

Being empathic is not the same thing as being sympathetic. My patient knew that I did not approve of his act, but he did feel that I was supporting his efforts to understand and change his behavior.

Showing empathy means being *tuned in*. A person who feels he is being dealt with by someone who *understands* is more likely to cooperate. And understanding has another constructive effect. Even though a suspect knows an officer will play his part to see to it that the subject goes to jail, he nevertheless will feel he is being treated like a human being. The suspect may have had little experience of being treated humanely, and will appreciate it. This basic respect can have a profound effect on a suspect's view of the law, of criminal justice, and of the police.

6. *Communicate understanding*. It is important that you show the interviewee that you understand his situation. You may communicate this by a nod of the head, a smile, or a frown. Or you may communicate it verbally by rephrasing what the interviewee has just said. You might say something like, "What I guess you're saying is that you went along with them, not expecting that anyone would get hurt," or "What I hear you saying is that you aren't going to trust me with any information at all."

7. *Handle silence by attempting to formulate what is on the interviewee's mind.* Express for him why he is not talking. For example, you might say to a juvenile gang member, "I guess you don't want to say anything because your friends will get you if you do." In many cases, a person is unwilling to talk because he is frightened and distrustful of the interviewer. Putting his distrust into words can be helpful. "I suppose you feel I am against you." He may then be able to respond.

8. *Express acceptance of the interviewee's feelings.* Along with guessing what is going on in the interviewee's mind, state that you can understand the reason for his position. "I would feel pretty angry and scared if I were in your position." When a person feels that his reactions are understood and accepted, he is more likely to be open and cooperative.

9. *Ask open-ended questions.* Questions that allow for a varied response are a good way to lead into the interview. A statement such as, "Can you tell me something about how you see this whole situation?" is nonjudgmental, accepting, and opens a wide area for response.

Open-ended questions can also be asked in the following way: After the interviewee has expressed an idea or has agreed with an idea suggested by the interviewer, he can be asked what experiences he has had to make him feel that way. For example, "You probably don't want to talk because of your buddies," can be followed with, "Tell me what has happened that makes you feel that way." Because he has discovered the suspect's problem about talking, the interviewer can then show him ways in which he might be cooperative without putting himself in jeopardy.

10. *Clearly communicate alternatives throughout the interview.* Let the interviewee know that he does have alternatives: "You can continue to remain silent. In that case I won't be able to help at all." "I do not intend to talk with you if you continue to be insulting."

11. *Communicate what you know about a suspect.* Telling a suspect what you do know about his situation may direct him to an honest answer. If you ask, "Did you steal that car?" he is likely to say no. But if you say, "I am aware that you stole that car. Can you tell me something about why you did it?" he is more likely to think and answer productively.

12. *Use appropriate timing.* Time your responses, some of which will be verbal, some nonverbal. How do you know when to pursue a line of questioning and when to change it? Pursue it when the interviewee shows signs of openness. Such cues include the following:

a) The interviewee discusses something new rather than repeating the same information.

b) He displays "open" body signs, such as leaning forward and listening attentively. If the interviewee moves parts of his body that "enclose the person"—if he extends arms that have been folded over his chest, if he uncrosses his legs—he is probably becoming more cooperative. Sometimes someone may go so far as to imitate the interviewer unconsciously. Such behavior shows an identification with the interviewer and indicates a willingness to follow him.

Change your line of questioning when the interviewee shows signs of resistance. These signs are generally the opposite of signs of openness, and include behavior indicating anger—tightly clenched mouth, head thrust forward belligerently, body turned away, repetition of the same statement, silence, "enclosure" of the body. When you encounter resistance, change to a nonthreatening subject—something you know the interviewee will be willing to discuss. You might refer to general topics or to what others think about something. For example:

"Do most of the kids you know think it's a bad idea to talk to a cop?"

"Are things worse in the neighborhood now than they used to be?"

"Do you find that teachers are generally pretty rotten?"

You can then lead back into a more productive area. Taking a break is also a useful way to turn an unproductive interview around. Another technique is to "reverse"—to tell the suspect that he is really smart not to talk and he shouldn't say a thing. He will probably look at you quizzically and may be more willing to talk.

By following these principles, you will ensure a greater degree of success in your interviewing, especially with resistant individuals. The rules are not always easy to follow, but continued evaluation of your interviews will enable you to improve your skills.

Traffic Problems

Police officers spend a great deal of time performing work related to traffic control.[2] The application of general psychological principles can help make this aspect of law enforcement easier and more effective.

In the United States, being "on the road" is a way of life. People will surrender furniture, clothing—even a mate—but they will hold onto their cars. A car represents power, mobility, independence. Indeed, most of us are unable to function without an automobile. We can neither work nor play.

The problems posed by the obsession with automobiles include crowding of highways (leading to irritability and consequent aggressive and impulsive behavior) and use of the automobile symbolically to serve and express emotional needs.

Crowding of Highways

On our streets and highways, crowding seems to bring out the worst of American characteristics. Americans become irritable; unlike the British, who will queue up and wait patiently for hours, Americans are impatient. They show their impatience by becoming competitive, trying to get the upper hand, often causing collisions. Many motorists feel they have to be first. They behave impulsively, expecting other motorists to get out of their way. If they don't, accidents result.

Using the Automobile Symbolically

Many tragic accidents stem from the symbolic use of the automobile. The symbolic role of the automobile is reflected in the names that manufacturers give to cars: Cougar, Jaguar, Mercury, Cobra, Phoenix suggest power beyond the reach of ordinary men. Americans too often view their cars as instruments to prove their manhood, or to express emotions of rage, depression, or weariness with life. They get into their cars after fighting with their wives or husbands, drive too fast and too recklessly, attempting to dominate other motorists. Some motorists play Russian roulette on the highway: "If I make it going eighty around this curve, fine; if not, I will simply die." Teenagers frequently rev their motors at high speeds to "show" that they are powerful. Sometimes they also play "chicken" on the highway (who will turn off first to avoid a head-on collision?) for the same purpose.

Other situations that cause loss of control by motorists are fatigue, illness, and drug effects. The National Highway Traffic Safety Administration estimates that 50 percent of all traffic fatalities are caused by drivers who are drunk. Fatigue is also a serious matter. Particularly in long-distance driving, motorists may become "hypnotized" by roads so straight that they provide no variety.

How to Cope

While a law enforcement officer can do little to change the basic conditions that cause accidents, efficient law enforcement—for example, keeping drunken drivers off the road—can reduce the trouble some drivers would cause. Stopping speeding motorists is another example. Generally, however, motorists will not take kindly to being stopped. Some may be courteous; others won't be.

In such situations, how can a law enforcement officer best exercise his authority? First, he must realize that the motorists will have a number of negative reactions to being stopped for a traffic violation. He will probably feel humiliated (driving is power, but *he has been stopped!*) and may be childish. Realizing this, the officer may find it possible to deal with insults and irritation in a calm and respectful fashion. If the officer says firmly, "I'm sorry I have to do this," he will tend to calm an irate motorist; whereas a brusque "Show me your license" may further inflame him. Similarly, refusing bribes can be handled tactfully. "Thanks for offering, but I'm not permitted to accept it."

Dealing with victims of serious accidents is a different problem, but it requires the same calmness and firmness. Although the most immediate concern is getting medical help, it is also extremely important that the victim be given psychological support. This is easier than it sounds. Simply let him know that you are there and are getting help for him; that you are working to make him comfortable. If he asks you, "How badly am I hurt?" you can answer truthfully and hopefully; say that he will be needing help, and that help is on the way. Remaining in physical contact with a person, such as holding his hand, can reassure him that you are indeed going to stay with him till further help arrives.

Dealing with survivors involved in a fatal accident is an even harder task. It may be best not to tell a seriously injured person that a loved one has been killed. It may be better to say something truthful but not too revealing, such as, "We are doing everything we can to help everyone in the car" or "I don't know yet how badly injured everyone is; let's concentrate on getting you out of this."

In notifying families of accident victims, it is important to be compassionate and truthful and to offer whatever concrete help you can (see discussion of dealing with families of victims of drug overdoses in Chapter 12).

Summary

Interviewing may appear to involve a basic conflict: that of being on the side of the interviewee while at the same time exercising the authority of the law. Following certain principles will help resolve this conflict. Honesty, understanding, empathy, and communication all are necessary if interviewing is to be effective.

Handling traffic problems is an important part of the the law enforcement officer's work. Traffic problems stem from Americans' dependence on automobiles as a means of transportation, and also from the symbolic use of cars to prove manhood, to compete, and to express aggressive or suicidal impulses.

Dealing with traffic offenders requires firmness and courtesy. Dealing with victims of traffic accidents requires physical and psychological reassurance that you are there to help.

Discussion Questions

1. Role-play an interview. Explain what you think your partner is saying. Ask him to tell you if that is correct. Repeat if necessary until you are able to understand the other exactly. Then reverse roles.
2. Discuss traffic accidents you have handled. What psychological state might have played a role in each accident?

Suggested Reading

Benjamin, A. D. *The Helping Interview,* 3rd ed. Boston, Mass.: Houghton Mifflin, 1981.

Gordon, R. L. *Interviewing Strategy, Techniques, and Tactics,* 3rd ed. Homewood, Ill.: Dorsey, 1980.

Hatcher, H. A. *Correctional Casework and Counseling.* Englewood Cliffs, N.J.: Prentice-Hall, 1978.

Kamisar, Y. *Police Interrogation and Confessions: Essays in Law and Policy.* Ann Arbor, Mich.: University of Michigan Press, 1980.

Leonard, V. A. *Police Traffic Control.* New York: C. C. Thomas, 1971.

Rubinstein, J. *City Police.* New York: Ballantine, 1974.

CHAPTER 6

Understanding Perception and How It Affects You: "Now You See It; Now You Don't"

Perception is a key problem for criminal justice professionals, because so much of the process depends on what people have seen or heard, or what they *think* they have seen or heard.

Consider a group of boys corner-lounging. Are they up to something, about to start trouble—a gang fight, a robbery, some muggings? Or are they just passing time?

Or assume you are dispatching. A woman calls. She sounds upset, but not hysterical. She says she's bleeding and needs an ambulance. How do you perceive her call? As an emergency that is important enough to take a car off a burglary check? Or as a routine need for transportation?

You see a man hurrying through the dark. A likely robbery suspect? Or someone late for work? While it would be counterproductive to stop a man peacefully going about his business, it would be equally so to allow a suspect to go on his way.

Or maybe you arrive after a shooting. A crowd has gathered, and some people are ready to tell you who did it. "He was tall, about two hundred pounds." "No, medium height, dark, sort of slim." "There were two or three of them, not one." Is someone lying?

Or consider a court scene in which a witness is describing an accident that happened two years ago. How reliable can his testimony be? If someone positively identifies a suspect, is that sufficient?

Who perceives what? And how can you tell when the perception is the "real thing"?

Perception Defined

First of all, let us define perception. We become aware of our environment through our senses—sight, hearing, touch, smell, taste. These are the raw data of perception. What we do with these sights and sounds—our interpretation of them—is perception. The fact that seeing and perceiving are two separate processes becomes clear when we consider the blind person who regains sight late in life. He is able to see, but not to perceive, and he does not understand the visual patterns that come to his brain. This is true for all of our senses, which simply bring us messages that require the interpretive process called perception.

Figure 6.1

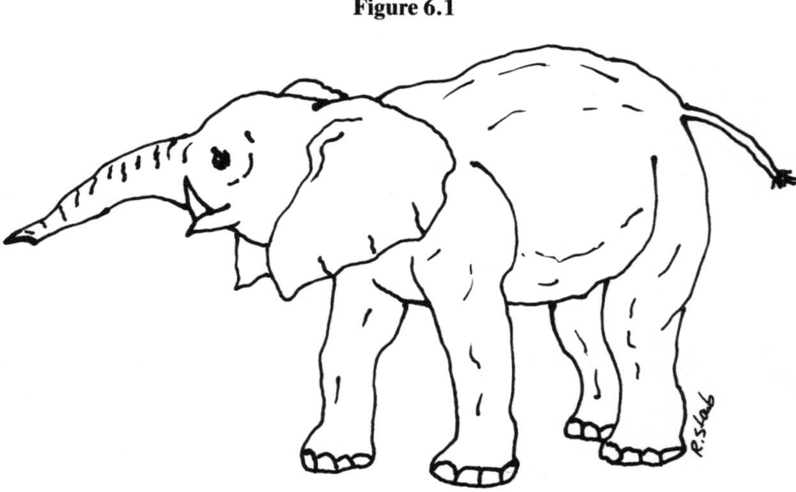

Perception Problems

Is the honest witness always accurate? Let's do a quick quiz to see how much you know about problems of perception:

1. Does everybody perceive objects in the same way? If you think of the examples already mentioned, you will correctly guess that the answer is no. Each person interprets objects on the basis of past experience.

Of course, if an object is clear-cut, almost everyone will interpret it in the same way. What does Figure 6.1 look like to you?

Almost everyone will describe it as an elephant. But how about Figure 6.2?

Figure 6.2

This is no longer clear-cut. Different people will "see" different objects or persons in this form.

2. When you see something, are you always consciously aware that you are seeing it? Again, the answer is no. Sometimes your brain records a scene without recognizing that it has done so. Only later do you realize that you have "recorded" the scene. For example, if you find out that a house has been broken into, you may remember seeing someone in the area who looked as if he didn't belong there. At the time you did not think about it. You had to wait until the memory fit into an intelligible pattern of facts.

In many situations persons are not aware of some of the events taking place. For example, did you ever notice that in an accident, or after a crime, the victims do not seem to be *aware* of being hurt? In these cases, they are not paying attention to their injuries because they are in such extreme danger. They are attending to immediate problems. Once in the hospital, they may faint or otherwise register their reactions to the injuries. An unfortunate example of this kind of inattention is that you—or a potential witness—may be at the scene of a crime but not perceive what has happened.

These examples are explained by the principle of selective attention. We can attend only to a few happenings at any one time, and we select the ones that seem most relevant. An experienced police officer will survey a scene and attend only to that which is out of the ordinary, becoming alert to a part of the situation requiring action. A motorist will attend to what is happening in the lane in which he is traveling, ignoring traffic going in another direction across an island, but he will attend to oncoming traffic if the road has no island, or if another car is driven peculiarly.

3. Once you have noticed something, will you remember it as well in two weeks as you do today? If you've tried, you probably have the answer—another no. Memory fades quickly. Details are lost within a very few moments after observation.

It is, therefore, of the utmost importance to record what you see as quickly as possible. Tape recorders can be used for interrogations. At the scene of an accident, it is important to write down as many details as you can as soon as possible.

4. If something happens quickly, can one perceive it as well as if one has had a chance to study it? Unfortunately for criminal detection, no. A fleeing burglar does not give an officer or bystander much of a chance for accurate perception. This fact can lead to embarrassing, sometimes tragic, errors, when men have been sent to jail on the basis of eyewitness identifications—only to have someone else confess to the crime years later. In some cases, the two men have been look-alikes. Sometimes, however, they have simply been misperceived by otherwise honest and well-intentioned witnesses. Persons have been convicted of murder on the basis of what other people think they have seen. A suspect may have been somewhat similar in appearance to the criminal. Because he was of the same general build (tall, thin, fat) or of a particular race, he was identified as the criminal.[1]

5. Do you perceive people and other things as well when you are not familiar with them? Have you ever heard statements such as, "All Chinese people look alike" or "All elephants look alike"? You may well agree with those statements. But do all your children look alike? Or your aunts and uncles?

The more important an object or person is to us, the more likely we are to notice the details. If we are interested in revolvers, we will know many things about different makes and calibers of revolvers. On the other hand, if we are not interested in art, a Ming vase may look like just another vase to us. Similarly, a patrol officer in a familiar district will know what sorts of people are likely to be where; in a small town, he will know most of the people individually. He will notice if something is not as it should be. This familiarity is extremely important and is a good reason why officers should not be moved around too often. Intimate knowledge of an area and the people in it is essential for accurate perception of events, and this happens only if the area or category is important to us.

Similarly, a person is more likely to make a correct identification of a person who is generally familiar to him. A white person might assume that any black who fit a general description of his assailant was actually the criminal. But if asked to identify someone of his own social class, age, and race, he is likely to make finer differentiations of hair and eye color, type of dress, and so on.

Therefore, perceptions of witnesses must be evaluated carefully. If a fifty-year-old says some kid broke into the empty house, is he as likely to know the difference between "some kid" and the one who actually did it as a youth worker, or another kid? Someone interested in kids will notice details of dress, walk, and mannerisms of which the uninterested fifty-year-old has no awareness.

6. Does strong emotion help or hinder perception? The answer is both. In a crisis, one will recall some aspects of the situation with great precision. But one will lose a host of other details.

When we are very anxious or frightened, we tend to develop "tunnel" vision. We act as though we are wearing blinders. In almost every serious situation we see just those aspects that seem most important to us. Two conclusions may be drawn from this information: (1) the officer must discipline himself to notice routinely those details that most people would forget; and (2) he must realize that witnesses will have a hard time telling an officer or the court exactly what they have seen, especially in a serious, frightening situation.

7. At this point, the reader will be able to answer the following question correctly. Is it true that an honest witness will always be able to describe exactly what happened?

Obviously, some or all of the problems discussed may intervene to prevent the witness from being truthful. He may have seen the event too quickly. He may have been unfamiliar with the situation. He may have waited too long before trying to recall it. The situation originally may not have been clear, or he may not have been paying attention.

Unfortunately, one must conclude that there are many difficulties in identifying and describing criminal and other law enforcement situations.

How Are Situations Misperceived or Misremembered?

The ways in which situations are misperceived and misremembered relate to the fact that we all tend to interpret what we see and hear in terms of previous experience.

How might this apply? Suppose, for example, that your experience has taught you that most crimes of vandalism are committed by young people. You see a somewhat stooped distant figure breaking chairs outside a furniture warehouse, but your immediate reaction is that it can't be an older person, even though it looks like one. Older persons don't do such things. You may have misinterpreted. If you could get a good look, you might see that the vandal definitely was a mature person, and your awareness of this reality would correct your past misperception. When not able to get a good look, you will let your past experience interpret that fleeting image. You may be wrong.

Such misinterpretations occur frequently under the kind of conditions that make perception unclear—too rapid a look, lack of attention, unfamiliarity with a situation, an unclear image (as in the dark), and the other problems we have discussed.

Other kinds of misinterpretations come from people's needs and motivations. If you have been searching frantically for a rapist, it is easy to decide that a strange man standing around must be the one. You want to find the assailant, and the suspect could as well as not be the criminal. Again, the perception is not clear.

Try a simple experiment with an unclear image. Look at the word in Figure 6.3. What is it?

Figure 6.3

Whether you see the word *food* or *good* depends on whether or not you are hungry. The first letter is unclear; it could be a *g* or an *f*. Your perception depends on your needs at the moment.

Here is another example. Look at Figure 6.4.

Figure 6.4

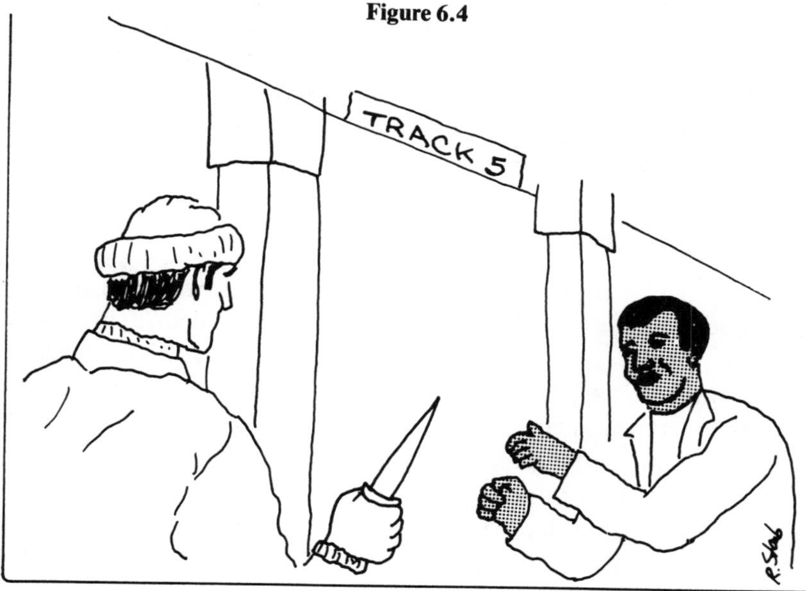

Would it surprise you to know that most people remember pictures such as this in a distorted way? Most people remember this illustration as showing a *black* person with a knife.

People naturally remember things in ways consistent with their beliefs and motivations. If they feel blacks are more likely than whites to be criminals, they will change a perfectly clear image and remember the white man as the victim.

It is especially important for police officers to be aware of this tendency. For themselves, they must try to remember the things that contradict as well as those that fit their ideas, goals, and past experiences about the world.

It is equally important to remember that people can consciously be honest witnesses and yet distort perceptions to fit their preconceptions of the kind of person committing a particular kind of crime. You might check yourself out by asking the questions: Who commits muggings? Who commits rapes? Who commits fraud? Who steals? Who sets fires?

While your answers may be right most of the time, it is the exception that would arrest your attention. Work with human beings is never boring, because there are always exceptions to our general rules of interpretation.

You can see why defense lawyers and prosecutors alike are concerned about the kind of people they have on their juries. The jurors' moral values and sympathies will affect their decisions; their perceptions of what happened originally also will reflect their experiences and motivations.

What Is Remembered?

A number of other perceptual principles can be useful in predicting whether a situation will be remembered accurately. Some of these principles are important for those designing highways and highway directions, or in analyzing why highway accidents occur. Others are of importance in ordinary police work.

Those things most likely to be remembered have a number of characteristics in common:

1. They are in sharp contrast to their surroundings. This may be because they are larger, of a contrasting color, or of a very different design.

This is part of the *figure-ground* concept. When you look around, some objects or persons stand out. Others are part of the background. Those that stand out are called the "figure" part of the image. The rest is called the "ground."

What is figure, and what is ground, can be very important for a law enforcement officer. It is, of course, clear that a police car can be "figure" for anyone committing an offense. Similarly, the experienced police officer will ignore what is figure to most people—such as a flashing sign—and look for what is happening in a dark alley.

In other words, he must *relearn* ways to perceive and focus on the important things. These may be objects or events that are "ground" for other people.

2. Brightly colored objects are easily perceived. Yellow and orange are very easy colors to perceive and therefore are useful for highway markings and directions.

3. Stimuli that change are more likely to arrest attention than those that remain the same. Highway engineers have caught onto this by designing flashing warning signs. Many accidents are caused by the monotony of modern superhighways. Drivers become stupefied or hypnotized by the sameness and need something to wake them up. The flashing signs help keep people awake. Truck drivers are particularly susceptible to this problem.

4. Clear-cut simple objects or designs are more easily perceived than ambiguous or elaborate ones. Unfortunately, most of the important things police officers see are ambiguous. However, highway signs can be made in clear-cut designs that become familiar to all drivers.

This principle is important in understanding the accounts of witnesses or officers.

Most people prefer clear-cut images. This is why an image that is unclear will be remembered as clear. For example, ○ becomes a clear-cut circle.

Similarly, stories passed through a classroom end up not only fitting each teller's preconceptions, but becoming much clearer, with most details omitted and a few details emphasized.

It is not difficult to see what this could do to an account of a crime!

Other Perceptual Distortions

Perceptual distortions can be very striking: for example, a stick appears to bend when we put it in water, or a mirage on the highway looks like a pool. These misperceptions come from tricks played on us by our visual apparatus.

Other misperceptions are more serious. Drivers are not only

subject to boredom and inability to pay attention; they are sometimes victims of another type of perceptual distortion—interpreting incorrectly something they see. Truck drivers are often subject to this type of distortion, perhaps swerving to avoid something that, after ten hours of driving, looks like a person but is in reality the shadow of a tree. Soldiers sometimes shoot at objects that they may see as threatening attackers, but that may turn out to be tumbleweed or bits of debris blowing in the wind.

Anyone concentrating intensely for too long a period of time is subject to such misperceptions, and dangerous situations can result. During the Newark riots, an inexperienced guardsman mistook a lighted cigarette for gunfire. He shot, others shot, and a number of innocent persons were killed.

A more extreme form of visual distortion is a hallucination. When a person hallucinates, he sees or hears something that is not present, such as visions or nonexistent voices. Usually only psychotics have hallucinations, but persons who have taken drugs called "hallucinogens" (such as LSD) may be subject to such often frightening apparitions. Persons who are feverish, alcoholics, or deprived of sensory input (as in solitary confinement) may also hallucinate.

Anyone hallucinating is in need of emergency care. He may behave in a bizarre way because of what he thinks is happening. Most persons who hallucinate are harmless, but they may get themselves into dangerous situations. This is especially true of otherwise normal persons hallucinating because of drugs or other toxic substances. Such people should be hospitalized or otherwise carefully supervised until the toxic element wears off. Although only a very small percentage of all seriously disturbed persons are dangerous, the possibility of danger is also a consideration in dealing with a psychotic person, because he perceives his fantasies as real.

Another serious problem related to perception is the complete inability to remember anything that has happened, often after a head injury.

Much less frequently, an officer might encounter someone with a rare problem called *amnesia*. The amnesia victim will not remember who he is or how he got there. An emotional problem, amnesia usually strikes individuals who have serious stresses in their lives and do not know how to cope with them. Their response is to escape by literally forgetting their identity. Such persons need psychological help and should be referred to a hospital or community clinic or social agency. However, such a problem is more frequently encountered on the late, late movie than in an officer's work.

A more frequent problem is the person who is wandering about unable to remember where he lives. This individual is usually an older person suffering from brain damage. Such memory loss may occur in the small group of aging individuals with *senile dementia.* These individuals become disoriented and may not remember their address or where they are. Usually someone will notice their absence and call the police, who can then help the individuals get home. If not, the older person needs to be handled as lost and given temporary hospitality until he is found.

Dealing with Problems of Perception

What can you, as a criminal justice professional, do to deal with perceptual problems?

Here are three general rules:

1. Train yourself to be attentive to cues that you have learned are important. They vary with the situation and frequently involve picking up unusual detail. Consequently, you must *know* what is usual in a particular kind of situation or area. Loud screams may be common in certain areas, but a slightly different quality of sound, or silence, may mean trouble.

2. Observe as much as possible about a situation. Again, to do so you need to draw on past experience. If you are in doubt, you must explore in order to be able to observe more. You may need to give yourself time to look at a situation.

3. Record anything about the situation that might need later expansion or follow-up. Many police officers do this mentally. If you do intervene in a situation, you need to follow up the intervention by recording as many details as possible, even if they seem unimportant, or are not requested on your report form.

Later, review the situation with others who have observed it or have had similar experiences to see what you missed.

Aids to Memory

Let's say that you saw something suspicious but cannot really remember what happened. Does it help to "try" very hard to remember? Or when a witness does not prove to be very helpful, should you insist on his *remembering*?

No! The reason is that memory involves two processes – storage and retrieval. Your eyes, ears, and other perceptual organs record everything that you have been aware of, but finding the record is another matter. As in computer storage, you must use the right formula to retrieve it.

Two tricks can help you do this:

1. Put yourself (or the witness) into a situation similar to the one you are trying to retrieve. Taking criminals back to the scene of the crime to remember what happened is an example. If you want to remember something about a situation, take yourself back in memory, or cruise over to a similar area. Don't try too hard to remember. Just let your mind wander.

2. Free-associate. Trying hard to remember is usually impossible, but letting your mind wander will peel off inconsequential layers to lead you to what you want. Letting yourself free-associate means allowing anything at all to pop into your head. Keep doing this. After a time, you will find that what you want to remember will appear.

You can do this another way. Just don't worry about it. Usually sometime during the day or night, what you want to remember will pop into your head.

The main principle is not to try directly. Under hypnosis or "truth drugs" (such as sodium amytal) people remember things that are not available to them consciously. Some psychologists have likened memory to an onion, with many layers. When we peel off some of the layers through free association or drug action, we get to the layer that has recorded what we want.

Of course, it is possible to retrieve information *only* if we or the witness initially "recorded" or perceived what happened. These methods help only when we have recorded but do not remember having done so.

Summary

Perception can be full of problems and distortions. What we perceive depends on how clearly we see it.

This in turn depends on the clarity of the stimulus originally, how good a look we had, whether the stimulus was disguised as part of the "ground" or whether it contrasted, whether it was clear-cut or ambiguous, our familiarity with it, and our interest in it.

Perception also depends on past experience, which tells us how to interpret something, and our motivation.

Perception depends on our psychological and physical state. If we are tense, fatigued, or under drug influence, our perceptions can change. We can think things we see are something else (illusions) or see things that aren't even there (hallucinations).

If our motivation makes us want to see something, we sometimes distort what we see. If we want to see a certain kind of person committing a crime, that may be what we "see." If we are anxious and afraid, we may "see" ordinary persons as menacing figures.

Even if we can perceive accurately, memory plays tricks on us. We distort what we remember even more than we distort what we perceive. We make our memories simpler and clearer, and we remember them in ways that fit our past experiences and desires.

Understanding perception is important in the process of describing a crime as well as making judgments about responsibility for a crime. It is therefore essential that officers observe accurately and record their observations as quickly as possible. Otherwise perceptions will become subject to poor memory and further distortion.

It is equally important for those involved in making judgments about who has committed a criminal act to be aware of these perceptual problems. Since an officer conducts the first (though informal) "trial" in making his decision whether or not to arrest someone, he must be clear about whether he is certain that the person committed the criminal act or not. If the officer is unsure, he should not be afraid to arrest someone, but must clarify his uncertainties to others.

Such fairness, while it may allow some criminals to slip through the net, can help improve the image of the police as concerned about justice. We need not always *be* correct, but if we understand perception, we can *know* that we are not always correct and why.

Discussion Questions

1. Why are witnesses to a crime inaccurate in their descriptions of what happened? In what ways are their perceptions distorted? What can be done about these inaccuracies?
2. What perceptual problems affect drivers? Can you think of any solutions?
3. Describe an incident that you have seen to the person nearest you. Have that person describe it to the next person until the description goes around the room. How do the accounts of the first and last persons differ?

Suggested Reading

Basinger, L. F. *The Techniques of Observation and Learning Retention: A Handbook for the Policeman and the Lawyer.* Springfield, Ill.: C. C. Thomas, 1973.

Brown, J., ed. *Recall and Recognition.* London: Wiley, 1976.

Clifford, B. R., and Bull, Ray. *The Psychology of Person Identification.* London: Routledge & Kegan Paul, 1978.

Held, R., ed. *Perception: Mechanisms and Models, Readings from Scientific American.* New York: W. H. Freeman, 1972.

Henshel, R. L., and Silverman, R. A., eds. *Perception in Criminology.* New York: Oxford University Press, 1979.

Kaufman, L. *Perception: The World Transformed.* New York: Oxford University Press, 1979.

Loftus, G. R., and Loftus, E. F. *Human Memory: The Processing of Information.* Hillsdale, N.J.: Lawrence Erlbaum, 1976.

Miller, G. A., and Johnson-Laird, P. N. *Language and Perception.* Cambridge, Mass.: Belknap Press of Harvard University, 1976.

Saks, M. J., and Hastie, R. *Social Psychology in Court.* New York: Van Nostrand Reinhold, 1978.

Yarney, A. D. *The Psychology of Eyewitness Testimony.* Riverside, N.J.: The Free Press, 1979.

CHAPTER 7

Reward and Punishment

Since the entire correctional system is based on reward and punishment, primarily punishment, it is important for those in the area of criminal justice to know something about how reward and punishment work. While this knowledge may not enable you personally to decrease crime, it will help you understand why delinquency "runs in families" and why the criminal recidivism rate is so high. Psychologists have made many studies of reward and punishment, the results of which may surprise you.

Reward

The image of reward is usually that of candy for a child, but the word reward has many different meanings.

Intrinsic versus Extrinsic Reward

One type of reward is *intrinsic* reward, a reward gained just by doing something we like. Why do people go fishing? Or skiing? Or bowling? We could think of fishing as a chance to get fish to eat. But clearly, skiing and bowling don't bring us anything special. We are not rewarded from the outside. We are rewarded because we enjoy the activity in itself. Why do people enjoy being at the local bar? Certainly not for the hangover or the empty pocket. They spend hours at the bar because it is intrinsically rewarding to them. They enjoy it.

On the other hand, *extrinsic* rewards come from the outside. Perhaps you are doing criminal justice work because you enjoy it. But let us assume that you do not; or let us consider a factory worker who does not enjoy his work. Why is he working? The answer is easy: for the paycheck. The paycheck is not part of the activity; it is something that comes from the outside, something that someone else gives the worker as a reward for his work. It is an extrinsic reward. Other extrinsic rewards include good grades for schoolwork and vacation trips for sales personnel who exceed their quotas.

So far, in talking about extrinsic rewards, we have been talking about material rewards—tangible things you can pick up and look at. Money, for example, is a material reward.

Another kind of reward that psychologists consider important is *nonmaterial* reward. Of nonmaterial extrinsic rewards, approval and affection are probably the most important. The mother who smiles at her child after he washes his hands is giving him this type of reward.

Many rewards we receive throughout life are of this nonmaterial, extrinsic nature (Figure 7.1). Sometimes we even reward ourselves in this way by thinking, "Hey, there, you've done a good job!" Or, "Dad would really think that was a good piece of work." Experiments have shown that, even when we do not care about another person particularly, we will change our behavior to gain his approval. This has been demonstrated with experiments using nods of the head when a subject says a particular word or group of words. For example, if I nod my head every time a subject says "he" or "she," I will soon find that the person's conversation includes more personal pronouns.

Figure 7.1
Rewards

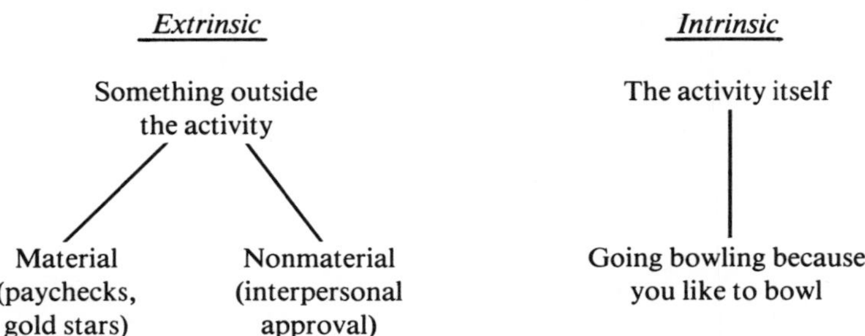

Reward Schedules

Now let us look at rewards in terms of time. Is a person rewarded every single time he does something? Is he rewarded at regular intervals? Is he rewarded by the amount of work he does? Or is he rewarded irregularly? A very important factor is that different *schedules* of reward produce different consequences.

For example, a man who does piecework in a factory is rewarded for the *amount* of work he does. Usually he will work harder as a result. An even better example is the salesman who is working to build up a clientele. He will often work extremely long hours because he is rewarded for each sale.

Contrast the salesman with a postal worker who gets paid every two weeks, regardless of his output. He will probably leave his job at the stroke of five and never arrive earlier than nine. He will take full advantage of coffee breaks. People whose salaries do not depend on the amount of work they do often work less hard than people paid for quantity of output.

Another factor in reward effectiveness is whether a person is rewarded regularly or irregularly. Can you think of any examples of regular and irregular rewards?

First of all, salary is a regular reward. You get it every week, every two weeks, or every month.

What about rewards given at irregular intervals? Can you think of examples? What about the man in business for himself? Some of the time he is rewarded by making money; sometimes he is not.

Figure 7.2
Reward systems

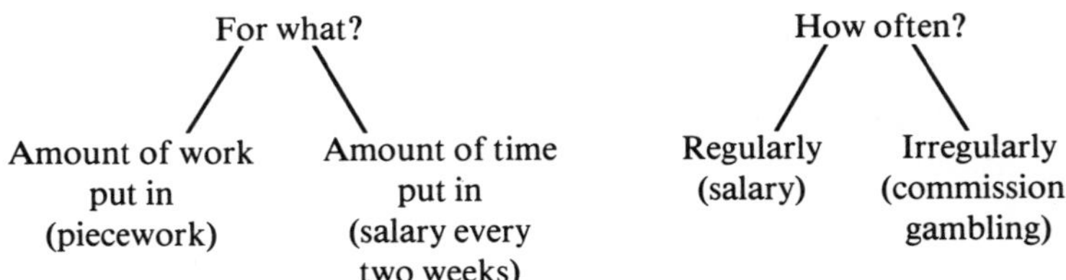

His rewards are irregular, but he continues to work hard. A more striking example is the gambler. He does not know when he will be rewarded. But he keeps gambling—for days, months, years. He is waiting for the reward that may come any day!

Another area in which irregular rewards are very important is child-rearing. Do you know any mothers or fathers who *regularly* reward their children every time they hang up their coats? Or go to bed without fussing? Or do their homework on time? Probably not. And it is not necessary. Children work for rewards given them at irregular intervals.

We do not have to look far to see examples of irregular rewards for adults. Adults do many things to receive the approval of, or attention from, the people around them. This approval comes only occasionally, but we keep working for it. In fact, irregular

Figure 7.3
Schedules of rewards

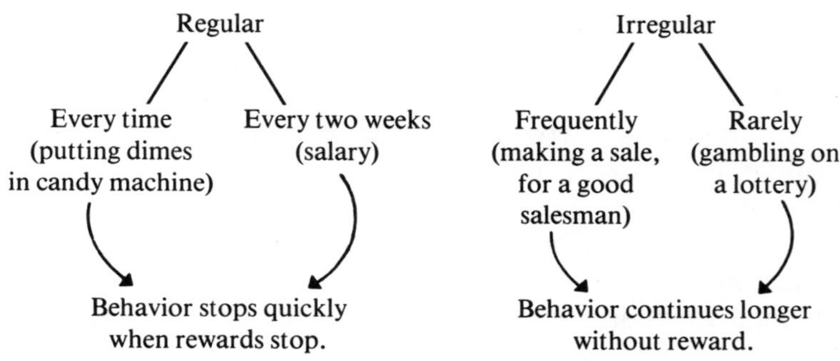

rewards are often more effective than regular rewards because a person continually anticipates that the reward will come. He is hopeful. When the adult believes there will no longer be a reward, he will stop working for it. However, if rewards have been coming to him at irregular intervals, he will continue for a long time before he gives up. The time is much longer than if regular rewards were suddenly shut off.

Effect of Rewards on Behavior

The tendency of human beings to work for rewards has important consequences in relation to undesirable behavior. Behavior that is punished only some of the time will continue because it is also *rewarded* some of the time. The boy who steals cars *sometimes* gets away with it; so he continues to work for his occasional reward (the fun of stealing a car without punishment). This is true of most delinquent behavior. The behavior has rewards for the individual, and if he is not punished *immediately every time* he misbehaves, he will continue for a long time—trying not to get caught.

Reward and Antisocial Behavior

What can we do to stop antisocial behavior if it is intrinsically rewarding? This question might be easier to answer if we consider some reasons why people engage in undesirable behavior. Here are three possible reasons.

1. Other, more rewarding activities are not available. It is difficult for a person to stop doing something he likes without somehow filling the void. Suppose you are in the habit of spending Friday nights in the local bar. You find this habit rewarding, but your doctor tells you it is hurting your health. If you stay home and watch not-very-interesting television, you probably will soon find yourself back at the bar. But if, instead, you do something else that you enjoy—perhaps go bowling—you will find it much easier not to drink.

Finding equally satisfying activities is difficult. You need to analyze all the satisfactions you received from the previous behavior and find substitutes for them. In the example presented above, seeing friends at the bar, escaping work you should be doing at home—these might be additional satisfactions for which you would need to find substitutes. This is why it is often necessary for people with serious problems—alcoholism, drug addiction, delinquency—to develop a whole new style of life.

People who are not delinquents or criminals have learned to find satisfactions in ways that are approved by society. Similarly, they confine their "bad behavior" to actions that are not punishable by law.

2. Criminals do not value the approval of others because this type of reward has not been available to them in the past. If they have grown up receiving little love or attention from parents, and regarding society as punishing, they will look only for material gains for themselves. According to some studies, children of alcoholic parents became delinquent more frequently than other children.[1] While the reasons for this were not established, it is likely that alcoholic parents do not provide many rewards for their children; that they are punishing; and that they provide examples of impulsive, self-seeking behavior. The child decides it is better to fend for himself.

Frequently other adults in the delinquent's life are equally unable to provide interpersonal or other rewards for good behavior. A great deal of evidence suggests that schoolteachers punish lower-class children more frequently and more severely than middle-class children.[2] These lower-class children are likely candidates for delinquency. This is why police programs that provide children with rewards from the adult society are beneficial. They teach children that behaving in nondelinquent ways can be rewarding. If a child really believes this, he may also learn to value the approval of law-abiding adults.

3. Criminals have not learned to wait for rewards. Seeing something in a store and taking it—an increasingly common habit of even primarily law-abiding citizens—is impulsive behavior. It signals an inability to wait for rewards.

On the other hand, getting an education, learning about something new under difficult situations, and saving money for books or tuition indicate a willingness to wait for rewards. Saving money for a down payment on a home; giving up buying sports equipment to make payments on a mortgage; giving up things *you* want in order to buy the kids shoes—all these behaviors indicate an ability to wait for rewards. Sometimes we may wonder about our behavior, or get depressed, but we continue because we have some hope that eventually we will be rewarded. Our children's happiness, our neighbors' respect, and the knowledge that we are doing what is best for our family—all are interim rewards that keep us going. (See Figure 7.4.)

Figure 7.4

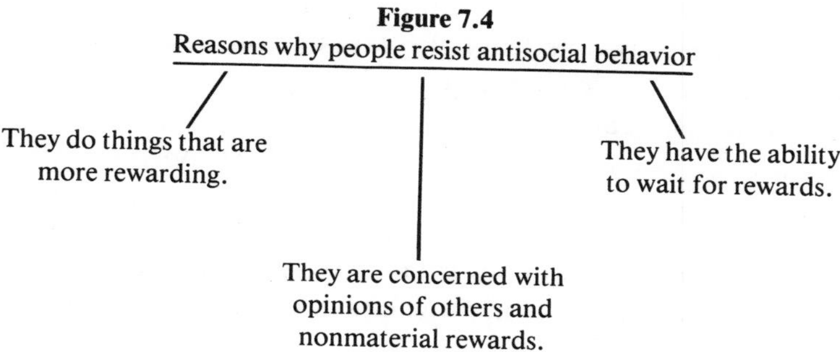
Reasons why people resist antisocial behavior
They do things that are more rewarding.
They are concerned with opinions of others and nonmaterial rewards.
They have the ability to wait for rewards.

Why is it, then, that some can wait and some cannot? The answer is relatively simple. It lies in the way we were brought up and also in the way we live now. If in both cases we have received rewards that we have worked and waited for, we are likely to repeat the behavior that produced the rewards.

Parents who give their children the chance to work for something they want are less likely to have delinquent children than parents who give their children rewards unrelated to behavior.

Suppose a child asks for a bicycle. Parents can use this request to help the child learn that it is worthwhile to work and wait for the bicycle. Parents of future delinquents, however, might give the child the bicycle when he comes home with a bad report card. The child does not learn that he can work for what he wants. The bicycle appeared without his having achieved something. But if, on the other hand, a parent helps the child find extra tasks at which to work to earn the bicycle, he learns to work and wait.

As adults, those of us with reliable incomes and reliable avenues for promotion are much more likely to wait and work than those who feel that rewards are given arbitrarily. The hard worker who thinks he may be fired for no reason other than a slow-up in the economy will gradually learn that it doesn't pay to be diligent. The woman who saves a dollar or two from each paycheck to buy some chairs—and then finds she must spend it for food when her husband is laid off—will soon learn that it doesn't pay to save.

This is probably the reason why current welfare systems discourage people from working. On the other hand, welfare programs that allow people to be rewarded for working—that is, programs that allow welfare payments to persons who supplement their welfare income by working—seem to teach people that work *is* rewarding. These people leave the welfare rolls as quickly as they can, while families in traditional welfare programs may remain on the rolls for generations.

Punishment

So far, our discussion has been concerned with reward. Yet for the criminal justice system, punishment is a much more important area.

What can psychologists tell us about punishment? How effective is it? Is it true that sparing the rod will spoil the child? You may already have ideas about the answers to these questions, but let us look at some of the suggestions that psychology can offer.

Intrinsic versus Extrinsic Punishment

First of all, is there such a thing as intrinsic punishment? It is clear that there is if you look at the many tasks you find intrinsically punishing. Cleaning out the cellar, filling out reports, writing term papers may all be punishing tasks for you. You will avoid them if possible. If someone else pushes you to do any of these tasks, you will probably resent that person. If, however, *you* decide that the cellar is no longer useful, that your desk is cluttered with unfinished reports and you are uncomfortable about it, or that you will be one step closer to a degree if you write the term paper, you will probably complete the task with pride rather than resentment.

Resentment results only if we feel forced to do something without adequate reason. If we see filling out reports as a necessary part of record-keeping, we will not feel resentment. If we see it as a job imposed by a not-very-bright bureaucrat, we will be resentful. Angry, or even delinquent, behavior may result when people feel forced to do something they find unrewarding and for which they see no good reason.

Punishment may also be extrinsic. If you do not fill out required reports, you may be fired or transferred to a less desirable post. Parents may beat their children. Such punishments may be regarded as objective and therefore material in contrast to the punishments involving interpersonal, emotional consequences. A frown, a kiss withheld, a lack of interest on the part of a loved one—all may be labeled as extrinsic, nonmaterial punishments. Extrinsic, nonmaterial punishment is more effective than extrinsic material punishment. In child-rearing, for example, many studies have demonstrated that punishing children by withholding affection or approval is more effective than material punishment, such as beatings. People who have lived with someone who stopped talking to them when angry describe this silent treatment as extremely disturbing.

Timing of Punishment

To be most effective, punishment must accompany the act it punishes. Few people continue to burn themselves after once touching a hot stove, since the punishment is immediate. Contrast this to the knowledge that one is more likely to get lung cancer years hence by smoking. This knowledge of future consequence stops few smokers, though a rasping cough may be more effective. Workable programs to stop alcoholism have included the use of Antabuse, which makes a person nauseous immediately after taking a drink.

Typically, however, punishments related to the criminal justice system are not immediate. For example, a person who receives a traffic ticket for speeding is more likely to associate punishment with *getting caught* than with speeding. The person who has an accident is more likely to slow down than the person who gets a ticket. Stopping behavior before it occurs is even more effective than allowing it to occur and then punishing it. In this regard, the speed bumps in roads that slow down motorists are more effective than other methods. Stopping a child from reaching for a cookie is more effective than punishing after he has had the enjoyment of eating it. After experiencing something he enjoys, a person is likely to do it again because he does enjoy it. It is difficult to stop this behavior through punishment.

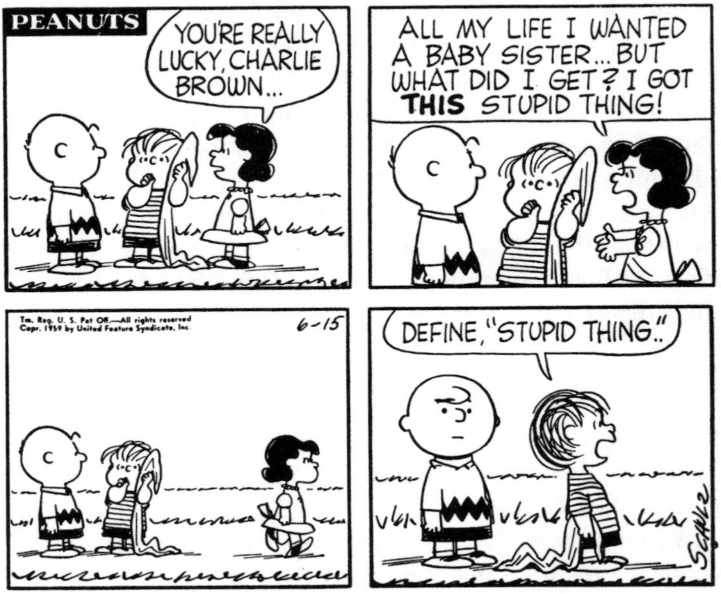

Figure 7.5 Lucy's punishments of Linus do not make it clear to him what he can do to be rewarded. Linus deals with them as best he can.

Source: Charles Schulz, *You're a Winner, Charlie Brown!* (Greenwich, Conn.: Fawcett Art Books, 1959). Copyright ©United Features Syndicate, Inc.

Conditions for Effective Punishment

To be effective, punishment must meet several criteria:

1. It should be immediate. Punishment is a determinant of learning, and learning is based on immediate associations. People quickly learn to get out of the way of heavy falling objects, since the punishment is immediate. Punishment is not immediate in the case of almost any crime or misdemeanor. It is days or even months before the traffic offender pays a fine or loses his license.

2. It must be a meaningful deterrent. Hijackers are frequently suicidal. Telling them that they may be put to death will therefore not deter them. Since they want to die, they do not fear such punishment. On the other hand, a large fine could be a meaningful deterrent for someone with a limited income.

3. It must lead immediately to the desired behavior. Laboratory experiments have clearly demonstrated this fact. For example, an experiment may give subjects a choice of two different buttons to push. Pushing Button A produces an electric shock. Pushing Button B does not. Subjects will quickly learn to push Button B. It is much harder in real life to produce punishment that leads immediately to desired behavior.

4. It must be reasonable. People usually do not resent punishment for disobeying traffic lights because they know that traffic lights are necessary to prevent accidents. However, many people resent tickets for speeding because they feel that speeding is not dangerous.

Punishment generally appears reasonable if it involves natural consequences. I know that I will be hurt if I dive into a shallow pool, so I do not do it. I do not resent the natural consequences of an action. Being asked to pick up a glass I have broken would seem similarly reasonable.

5. It must represent a real loss. Much punishment that works in families is love oriented. The child feels that his parents love him, and he wants them to approve of him. The potential of real loss is one of the essential ingredients for punishment to work. Threat of loss of approval can, in fact, work even too well, intimidating the child.

Conditions for Ineffective Punishment

Punishment, especially if arbitrary or unfair, may have negative effects:

1. Arbitrary punishment causes confusion. In general, punishment does not indicate to the person what he *should* do. If you have ever been expected to do something that you didn't know how to do, you will understand the problem it presents. In such circumstances, the more a person is punished, the more upset he becomes. He may want to do the right thing, but he doesn't know how. Many

sociologists believe that this kind of confusion is characteristic of many delinquents. If they knew how to get a car legitimately, they wouldn't continue to steal cars. Punishing them doesn't show them the correct behavior. It teaches them (1) to try to avoid getting caught and (2) to hate the people who punish them.

2. Punishment may unduly emphasize the punished behavior. Punishment tends to reinforce the undesirable behavior, making the person more likely to repeat the behavior. The punished act becomes forbidden fruit. It is similar to the desire you may have for ice cream when you are dieting. The more you tell yourself you shouldn't have it, the more you are likely to succumb to temptation.

It is therefore more effective to ignore behavior than to punish it. The best way to prevent a child from engaging in an activity is to set up a situation in which he will not be tempted.

3. Arbitrary punishment may cause anger. If punishment seems arbitrary and unfair, most people become angry at the punisher. An angry person is more likely to behave antisocially.

An example is offered by a mother who complains that "Johnny is such a bad kid" that she just can't do anything with him. So she beats him and beats him and takes away privileges. Nothing works. Johnny gets more and more angry and looks for any way to get even—even if he has to suffer at the same time. Again, a vicious cycle is set up. His mother would be less mystified if she realized that punishing bad behavior is less effective than rewarding good behavior.

4. Punishment may cause guilt. While guilt is important in preventing a person from going down the wrong path, it often has unexpected consequences. Persons who feel guilty about their behavior also may be badly affected by punishment. They feel bad at having done something wrong; so they look for punishment. But punishment makes them angry. Then they feel guilty about being angry and they look for punishment for that. The way to get punishment is to do something wrong. The result is a vicious cycle.

If a person feels guilty about certain behavior and knows how to behave in a better way, his guilt becomes an effective stimulus for behavior change. If, however, a person feels guilty but doesn't know what to do, he will probably seek further punishment in order to relieve his guilt. He does this by doing something else that is wrong.

Reward versus Punishment

Why is reward so much more effective than punishment in changing behavior? Reward is effective for several reasons: it does not cause confusion; it teaches the desired behavior. It shows that the desired behavior is pleasant. As a a result, a person does the desirable things, sometimes unconsciously.

In contrast, punishment tends to make a person repeat undesirable behaviors, unless someone is present and threatening punishment. This is because punishment makes a person think about *not* doing something. You can see how this works by telling yourself not to do something. Tell yourself not to scratch your ear for the next ten minutes. You will find yourself thinking about scratching your ear to a much greater extent than you otherwise would have. When ten minutes are up, you are much more likely to have scratched your ear than if you hadn't been telling yourself not to.

Remember the story of the mother who cautioned her children, "I am going out. Now, whatever you do, don't put beans up your nose." The end result was predictable. Anyone who has worked with emotionally disturbed or delinquent children is familiar with the consequences of repeated warnings not to do something. For example, a young girl had been questioned closely about her possible sexual activity with boys since she was seven. Her later promiscuity was as predictable as it was troublesome.

On the other hand, if troublesome behavior can be ignored, and actions approximating the desired behavior are rewarded, persons begin to repeat desired behavior. For example, pigeons can be taught to play Ping-Pong simply by rewarding behavior that brings them closer and closer to effective motions, ignoring ineffective movement. The same principle works with children.

Why Punishment Is Often Used

Since reward is much more effective than punishment in changing and influencing behavior, why do people so rarely reward others? This is because it is easier to punish than to reward. Punishing someone else lets off steam, which makes us feel better. Furthermore, few of us take action when we are pleased with the way things are going. It is when we are *displeased* that we want to do something. What we often do is look for someone to punish.

For example, when we do not know how to solve a problem, we become frustrated and angry. If we become sufficiently angry, we may try to punish someone in an effort to relieve our anger. An example of this mechanism can be seen in New York State's imposing the penalty of life imprisonment for anyone convicted of pushing drugs in the 1960s. The law was promoted by the governor because he felt frustrated and anxious about the drug situation. Instead of trying a new approach to the problem, he reverted to the simplest solution—punishment.

Reward, Punishment, and Criminal Justice

A knowledge of the principles of reward and punishment can help criminal justice professionals in a number of ways. First, it will help them realize that it is better to ignore trivial infractions than to punish them. For example, many persons become extremely provocative after being arrested. Punishing them for their behavior may seem right, but it makes for more problems in the long run. If their provocations are ignored, the individuals are less likely to continue their annoying behavior.

Second, it will help you steer an offender into more productive behavior. Parole officers can guide their clients into constructive programs. Volunteer programs can help assure that clients go to work. Community-police programs can be geared to present constructive activities to youth. Third, it will help professionals to realize the importance of spending time constructing situations in such a way that problems can be prevented rather than reacted to. This sometimes can be done through active community-relations programs as well as through individual actions.

The Effects of Our Prison System

Our society punishes offenders through an outmoded penal system. Few prison authorities believe it is a good system, since it teaches inmates more about antisocial activities than about living productive lives. Recidivism is high, and even the best of prison systems tend to help the individual learn to be a good prisoner rather than a good citizen.

What then can be done? The answer is not simple; it involves the application of the principles discussed in a fairly rigid, complex system. Many correctional researchers believe that only 1 or 2 percent of our prison population cannot be rehabilitated. For the other 98 or 99 percent, many new programs have been instituted. These programs include alternatives to prison, referral of suspects to community agencies for rehabilitative services even before they are brought to trial. Some have been successful, some not. A major problem seems to be finding agencies and staff that not only believe in the programs but have competency and support to provide adequate direction.

However, as long as our major way of protecting citizens is to keep criminals in our present correctional system, the job of the entire criminal justice community will be difficult.

Summary

Reward may be extrinsic and intrinsic, material or nonmaterial, regular or irregular. All these considerations affect how hard people will work for reward.

People exhibiting undesirable behavior generally do not have other activities that are more rewarding, do not value the approval of others, and have not learned to wait for rewards.

Punishment also may be extrinsic or intrinsic, material or nonmaterial, regular or irregular.

To be effective, punishment must be immediate, meaningful, reasonable, lead to correct behavior, and represent a real loss.

Behavior that is punished only part of the time will continue because it is also rewarded part of the time. Such arbitrary punishment can cause confusion, anxiety, undue emphasis on the forbidden act, anger, and guilt. Ignoring undesirable acts and rewarding desired behavior are frequently more effective.

The police officer will find his work easier if he ignores deliberately provocative behavior, explains options and consequences clearly, and works toward preventative rather than punitive programs.

The high rate of recidivism indicates the ineffectiveness of our current prison system in administering either punishment or reward. Alternative programs need to be freely encouraged and critically evaluated.

Discussion Questions

1. What material rewards motivate police officers (correctional officers)?
2. What nonmaterial rewards motivate police officers (correctional officers)?
3. What kind of rewards could be used to improve performance?
4. Describe a possible police-community relations program. What kind of rewards could be used to motivate teenagers to participate?
5. In what ways can you use theories of reward and punishment in interrogation?
6. How could a probation officer use rewards to influence his clients?

Suggested Reading

Barnett, R. E., and Hagel, John III, eds. *Assessing the Criminal: Restitution, Retribution, and the Legal Process.* Cambridge, Mass.: Ballinger, 1977.

Berkson, Larry C. *The Concept of Cruel and Unusual Punishment.* Lexington, Mass.: Lexington Books, 1975.

Burton, A. *What Makes Behavior Change Possible?* New York: Brunner-Mazel, 1976.

Chorover, S. *From Genesis to Genocide: The Meaning of Human Nature and the Power of Behavior Control.* Cambridge, Mass.: MIT Press, 1980.

Dodge, C. R. *A World without Prisons: Alternatives to Incarceration.* Lexington, Mass.: Lexington Books, 1979.

Poser, E. G., *Behavior Therapy in Clinical Practice.* Springfield, Ill.: Thomas, 1977.

Skinner, B. F. *Beyond Freedom and Dignity.* New York: Alfred A. Knopf, 1971.

Sullivan, D. *The Mask of Love: Corrections in America—Toward a Mutual Aid Alternative* (National University Publications, Multi-Disciplinary Studies in Law). Port Washington, N.Y.: Kennikat, 1980.

Van den Haag, Ernest. *Punishing Criminals.* New York: Basic Books, 1975.

Van Hirsch, A. *Doing Justice.* New York: Hill & Wang, 1976.

CHAPTER 8

Understanding Socioeconomic Class Influences

An understanding of socioeconomic class influences is one of the most important tools of understanding and prediction a criminal justice professional can acquire.

Although our society attempts to provide equal opportunities for all, we have not been successful—nor have we always tried to be—in establishing a society in which all are equal. As a result, life-styles for various groups differ radically. Where people live, how they live, what they read, what they eat, how they raise their children, what they do for recreation differ in accordance with their socioeconomic class.

For example, Richard Parker (*The Myth of the Middle Class*)[1] cites grim statistics on the extent of poverty and the continuing accumulation of wealth by the few (1.5 percent of the population receives 24 percent of the total national income). Our attitudes toward varying occupations also document the continued existence of social status in America, with judgments remaining the same through the years.

Therefore, knowing the socioeconomic class of an individual can help you predict much of his behavior. What newspaper he reads, what television shows he watches, whether he is likely to have a gun in his house, whether he will respond to an officer's knock on the door with violence or politeness can be predicted with some accuracy from a knowledge of the socioeconomic class to which he belongs.

The Socioeconomic Classes

Dividing our society into socioeconomic classes is simply a way of describing where a person fits in the status hierarchy—at the bottom, at the top, or somewhere in the middle. It is basically what you and I are talking about when we describe a person's position in the community. He may be thought of as wealthy, poor, or somewhere in the middle. Sociologists rank people according to what other people think of them. By trying to find out what goes into these judgments, they can then figure out why someone is ranked by others at a low or high level. How important is money? Occupation? Education? The kind of house a person lives in? The neighborhood? The clubs he belongs to?

These are indeed the important factors in ranking people. However, no one factor is decisive. Persons with education tend to be given higher ratings than persons without, though their incomes may be low. A carpenter may make as much money as a teacher, but the teacher has higher status. A physician or lawyer has high social status, even though some physicians and lawyers do not make high salaries. People living in expensive neighborhoods with spacious grounds and large houses tend to get high ratings.

The source of a person's income is also important. A person who gets his income from stock dividends has higher status than a man who goes to work in an office—even an executive office. The length of time a family has had money also has a bearing on its status. To belong to the upper upper class, a family must have had status for generations. Often this means that such a family has little money but high status, since estates may diminish over generations.

Within each socioeconomic class, life-styles are similar and predictable. Attitudes and recreational interests seem to go with particular socioeconomic classes. This is because people influence one another. If all my friends are going bowling, I will go too. People from a socioeconomic class share attitudes because they have been similarly educated. As a psychologist, I have been educated to value certain ideas and attitudes. As a criminal justice professional, you also have been educated to value certain ideas and attitudes. Our occupations—which define our socioeconomic class to some degree—also make it more likely that particular recreational activities will be followed. If you are working physically all day long as a patrolman, you will be unlikely to want to go on a hike on your day off. If you are sitting at a desk, you will be more likely to want to go jogging. Expense also enters into recreational pursuits. It is unlikely that I will ever become a polo player, since polo requires wealth. Skiing is less expensive, but more expensive than patronizing local facilities for baseball, bowling, or skating. My financial status will clearly determine attitudes. If I have a portfolio of stocks and bonds, I will be interested in obtaining tax breaks for business. If I am barely making ends meet, I will be much more concerned with the price of food.

Combining factors of occupation, education, living area, income, and source of income can produce a categorization of three classes. Although there is little to make one believe that one class is inherently better than another, the terms "lower," "middle," and "upper" are applied to groups of people. These categories reflect very different attitudes of other people in society toward these socioeconomic groups. Not only are the terms lower, middle, and upper applied, but further subdivisions of each of the three classes into a lower, middle, and upper segment are used. This suggests intense concern in our society with status. Differentiations include describing a lower lower class that consists of people who are chronically unemployed and therefore at the bottom of the social structure. We describe the upper segment of the same class as having regular but unskilled or semiskilled jobs. The middle class is similarly separated: most lower-middle-class persons have white-collar jobs; most upper-middle-class persons have professional or managerial jobs. This is true even though most people identify themselves as middle class. The top segment is divided mainly on the basis of whether wealth is earned or inherited (see Figure 8.1).

Figure 8.1
Social class in America

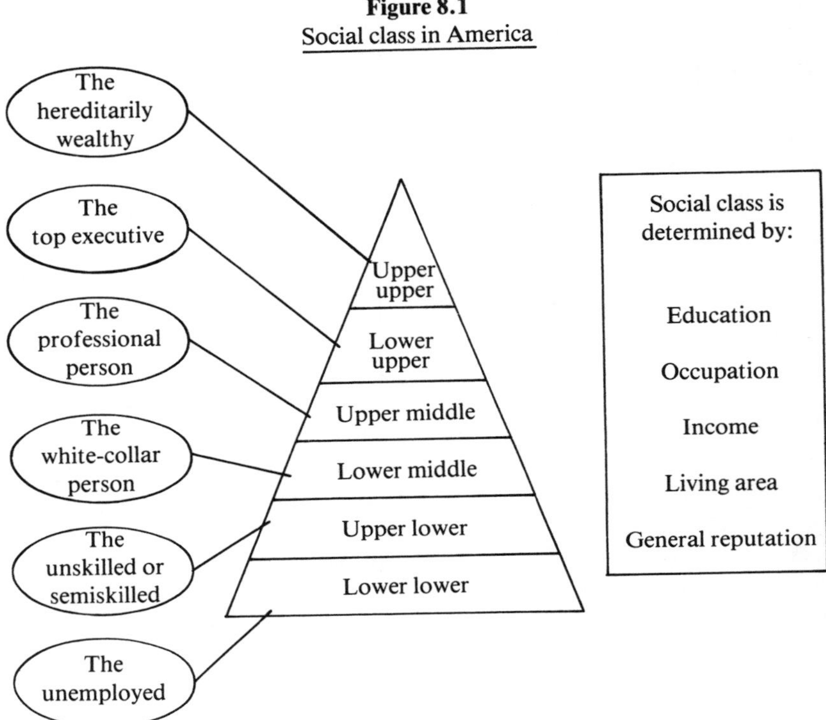

Other ways of stratifying society include doing so by occupational groups. Professional, business, semiprofessional, white-collar, blue-collar are terms frequently used to designate subgroups in our society.

Occupational Differences

Basic occupational differences partially define each class. Lower-lower-class persons typically are either unemployed or employed at occasional, unskilled jobs (see Figure 8.2). Their employment is irregular. They are the first to be laid off in a recession, the last to be rehired. They are the most poorly paid and are subject to the numerous setbacks that go with irregular employment. For example, if an unskilled worker is ill, he doesn't get paid. If he has problems and takes time off from the job, he may be fired. If new groups of people (such as immigrants) swell the labor market, his wages go down. Lower-lower-class persons have little to lose in clashes with the police. Further, their lives have often been filled with violence. Some of them may be violent, physically and verbally, with representatives of the criminal justice system.

Figure 8.2
Lower-lower-class employment

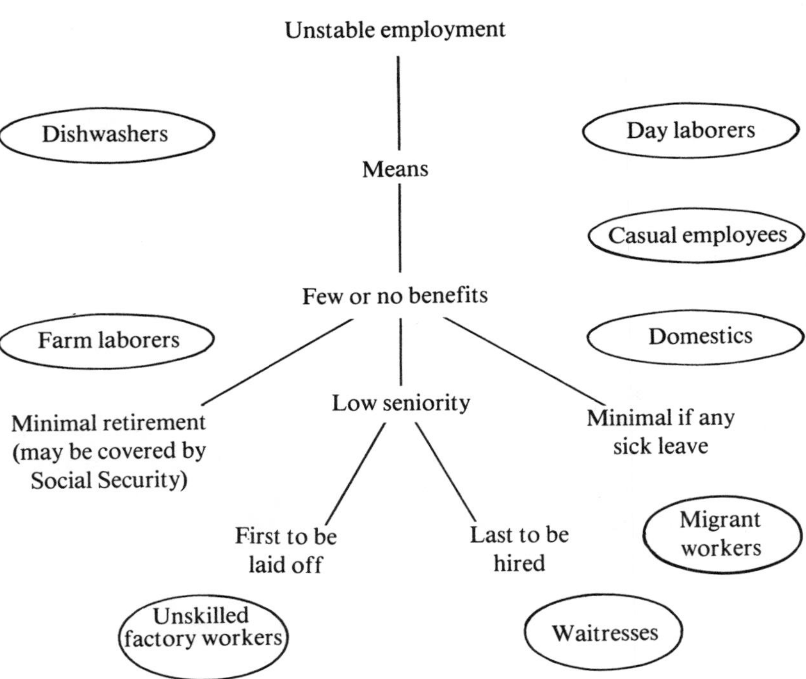

Upper-lower-class workers, or blue-collar workers, have more to lose by clashes with the police than lower-lower-class workers (see Figure 8.3). Their marginally acceptable status makes them insecure. Although people of this class are familiar with violence, they work hard to follow accepted standards of behavior. The police officer should find it much easier to keep a mutually respectful interaction with people from the upper lower class than with people from lower-lower-class backgrounds, although "independents" such as truck drivers may be tougher than others.

Figure 8.3
Upper-lower-class employment

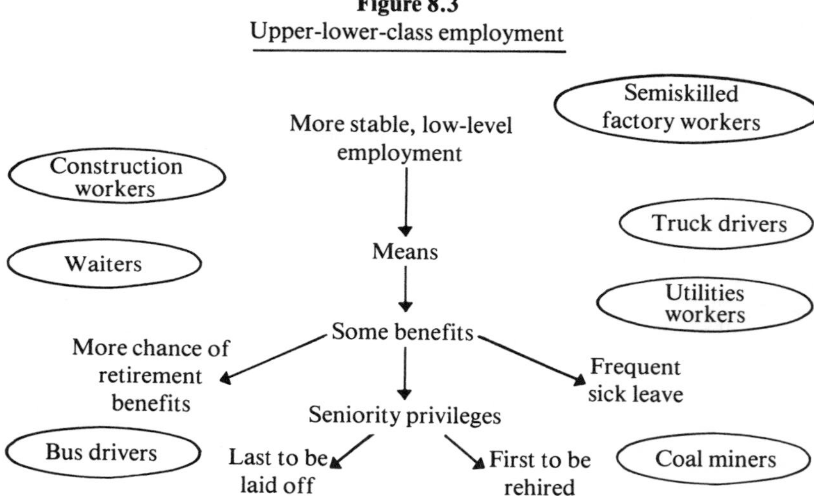

Persons coming from the upper lower class are more likely to resort to violence than white-collar workers, who constitute the most typical members of the lower middle class. The latter work at office jobs as clerks or secretaries or in lower management positions. Middle-middle-class positions include such jobs as public school teacher, salesman, and policeman. As you can see, the middle middle class includes in its ranks persons with at least a high school education and sometimes college (see Figure 8.4).

Persons in this group have worked hard for respectability and rights. They are less insecure about their rights than persons in the upper lower class. They expect to be treated with courtesy. Difficulties with the law are considered shameful. They want to keep such problems as quiet as possible.

However, many lower-middle-class persons have had little training in problem-solving. If pushed, they may resort to name-calling and physical aggression in their dealings with each other. This does not apply to the more educated, or middle middle class.

The upper middle class includes such professionals as doctors, lawyers, middle management people, and proprietors. These persons have a higher degree of education or more capital and income than persons in the lower middle class (see Figure 8.5).

Figure 8.4
Lower-middle- to middle-middle-class employment

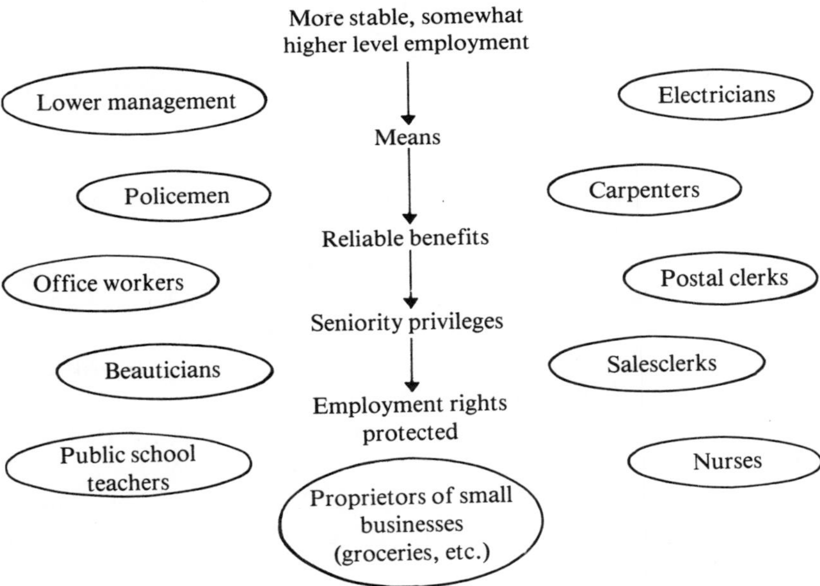

This group poses interesting problems for criminal justice personnel. While arrested less frequently than those in lower socioeconomic classes, persons from this group are more likely to resort to whatever legal means are possible to fight arrest. When dealing with upper-middle-class persons, it is important to be aware of appropriate legal procedures. While persons from this group will not be assaultive, they will not show the kind of respect you might wish. Be courteous and act within your prerogatives. Such persons

Figure 8.5
Upper-middle-class employment

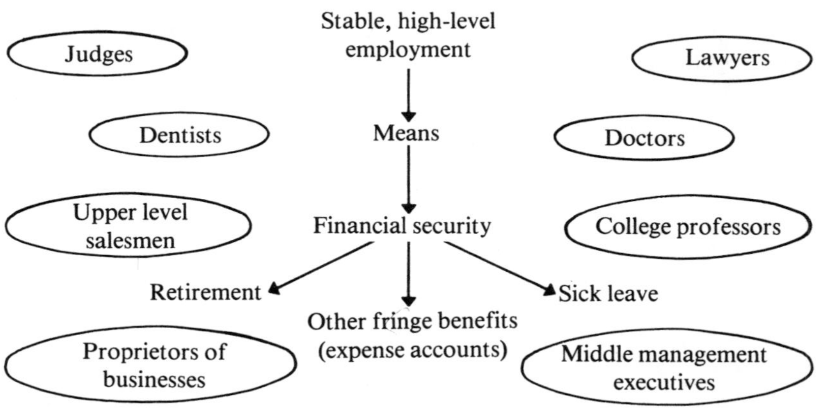

are more likely to be involved with the criminal justice system via white-collar crime.

The two upper classes—lower upper and upper upper—are only slightly differentiated occupationally and financially. Upper-upper-class persons may more frequently own large businesses or do no work, having sufficient income from corporate profits and stock holdings. However, lower-upper-class persons are similar to the upper middle class in engaging in professional, upper management, and business ownership activities (see Figure 8.6).

Members of the upper class are even more likely than upper-middle-class people to use their power to prevent legal interference in their affairs.

Income Differences

It is probably meaningless to pinpoint exact income criteria for the social classes since real money values change so quickly. It is possible, however, to discuss class differences in terms of what typical members of each class can buy.

As suggested earlier, the lower lower class has the least ability to obtain material goods. Income is unstable. A large proportion of

Figure 8.6
Lower-upper and upper-upper-class employment

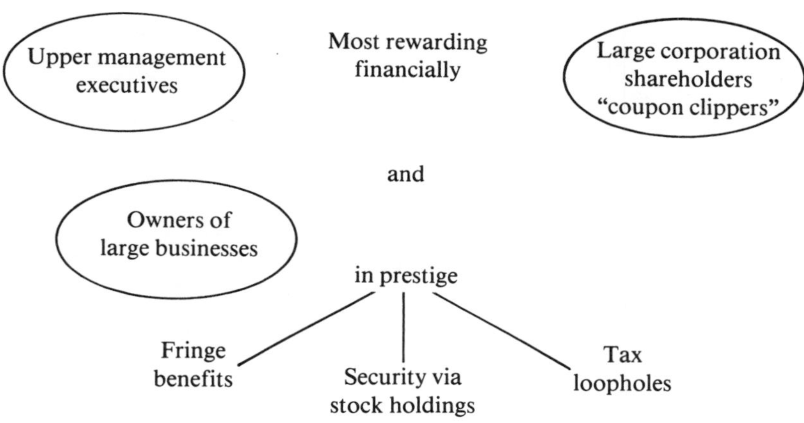

lower-lower-class persons subsist on welfare. Homes are rented; evictions are frequent; and lower-lower-class persons live in the worst sections of town, in the slums and ghettos. Clothing is of poor quality, and larger items will be purchased for above-average prices. These items—furniture, TV sets, stereos, and such appliances as refrigerators, washing machines, and freezers—are purchased on the installment plan. They are frequently repossessed, leaving the family with a bill and no goods.

Persons from the upper lower class, in contrast, usually manage to have neat, though substandard, homes in somewhat better, working-class neighborhoods. Frequently, working-class families laboriously save enough money to purchase their homes. They can do so because their employment is steady. They too buy appliances on installment plans, but they usually can meet their payments. Their furniture, clothing, and automobiles are nevertheless of low quality, and worn items are replaced slowly. The family portrayed in the television program "All in the Family" (with Archie Bunker) was a good example of an upper-lower-class family.

Lower-middle-class persons have a somewhat higher income. They may be able to live in suburbs with attractive, well-kept homes. Although money is always short, lower-middle-class persons are usually able to keep their families well clothed and their homes furnished "respectably."

Upper-middle-class persons, while not "wealthy," tend to have enough money to live not only "respectably" but with many luxuries. Houses are moderate-sized to large, well kept, and furnished with better-quality items. Clothing is not only suitable, but well made and fashionably styled.

Lower-upper-class persons tend to be the wealthiest of all, since the class above them, the upper upper class, usually derives status from "old wealth"; old wealth sometimes diminishes, leaving a family with more status than money. Housing for lower-upper-class persons is in attractive and usually exclusive neighborhoods. Houses are large and well kept. Luxuries are available and evident in styles of clothing, leisure activities, automobiles, and so on.

Attitudinal Differences

One major reflection of class membership is a person's attitude toward himself and others.

The upper-class person, and to a lesser degree the upper-middle-class person, has had many experiences that give him confidence in himself. He is treated courteously by salespersons, waited on quickly in restaurants. In many other situations, he is accorded better treatment than others. He avoids many of the difficulties of life with which others must cope. For example, when the upper-class person travels, he travels first class. What is the difference between first-class travel and other types of travel? Anyone who has had to make trips by bus—waiting in crowded, stuffy, unpleasant bus terminals—knows the difference. Anyone who has had to travel by subway or wait on a street corner in freezing weather knows the difference. Limousines transport upper-class persons to their destinations. Private airplanes are sometimes available. Even on commercial routes, accommodations for first-class passengers duplicate a comfortable and luxurious home setting.

When the upper-class person becomes ill, the best facilities in the country and sometimes the world are mobilized. Treatment is given with courtesy and deference. Contrast this treatment with that of a lower-lower-class person, who must wait in a crowded, stark outpatient clinic for hours and sometimes days. When this patient is finally seen, he frequently is treated not as a person with feelings, but as an object to be handled.

Consider a shopping trip for clothing by the upper-class woman. If she does go to a store (many upper-class persons have clothing brought to them for selection), she will arrive in a carpeted, uncrowded area where she can make her selections while salespersons assist. If she has young children, she leaves them at home with a servant. Women from most of the other classes must battle crowds and look for bargains. The bargains they find are often of poor quality—not really worth the money. The upper-lower-class or lower-middle-class mother typically shops with several children—exhausted and crying by the end of a day. She returns home tired, screaming at the children, clutching several bags, and wondering whether she will have enough money left for the rest of the week's groceries.

As a result of such pleasant or unpleasant experiences, individuals begin to think of themselves as having, or not having, real merit. It is undemocratic, but nevertheless true that we usually rate ourselves the way other people rate us. If we are treated well, we think, "I must be a pretty nice person." If we are treated badly, we think, "I guess there must be something not very good about me." (See Figure 8.7.)

At the time of this writing, numerous articles have described the attitudes of many Americans toward poverty: If people are poor, it must be because they are unworthy. Poor people believe this, too. *It is not true.* People are poor or wealthy for a variety of reasons, one of the major ones being who their parents were. But as long as people believe the poor are unworthy, they will look down on them. Upper-class children will continue to believe that they are better than lower-class children. Black children will continue to regard themselves as inferior to white children. When they are as young as three or four, black children prefer white dolls to black dolls, saying they are prettier. But low self-image is frequently seen in lower-class white children as well. Lower-class parents tend to say to their children, when they are treated less well than upper-class children, "Don't pay any mind to that—you're just as good as they are." But the very statement that "you're just as good as they are" gets the message across—other people think you aren't![2]

In addition to this rather general feeling that "I'm a good per-

Figure 8.7
Attitude toward self

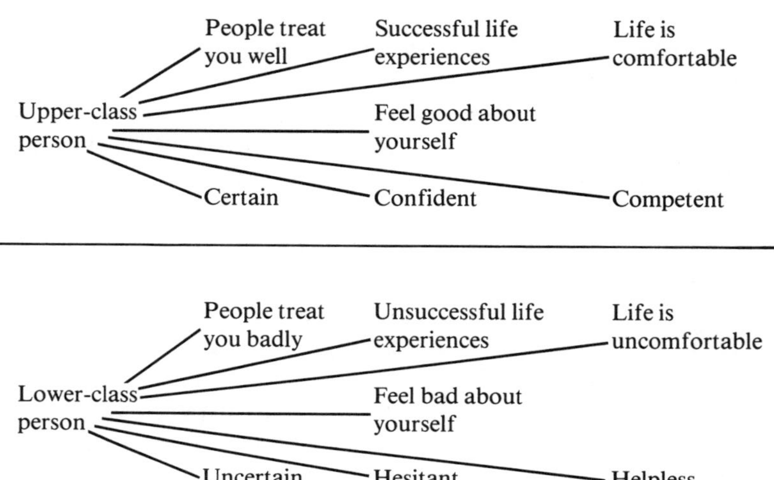

son," members of the upper class tend to have a feeling of competence ("If I can manage things well, I must be capable"). Upper-class children get better grades in school. Without realizing it, teachers give better grades to children who are well dressed. They even tend to perceive them as getting along better with other children, having fewer problems, and so on. So the upper-class child will *feel* he is a better student. And if he should get into a scrape with teachers—or the law—he knows that his parents can bail him out.

All this leads to feelings of self-assurance and success on the part of the member of the upper class. He expects to be treated well. He will politely let others know if he is displeased with them. He does not need to be a street fighter to be successful. If he wants something changed, he can take action, often by making a few casual and friendly phone calls, since the center of power is usually in the hands of upper-class persons like himself. This does not mean that he has no problems; merely that routine elements of life are made easy for him. In fact, sometimes the upper-upper-class person experiences difficulties stemming from the ease with which he receives all the good things in life. If he has never had to work for anything, he may feel incapable of having or achieving goals.

The upper-middle-class person partakes of some of this feeling of competence.

In contrast, lower-middle-class and upper-lower-class persons often develop feelings of uncertainty, unworthiness, and helplessness even though they do not experience the degree of worthlessness felt by lower-lower-class persons. The working-class person or the white-collar worker sees himself as someone worthy of some respect and concern by others—if he is careful and "minds his manners" in all regards. He may be poor, or close to it, but he is respectable. He will dress carefully for special occasions in clothing similar to that worn by upper-class persons. He can get into a shiny automobile, which he lovingly cares for. He can survey the world and say to himself—as his parents may have said to him—"I'm just as good as anybody." If he is careful not to spend his money impulsively, he can acquire those things he considers most valuable—a home in the suburbs, a late-model car, and a college education for one or more of his children.

The lower-lower-class person, however, views himself as unable to get ahead in the world. All around him he sees products and possessions that are supposedly essential to a good and happy life. But with no job, he cannot make the money needed to buy these things. Even if he gets a job temporarily, the money is quickly gone. A lower-lower-class person may save diligently, only to have the money gone in days or weeks when he loses his job. There is little reason to develop a habit of saving. It is small wonder that lower-class persons spend money the way children do—quickly and impulsively for something that appeals.

It is small wonder, too, that children of lower-class families frequently steal what they can. When they do get into trouble with the law, they are treated badly compared to the way upper-class children are treated; and they are much more frequently sent to reform schools, where their feelings about themselves deteriorate further.

Personality Differences

All these differences in experience lead to differences in personality.

Contrasting the two ends of the social ladder, the upper-class child lives in a relatively safe and protected world. He is encouraged to learn. His education differs from that of the lower-class child in that it teaches him to make fine discriminations, to understand complexities. Understanding these complexities allows him to develop useful problem-solving skills, which in turn enable him to become even more competent and capable.

Because he feels worthwhile, he can be tolerant of others. (People who feel positively about themselves tend to think of others positively.) Because he is not threatened economically, he is not worried that other groups will deprive him of his means of subsistence. He is therefore less likely to be prejudiced or to discriminate against others.

In contrast, the lower-lower-class person's life is consumed with trying to obtain the bare essentials. He sees himself as helpless to change his condition; and in most cases he is. Without the tools to understand the world, without the position in society that makes getting ahead easy, his struggles will be largely unrewarded. The lower-lower-class person therefore tends to see things in terms of bare power. He does not expect to treat others well; nor does he expect to be treated well by others.

Differences in Treatment by Institutions

We have suggested that persons from different social classes are treated differently by others. Now we shall discuss briefly the differences in treatment by institutions—the criminal justice system, utilities systems, banks and other lending institutions, health care systems, and schools.

The Criminal Justice System. While it may not be true in your locality, it is generally true that the criminal justice system operates differently for different classes. Children of upper- or upper-middle-class families are rarely included in crime statistics. On the other hand, children of lower-class families account for an unduly large proportion of juvenile delinquency figures. Is this because upper-class children are less likely to be involved in antisocial behavior? As discussed more fully in Chapter 17, upper-class children commit the same kinds of offenses as lower-class children. While the frequency of their crimes is probably less, they are also less likely to be apprehended than are lower-class children, who are always likely suspects. If they are apprehended, upper-class children will more frequently be sent home to their parents with a warning. If they are booked, they are likely to be given a light sentence or placed on probation. Children of lower-class families are frequently apprehended and sent to reform schools—where they are given good training in how to develop criminal careers![3]

The bail system also has different effects on different classes. Some people regard the bail system as underlying most problems of the criminal justice system. Because middle- and upper-class persons are able to "make bail," their whole experience when apprehended is totally different from that of lower-class persons. Those with higher social status do not have to languish in jail; they therefore are better able to prepare a case. Usually they hire an expensive lawyer, who will have adequate time and money to prepare the case. The suspect can work for an acquittal—instead of pleading guilty to a lesser charge to avoid a more serious conviction. For lower-class persons who cannot make bail, the likelihood of an acquittal is remote. They have no money to hire a private lawyer. In civil cases, they will not be represented at all. In criminal cases, a public defender may be able to spend only a few minutes talking to them before the case is tried. Civil cases will be lost. In criminal cases, the arrested person will end up with a record—which can have serious consequences for his future.

Utilities Systems. Different treatment for different social classes is also reflected by utilities systems. I personally have been impressed by the different treatment I have received by the same telephone company, depending on my residence. When I lived in a lower-class area, I received threatening letters when I paid my bill only a few days late. In an upper-middle-class area, the bill could be left unpaid for months; the only repercussion would be a polite note asking whether payment had been "overlooked."

Banks and Other Lending Institutions. A similar situation occurs with banks and other lending institutions. A well-dressed individual who enters a bank and asks for credit will receive courteous attention. Frequently his loan will be processed immediately. A poorly dressed individual will be thoroughly investigated; frequently his loan application will be turned down. Lower-class persons may be forced to turn to small loan companies, which charge higher interest for loans. Frequently, they turn to "loan sharks," sometimes with tragic results, since such loans often are controlled by criminals, who may charge as much as 1,000 percent in repayment. As a result, the individual is in virtual slavery to the loan shark. Threats of physical harm may further keep the debtor in line, or he may have to participate in illegal activities.

Health Care Systems. Health care is less frequently available for the lower-class person; when it is, it is often of poor quality. I remember vividly the plight of a lower-lower-class client who was on welfare and pregnant. Although living in a large city, she was not eligible for any prenatal care. This was true even though it would have been less expensive to provide good prenatal care than to have later problems with mother and child. Yet the only care possible for this woman was emergency room treatment when she was about to deliver.

In general, emergency or clinic treatment is the only care possible for the person without financial resources. Mortality rates are much higher for lower-lower-class infants than for babies in other groups. Mothers must bring their sick children to pediatric clinics, but sometimes these clinics are a long distance away. It is almost impossible for a mother with young children, with no transportation and no money, to get to them. Older people are similarly unable to make use of medical resources, or they lack knowledge about how to find them. None of these problems beset the middle- to upper-class person.

Schools. Many reasons have been suggested for the pronounced social class differences in school success, an area of deep social concern (see Figure 8.8). Some people believe that abilities of children differ according to social class, but there are many other possible and probably more reasonable explanations.

One major explanation is that schools conform to middle-class expectations. Children are expected to be quiet, clean, and neat. The lower-class child is discriminated against because he does not conform to these expectations. He comes to school undernourished and overtired. Both these factors contribute to poor performance. Further, there is little in his environment to make him feel that school success is important. On top of that, he must learn a "new" language. (Recent studies suggest that most middle-class persons do not fully understand the "lower-class language."

Phrases that we consider ungrammatical may actually be more conducive to problem-solving, and more descriptive, than "correct" phrases.[4]) If a person uses "poor grammar," school personnel almost immediately categorize him as uneducated and probably unintelligent—if not immoral.

The teachers sent to ghetto schools are less experienced; they have poorer facilities with which to work. The lack of stimulation in the early environments of their pupils also adds to their educational handicap. In fact, many studies suggest that, without such early stimulation, children do not reach their full potential intelligence. The net result is that lower-class children—especially lower-lower-class children—usually drop out of school, while children higher on the status ladder stay in school and graduate, frequently going on to college and graduate school.

The subject matter taught to different socioeconomic groups is also quite different. Upper-class neighborhood schools tend to teach the complexities of the political process. Lower-class neighborhood schools do not. Problem-solving is stressed in the upper-class schools; obedience in the lower.

Child-Rearing Differences

As suggested earlier, there are major differences in child-rearing among the social classes. Middle-class mothers are attentive to

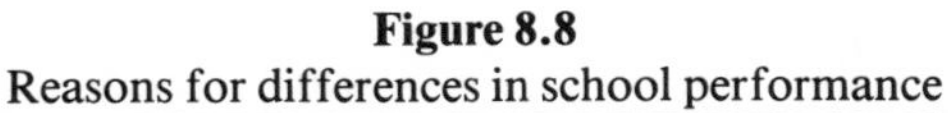

Figure 8.8
Reasons for differences in school performance

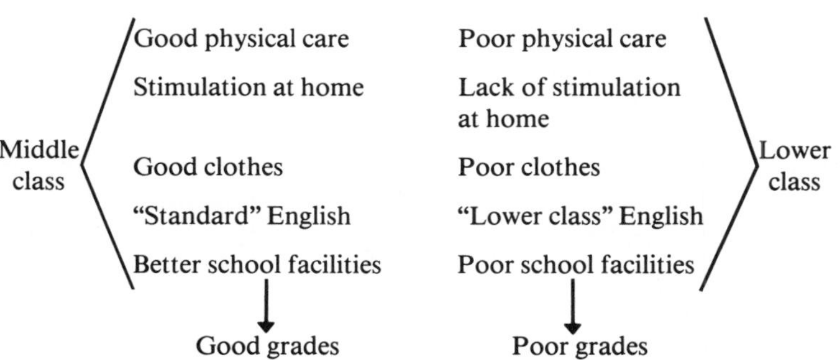

their children's needs, allow little freedom, and expect high achievement. Lower-class mothers are less attentive to their children's needs, allow them a great deal of freedom, and expect little in the way of achievement. In regard to freedom, the pattern is reversed for the upper middle class, with more freedom for children to come and go, though with attentiveness to achievement.

Patterns of communication of parents and children also change with social class. Middle-class mothers talk to their children a great deal. When they tell them what to do, they are likely to tell them why. Lower-class mothers talk to their children very little. They tend not to explain why the child should or should not do something.

Of all the social classes, the lower middle class is probably the strictest in regulating behavior. Lower-middle-class parents have a strong feeling that children must be respectful toward parents and other authorities. Upper-middle-class parents are not as worried about their status and therefore allow their children to get dirty, argue with them, explore, and question authority.

Child-rearing practices of upper-class families have not been extensively studied. A recent study by Robert Coles, however, suggests that such children feel "entitled" to privilege, pleasure, and a purpose to which they can devote their lives.[5] Their expectation that good things will consistently happen to them is confirmed, and they go through life with an easy acceptance of what they believe are their privileges.

Recreational Differences

While it is not possible to specify exactly which leisure activities are chosen by the different social classes, definite trends can be identified in the choice of recreational pursuits.

These trends are based on convenience, expense, and how well the activity complements the person's work. For example, if I live near the ocean, I can easily go swimming. But if I live away from lakes or ocean, I may have to join an expensive country club, and travel to get there. If I work hard physically all day, I might prefer to watch television.

The way I socialize will also differ. Arranging elaborate parties takes time and money. If I earn little, I will prefer to visit friends, or go to the local bar.

Identifying Social Class Membership

While the preceding discussion should give you some understanding of how and why persons of different socioeconomic class origin behave differently, it is useful to know some signs of class membership.

Just as in the play "My Fair Lady" Professor Higgins made great efforts to change the language usage and pronunciation of his charge, so can we identify different social classes by their language. Colloquialisms are more frequent in lower-class speech, such as "carry" instead of "go with" ("I'm going to carry her to the market") or "Man, you're jiving me" to express skepticism, "Who you talkin' to (boy or girl)" or "I'm in check with you" to express dissatisfaction or agreement.[6] Middle-class and upper-class membership is related to more uniform speech. There is more cursing in the lower class in single-sex company. Middle-class people curse less than in the lower and also the upper class, where cursing is used for emphasis.[7]

Sex roles are different in different classes. Equality is becoming more valued in our society generally, but middle- and upper-class families tend to adopt new social stances more quickly than lower-class families. In lower-class families, the norm has been for women to stay home if they can, though most must work. In middle- and upper-class families, income is sometimes needed, but there is an acceptance of work as a satisfying outlet.

Patterns of dress also differ. Upper-upper class persons tend to be conservative, probably because they have no desire to show off their status. Lower-upper-class persons usually wear designer clothing—expensive, elegant, impressive. Upper-middle-class persons tend to imitate the patterns of the lower-upper-class, but their clothes are less expensive and mass-produced. Lower-middle-class and upper-lower-class persons tend to dress less fashionably. The lower-lower-class person tends to imitate high fashion in an exaggerated manner.

Home furnishings follow the same trends, with furniture in the upper-class or upper-middle-class expensive, decorator planned, with experimentation in styles. Upper-middle-class homes are those most usually depicted in television advertising. Lower-middle-class furnishings are standardized more frequently, with a tendency to display sentimental articles and plaques. "All in the Family" depicted an upper-lower-class city home with both its shabbiness and cleanliness.

The trends may be summarized as follows: While the upper groups usually furnish their homes to please themselves, other groups try to imitate the social class above them. For example, the upper middle classes try to imitate the lower upper classes; the lower middle try to imitate the upper middle; and the upper lower try to be middle class. The lower-class person imitates upper classes in a manner easy to spot because it is overdone. Upper-middle-class and upper-class persons frequently attempt to be "different." The lower classes try to be "the same."

It is important to remember, however, that these characterizations are not absolute. There will be exceptions in all classes, and families on the borderline between two classes will usually display mixed characteristics.

It is also important to realize that persons who have moved from one class to another, who are mobile, display characteristics different from those described. Their behavior is likely to be a combination of styles, with new problems and/or benefits.

Meaning for the Criminal Justice Community

Understanding the problems and attitudes of persons of various classes will help in dealing with them. Knowing that the lower-lower-class person expects to be mistreated will help you realize that he is likely to try to mistreat you first. Knowing that the upper-lower-class person is concerned with respectability—but is likely to have few resources for dealing with problems—will help you help him. He can use help in seeing alternative solutions to his difficulties; but you must be tactful in your suggestions. Knowing that people at the upper end of the social strata will expect deference and sophistication from you will make it easier for you to do your job in dealing with them.

You must most of all realize that while all people are "the same," they are the same in different ways. Every individual wants to be respected, but this respect must be offered appropriately. Speaking a language that a person understands, demonstrating awareness of his difficulties and a feeling for his style of life will help you modify your behavior effectively. Understanding the similarities in social class behavior, as well as individual differences, will help you figure out what is happening in, say, a family fight. Then you can more easily decide what to do about it.

Summary

Socioeconomic classes in the United States are usually designated as upper, middle, and lower, with each class in turn divided into upper, middle, and lower segments.

Other ways of dealing with stratification are through occupational categories. Social class is usually determined by occupation, income, area of residence, general reputation, and education. Each class also displays differences in personalities, child-rearing practices, recreational choices, and personal habits.

Social class frequently determines how much respect an individual will receive—from other people, from institutions, and from himself.

Understanding the characteristics and attitudes of the various social classes will help in dealing realistically and effectively with them.

Discussion Questions

1. In what ways do your attitudes reflect a particular social class?
2. In what ways does social class affect the treatment of people who are arrested?
3. Do you think it is possible to adopt attitudes of a social class different from one's family of origin? What effect would this have on someone?

Suggested Reading

Beeghley, L. *Social Stratification in America.* Santa Monica, Calif.: Goodyear, 1978.

Bendix, R., and Lipset, S. M., eds. *Class, Status and Power: A Reader in Social Stratification*. Rev. ed. New York: Free Press, 1966.

Coleman, R., and Rainwater, L. *Social Standing in America*. New York: Basic Books, 1978.

Cooper, J. L. *The Police and the Ghetto*. National University Publications, Multidisciplinary Studies of the Law. Port Washington, N.Y.: Kennikat, 1979.

Davis, A., and Dollard, J. *Children of Bondage*. Washington, D.C.: American Council on Education, 1940.

Levison, P. *The Working Class Majority*. New York: Coward, McCann, 1974.

Lundberg, Margaret. *The Incomplete Adult*. Westport, Conn.: Greenwood Press, 1974.

Mills, C. W. *White Collar: American Middle Classes*. New York: Oxford University Press, 1956.

Parker, R. *The Myth of the Middle Class*. New York: Liveright, 1972.

Reed, J. A. "You Are What You Wear." *Human Behavior*, July, 1974.

Reiman, J. H. *Rich Get Richer and the Poor Get Prison: Ideology, Class, and Criminal Justice*. Somerset, N.J.: John Wiley, 1979.

Warner, W. L., et al. *Yankee City*. New Haven, Conn.: Yale University Press, 1963. (Classic statement on social class.)

Wright, E. *Class, Crisis and the State*. London: Shocken, Verso, 1979.

CHAPTER 9

Mental Illness

While there are almost as many ways to be mentally ill as to be mentally healthy, it is useful to understand the general meaning of such common terms as *crazy, neurotic,* or *psychotic.* With such knowledge, it may be easier to understand and make predictions about individuals whose behavior is strange. There are also legal principles related to mental illness; these principles become very important when a person is brought to trial. Another reason for understanding mental illness is that it helps us understand normal persons, as will be explained below.

Theoretical Concepts

Mental illness is a unique kind of animal. First, let us discuss what it is not. It is not an illness like the flu or measles (see Figure 9.1). It is not something with an easily identifiable cause. It is not something with symptoms that are the same for everyone throughout the course of the illness; nor is it something with a definite time limit. Causes and effects vary.

Some people feel that the term *mental illness* is misleading, since it tends to imply that emotional problems are like physical problems. Many people prefer to talk about "emotional difficulties" rather than mental illness. We, however, can use the more common term if we don't get bogged down by this thinking that emo-

Figure 9.1
Physical and mental illness

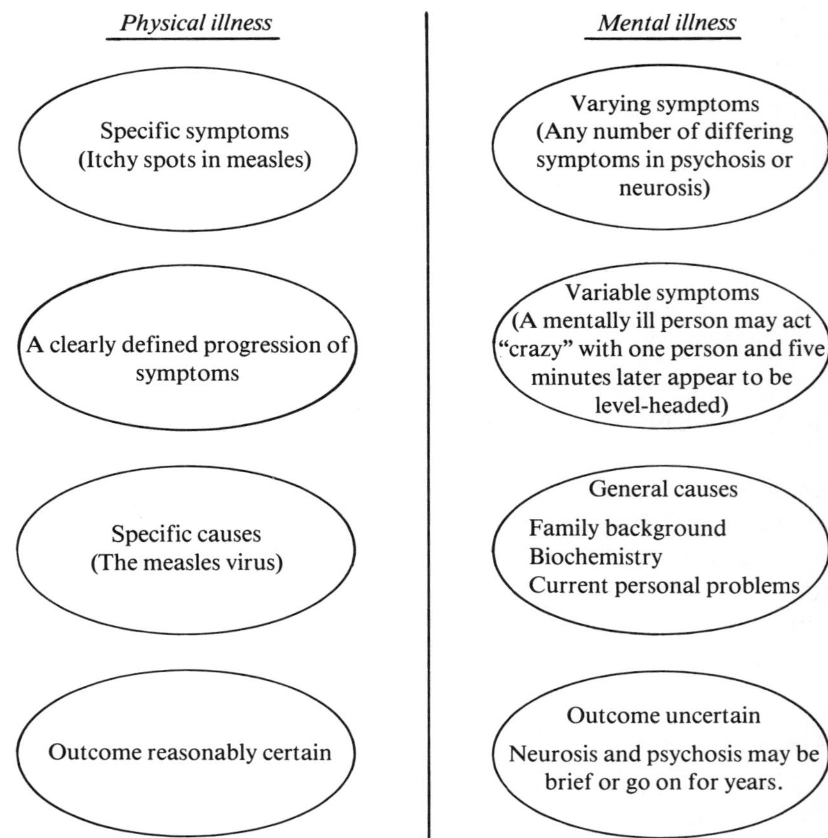

tional problems are like physical illnesses. In fact, the mentally ill have many of the same problems mentally healthy people do, but these problems are of greater intensity, or greater quantity, or both.

If we are to understand mental illness, it is important that we be able to see the similarities between the mentally ill and the mentally healthy (see Figure 9.2).

Figure 9.2
Mental health and illness

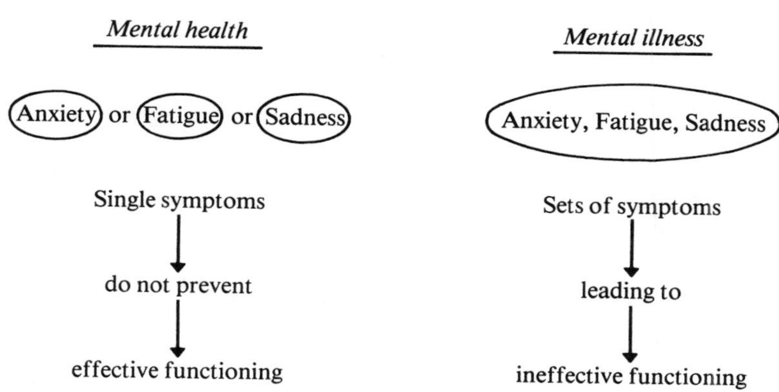

We must also be able to see the differences in order to avoid suffering from something called "medical students' disease." Medical students, when reading about the symptoms of various diseases, often see similarities with their own symptoms. Brain tumors are characterized by headaches. The student has a headache. Maybe he has a brain tumor. This "disease" happens to psychology students as well. For example, manic-depressive psychosis is characterized by up-and-down moods. Maybe you feel up some days and down some days. This mood swing may help you understand the manic-depresssive person, but it does not mean you are suffering from manic-depressive psychosis for the following reason.

Just as one swallow does not make a summer, one symptom does not make a disease. It is a combination of symptoms, making the person unable to function effectively, that comprises illness, including mental illness (again, see Figure 9.2). Abnormal functioning can be of various types (neurotic, sociopathic, psychotic). These types of functioning often overlap but are nevertheless distinguishable.

Normal functioning is extremely difficult to define. Roughly, it means that we solve our problems reasonably effectively, that we don't let our hangups get in the way of enjoying life. It means that we have people in our lives whom we love and help, and who love and help us. It means that we find our work satisfying.

Or normal functioning may mean that we are doing something about finding people and work that will give us satisfaction. It means we have goals in life. It means we are doing something about reaching our goals. It also means that we are functioning in a "whole" kind of way.

In abnormal functioning, people are unaware of how they feel, of what their goals and desires really are. Their motivation is unconscious. This means that they are like automobile drivers who are driving in one direction while wanting to go in another. Their actions and desires are not "put together," or integrated. Sigmund Freud was the first person to make this link with the unconscious widely known. His method of psychoanalysis helps people talk out and discover their hidden motivations and desires.

As an example of unconscious motivation, we might look at a boy who sets fires because in some way he receives sexual pleasure from his actions. He will tell you he does not know why he sets fires. He is telling the truth. If he knew why, he could then obtain sexual pleasure in approved ways. He would not be considered mentally ill. But because obtaining sexual pleasure is frightening to him he has "forgotten" (repressed) his desire for it. As a result, setting fires comes out as a symptom of his repressed desire. Symptoms are therefore expressions of goals that are not accepted (see Figure 9.3).

How can you tell whether behavior is a symptom reflecting repressed emotions or whether it is an expression of an ordinary desire or goal? One way is to see whether what a person says fits with what he does. If you have a friend who says he wants to change jobs but never takes the opportunity to look for another, his complaint is a symptom. Perhaps a friend of yours says he

Figure 9.3
Origin of symptoms

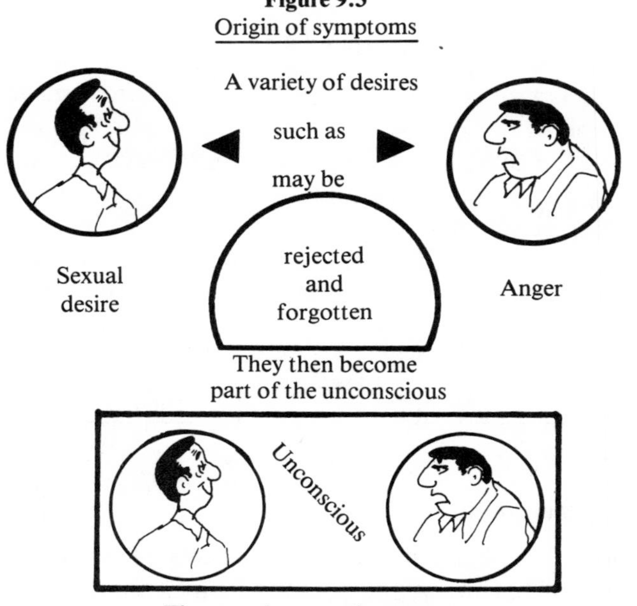

They sneak out and reappear as:

Symptoms
(which may be more or less serious)

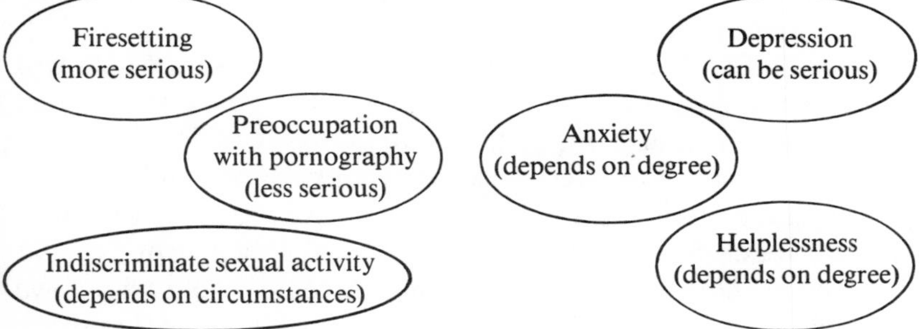

wants to be helpful, but instead he manages to make things more difficult. His behavior is a symptom (see Figure 9.4).

Figure 9.4
When is a behavior a symptom?

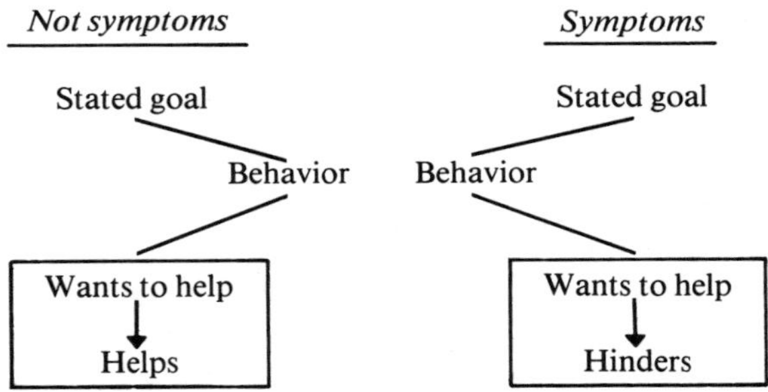

Abnormal Functioning

When goals and behavior or other aspects of personality are seriously out of harmony, the person is functioning abnormally and may be *neurotic, sociopathic,* or *psychotic.* Although the categories described here have been revised somewhat (see the American Psychiatric Association's *Diagnostic Manual of Disorders,* 3rd ed., 1980), they continue to represent a simple way of describing types of mental illness.

Neurotic functioning is not dissimilar to the ways in which you and I function, because there are some areas in which we, too, are not totally "together": our behavior and our stated goals diverge. For the most part, however, we know what we want, and we try to get it. If there are quite a few areas in which we are confused about what we are doing and why, then we are probably neurotic—or at least functioning neurotically in these areas. People who have hangups that keep them from doing most of the things that other people do may be more properly labeled neurotic.

Sociopathic functioning may appear similar to normal functioning. However, it involves a separation of goals and behavior from conscience. The most characteristic aspect of sociopathic behavior is the lack of real concern for others. Sociopaths do not have a conscience in the sense that you and I do. We shall discuss why this is so, and what it means, a little later.

Psychotic functioning is the least "together," the least oriented toward reality. Severe psychotics may live almost totally in a world of their own. They communicate symbolically, if at all. Many less severely ill psychotics, however, have areas in which they behave normally. Only in the most severe psychosis does the person seem totally cut off from society.

Neurosis

While most neurotic persons have a variety of symptoms, certain sets of symptoms are known as *anxiety neurosis, phobic neurosis, dissociative neurosis, depressive neurosis, obsessive-compulsive neurosis,* and *conversion neurosis.*

The person who suffers from an *anxiety neurosis* will feel fearful and upset. He will not understand why he is so worried. He may suffer from rapid heartbeat and excessive sweating—both physical symptoms of fear.

The person suffering from a *phobic neurosis* will try to avoid particular situations—perhaps elevators, airplanes, or high places. Instead of being vaguely anxious, he is frightened of something in particular, which he will avoid. However, what he is really frightened of is something different. Avoiding elevators does not alleviate the original fear. Instead, it may even make it worse. For example, a woman frightened of her own sexual impulses refused to travel on buses. She did not know why bus travel scared her; unconsciously she knew that if she went out she might meet young men and have to deal with her sexual impulses. By believing she was afraid of buses, she was able to hide her fear of sexuality from herself.

The *dissociative neurosis* includes cases of multiple personality, as in *The Three Faces of Eve.*[1] Persons with this type of neurosis may function as completely different personalities at different times. This is rare, however. Amnesia is another type of dissociative neurosis. An individual with amnesia may forget everything about his life. For example, a man was having an affair and could not bring himself to leave his wife or break up with his mistress. He was under increasing pressure from both. One night he bought a bus ticket to a distant city. Once there, he could not remember who he was. While this man was not aware of what he was doing, unconsciously he was escaping. You can see that almost anyone in a conflict situation would want "to get away from it all."

Depressive neurotics are people who are sad, tired, and feel worthless most of the time. While all of us feel depressed at times – frequently when we are tired – we usually recover in a few days. People who are neurotically depressed remain so. These people feel angry and helpless. They usually feel better if they can express their anger, but they are afraid to do so.

Obsessive-compulsive neurotics feel forced to think about irrational ideas or engage in irrational behavior. Lady Macbeth's continual hand washing is an example of a compulsive symptom. The person who feels forced to check again and again to see whether he has locked the house is suffering from a compulsive symptom. Compulsive people express their anxiety by doing the same thing over and over.

Conversion neurosis is less common today than it was in the early part of the nineteenth century. It used to be called *hysteria* and involved expressing symptoms through bodily disabilities. For example, a woman who was afraid she might use her hand to strike her father developed a paralysis of her hand and arm. This was not a true paralysis in the physical sense. However, the woman was not aware that she could use her arm. She would have become very frightened if someone had convinced her that there was nothing wrong with her arm.[2]

Sociopathy

For criminal justice professionals, sociopathy is the most important kind of mental illness to understand. *Sociopath* (or *psychopath,* an older term) is the word used to describe a person with the life-style of a criminal. Some sociopaths may become criminals because everyone else in the area engages in delinquent or criminal behavior. (In ghetto areas, for example, *not stealing* is considered antisocial behavior by most kids.) Others are criminals because they themselves have decided – for a variety of reasons – that criminality is more rewarding than a regular job.

Sociopaths are frequently described as having no conscience. Their relationships with others are distant.[3] The "con man" is a good example of this kind of sociopath. He is charming and intelligent and may lead a normal and successful life—if he gets away with his operation. I recall a con man who had written a large check, expecting it to be covered by another deal he was working out. The deal was delayed, the check bounced, and this particular con man ended up in a psychiatric reception center, disturbed to the extent of being labeled psychotic.

With the exception of sociopaths who are merely conforming to their environments, most sociopaths have had lives in which reward has been inconsistent and unpredictable. Frequently, they have been treated harshly and unjustly. The sociopath therefore ends up feeling that he might as well get what he wants. Those who reared him set no example of fair play, caring, and reward for good performance.

The author has collected early memories of sociopaths including such recollections as "the way my sister would punish me when I lived with them. I thought she did it unjustly." Or "the death of my boyhood friend from drowning in the bathtub, and how I blamed his mother." Or "the day my father hit me and knocked me out. My brother used to laugh at me because I could not be included in sports."

Psychosis

Psychosis is the mental illness we refer to when we talk about someone's being "crazy." What we mean is that he or she is unable to function in society. Psychotic persons are unable to live normal lives. They may be married or may hold jobs, but at some point they are not able to continue in their marriages or jobs. For example, the psychotic worker may one day complain that he must leave his job because his office is bugged, that his co-workers are all spies of the CIA, and that there is an international network attempting to nail him. This type of suspicion is distinguishable from realistic concerns. The individual inflates his own importance. A psychotic individual also may stop coming to work. He may spend more and more time daydreaming, alone in his room. He might begin to hallucinate, to see or hear things that aren't there. He may behave quite strangely when under the influence of such hallucinations. Some psychotics commit crimes that they say they were told to perform by "the voices." A few such persons are dangerous, although most psychotics are so withdrawn that they are less harmful to society than many normal people.

Legally, psychotic persons are those who, under the McNaughton or Durham rules, are considered not responsible for their crimes. These rules state that people who did not at the time of the crime understand what they were doing (the McNaughton rule), or had a mental illness contributing to the crime (the Durham rule), are not responsible. These rulings, however, are difficult, if not impossible, to apply consistently. They have come under a great deal of fire from mental health and legal professionals. New definitions are currently being developed of how a "criminally insane" person should be defined and dealt with.[4]

Psychosis is divided into two major types: (1) *organic psychosis,* resulting from physical disease or damage, and (2) *functional psychosis,* resulting from emotional problems.

Organic Psychosis. People who have accidents may be confused and disoriented afterward. This is because they have been brain-damaged. People with certain diseases also may become confused. Some older people suffer from what is called *senile psychosis.* It originates when, due to hardening of the arteries, insufficient blood circulates to the brain. The result is damage to brain cells. Senile persons may wander about, not knowing where their homes are. Their clothing may be in disarray. They may be unable to remember what has happened to them. Such people need constant care. Although many persons suffering brain damage from an accident recover their functions after a lapse of time, or with retraining, there is little hope of recovery for senile persons.

Another type of organic psychosis is *alcoholic psychosis,* sometimes appearing in older alcoholics. In younger alcoholics one frequently sees acute alcoholic psychosis, otherwise known as the DT's (delirium tremens).

Another type of psychosis is caused by drugs such as LSD (acid). Persons who have taken LSD sometimes become disoriented or frightened. They have ideas of grandeur (thinking they can fly, for example) and often have hallucinations (seeing things that are not there) or delusions (seeing something in distorted form). Visual distortions such as those described in *Alice in Wonderland* are common in drug-induced psychosis. These persons need constant attention until their brains clear.

Another organic psychosis comes from syphilis and is known as Korsakoff's syndrome.

Figure 9.5
Organic psychoses

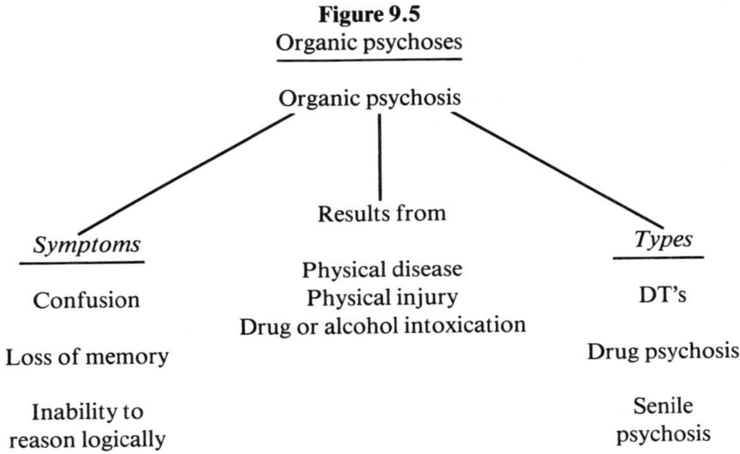

Functional Psychosis. The second type of psychosis is due to emotional disturbance. There are two major types of functional psychosis: *schizophrenia* and *manic-depressive psychosis.*

Schizophrenia is the most common psychosis; it is the illness most people think of when they speak of "crazy people." The man who walks down the street talking loudly to himself (sometimes we all mutter, but quietly) is schizophrenic. The woman who turns around three times at each corner before crossing the street is schizophrenic. While schizophrenia is not split personality, it does involve a lack of organization in the personality. Feelings, thoughts, and behavior do not cohere. However, if you understand the schizophrenic, you will find that his behavior has definite meaning. The woman who turns around three times at street corners is magically warding off danger. More normal people may carry a rabbit's foot or consult their astrology charts to reassure themselves.

The more frightened we are, the more we look for magical reassurance. This is the basis not only for many superstitions but also for many schizophrenic symptoms. Much of the violent behavior of schizophrenics is caused by terror and may be stopped by reassurance. For example, if you tell a criminal out for profit that you will not allow him to hurt you, it won't do much good. But telling a schizophrenic the same thing could be enough to change his behavior. A gentle, firm approach is necessary. The schizophrenic will feel that you are protecting him from himself.

Figure 9.6 shows some of the common symptoms of schizophrenia. Terror is common to all schizophrenics except those who feel nothing. Symbolic language is also common. Some of the other symptoms may or may not be present. While many schizophrenics hallucinate, some do not. Many schizophrenics have ideas of reference (thinking everyone and everything that happens is directed at them); some do not.

Figure 9.6
Symptoms of schizophrenia

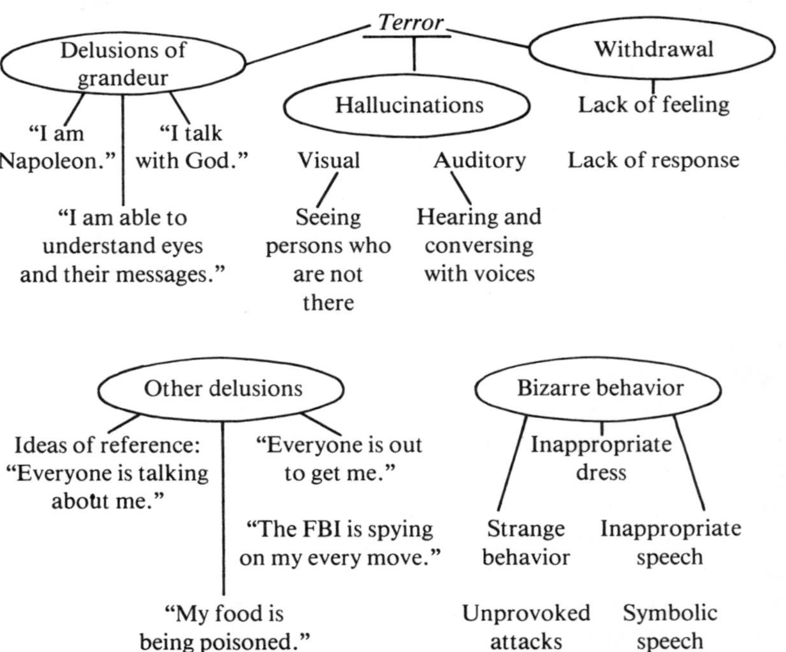

Manic-depressive psychosis is less common than schizophrenia, but easier to understand. For example, we all have mood ups and downs, gloomy Mondays, "the blahs"—and also times when everything seems great. Manic-depressive psychosis represents an exaggeration of these moods (see Figure 9.7). A variant of manic-depressive psychosis, depressive psychosis, is very similar. The difference is that the individual does not go through the "high" phase but instead is acutely depressed.

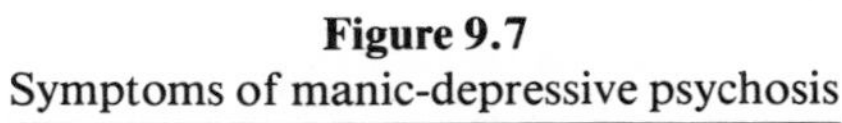

Figure 9.7
Symptoms of manic-depressive psychosis

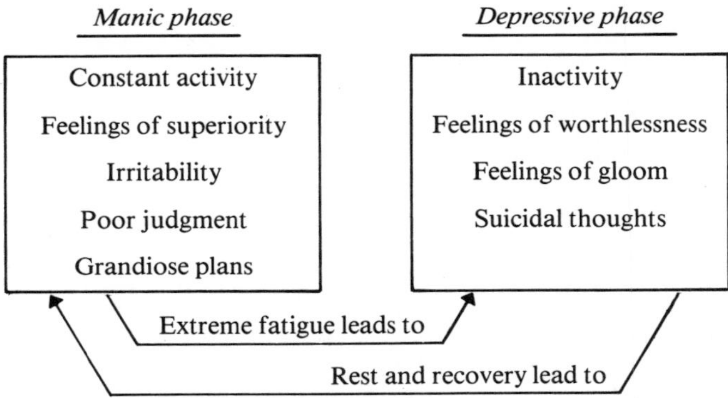

In the manic phase an individual, while seemingly normal, may build himself up to such a height of activity that he shows extremely poor judgment. Property, reputation, and job status all may be thrown out the window in his frenzy of activity. Such individuals need protection.

The manic phase ends when the individual eventually becomes extremely fatigued, discouraged, and depressed. He now expresses feelings of total worthlessness and sees no point in living. He becomes unable to function in his usual daily activities.

Depressions, whether neurotic (in which the individual maintains some degree of normal functioning), psychotic (in which he does not), or normal (in which the depression is neither very long nor very intense), are frequently self-limiting. This means that after a time the person begins to behave more normally. However, in the period of getting over a depression, the suicidal risk is greatly increased. This is because the individual now has more energy at his disposal while he feels worthless. He therefore may do something about his "worthlessness"—destroy himself.

Treatment of Mental Illness

Mental illness may be treated through the use of physical or psychological means. Physical means include the use of tranquilizing (calming) and energizing (activating) drugs and the administration of shock therapies. Psychological means include psychotherapy, in which an individual talks about his problem with a psychotherapist (social worker, psychologist, or psychiatrist), either individually or in a group. Environmental therapy is another way of helping disturbed individuals; usually it means putting the disturbed individual in a hospital. However, this is usually only temporarily effective, unless the hospital provides treatment in addition to environmental therapy.

Each means of treatment has advantages and disadvantages. Physical means—drugs or shock treatment—are easy to administer, but they leave many real problems untouched. Shock treatment may cause irreversible physical damage. This is particularly true when many courses of shock treatment are administered. Such treatment may lead to permanent memory loss and an inability to function adequately in career and family life.

Psychological means of treatment are aimed at changing the person's ways of thinking and behaving, therefore leading to a more permanent cure. These means are costly and difficult to administer; they require trained psychologists, social workers, psychiatrists, or other counselors; and they take a long time to be effective.

If, however, the cost to society of repeated mental illness is measured, providing psychological help may be cheaper in the long run. Further, professional help may be combined with that gained from self-help groups (Recovery, Inc., for mental patients; Alcoholics Anonymous for alcoholics; Gamblers Anonymous for gamblers; and so on), and money can be saved. It has also been found that sensitive, mature persons can be trained as paraprofessionals to aid and in some cases replace the more expensive professionals.

Dealing with the Mentally Ill

The criminal justice community may have to deal with the mentally ill in a number of ways: when the mentally ill become involved in criminal activity; when a patrol officer feels that a mentally ill person may cause damage to himself or others if left on the streets; or when relatives or others request that someone mentally ill be removed from the community.

A mentally ill person, when violent or when suspected of engaging in criminal activity, obviously falls under the jurisdiction of the law. When brought to trial, he may be pronounced unable to have recognized right from wrong or to have considered the nature and consequences of his act (the McNaughton rule) or he may have been judged (under the Durham rule) to have had a mental disease that substantially contributed to his committing the criminal act. In either case, if he is considered unable to be held responsible, he will be committed to a mental hospital for the criminally insane.

In dealing with such a person, recognize that he will speak to you in symbolic terms and out of tremendous fear. For example, a mentally ill person may tell me that the "sorcerers" are out to get him. This refers to his parents and their influence on him, but he cannot tell me this except symbolically. An understanding of symbolic language, while helpful in dealing with him, is difficult to acquire; a simpler technique is to "go along" with his craziness. For example, tell the psychotic person that you are there to protect him from his enemies. Before doing this, speak quietly and gently to him, to find out what his fears are. "Are you in any danger?" would be an appropriate question. Explaining clearly and truthfully what you are going to do, as a way of protecting him from whatever enemies he has acquired, will ensure his cooperation.

In emergency situations, speak firmly and confidently, telling the person you will not allow him to hurt others. Approach slowly, without making sudden moves, and then, if possible, hold him gently.

Bizarre behavior can be handled in a similar fashion. An appropriate way, without commitment, of handling someone who might cause difficulty to himself or others might be the following: tell the person he cannot do what he is doing and take him to the admission office of a state hospital for observation (most states permit a short period of observation). Be sure to explain to him what you are doing and why. If he talks to you symbolically, answer him in the same way. For example, a person terrified of being killed by "enemy forces" was told that he would be safe after having a circle drawn around him. An officer might tell such a person that a patrol car is a safe place, and that no one can get to him while he is inside of it. Other symbolic terms frequently used are the devil and God. Continuous physical contact of a reassuring nature is often necessary for such terrified people.

Continued emotional support is also important for people with drug-induced psychosis. Often such persons need to be in close physical contact: holding their hands or putting your arms around their shoulders will be reassuring in many cases.

Families who ask police to take away a disturbed relative must be informed that observation at a mental hospital is only a temporary procedure, that commitment must take place through a formal procedure. In some states two physicians signing commitment papers is sufficient; in other cases, where a patient wishes, court rulings may be necessary. Voluntary commitment is also possible in most hospitals; usually it allows the patient to sign himself out when he wishes to leave. The family also needs information about other sources of help, such as community mental health clinics or family service agencies. These agencies can offer long-range support to help the family deal with the problems caused by the patient. The community agency also will know of additional resources, such as halfway houses and other rehabilitative agencies that can supplement, or replace, hospital care.

Summary

Mental illnesses represent extreme responses to everyday problems. Normal people are aware of their problems, of how they wish to solve these problems, and of how they want to direct their lives. Neurotics are less aware of their goals and how to achieve them. Sociopaths are unable to accept the norms of society and thus act in criminal ways. Schizophrenics have broken with reality, communicating with others in symbolic terms.

Types of neurosis include anxiety neurosis, phobic neurosis, dissociative neurosis, obsessive-compulsive neurosis, and conversion neurosis.

Two types of psychoses are organic, caused by physical malfunction, and functional, caused by emotional problems. Organic psychoses include senile psychosis, stemming from circulatory problems in older people; alcoholic psychosis; drug-induced psychosis; and psychoses resulting from head injuries or brain tumors. Functional psychoses include schizophrenia and manic-depressive psychosis.

Persons may be helped to recover from mental illness through psychological or physical means. Psychological methods usually cause less damage and have longer-lasting results than physical methods, but the latter are easier and cheaper to administer.

Dealing effectively with the mentally ill requires an understanding of their terror and their need to fight imaginary assailants. Being sympathetic and talking to them in symbolic terms, plus using gentle firmness, can be extremely helpful.

Discussion Questions

1. In what ways are the mentally ill like normal persons? In what ways are they different?
2. Role-play a situation in which a mentally ill person is threatening his family with physical harm. Try to calm him down. See what works.
3. How can you tell what a person's real motives are? How are they related to symptoms?

Suggested Reading

Normal problems and solutions:

Baron, R. A. *Human Aggression*. New York: Plenum, 1977.
Berne, E. *Games People Play*. New York: Grove Press, 1964.

Berne, E. *What Do You Say After You Say Hello?* New York: Grove Press, 1972.
Fast, J. *Creative Coping*. New York: Morrow, 1976.
Jourard, S. M. *Healthy Personality*. New York: Macmillan, 1974.
Kangas, J. A. *The Psychology of Strength*. Englewood Cliffs, N.J.: Prentice-Hall, 1975.
Moustakas, C. E. *Loneliness*. Englewood Cliffs, N.J.: Prentice-Hall, 1961.

Mental illness:

Green, Hannah. *I Never Promised You a Rose Garden*. New York: Holt, Rinehart and Winston, 1964.
Lindner, R. M. *The Fifty-Minute Hour*. New York: Bantam, 1956.
Vonnegut, M. *Eden Express*. New York: Praeger, 1975.

Mental illness and criminal justice:

Bittner, E. "Police Discretion in the Emergency Apprehension of Mentally Ill Persons." *Social Problems* 14 (Winter 1967): 278–92.
Bromberg, W. *The Uses of Psychiatry in the Law: A Clinical View of Forensic Psychiatry*. Westport, Conn.: Greenwood Press, 1979.

Part Two

Criminals without Victims

CHAPTER 10

Understanding Criminals without Victims

Victimless crime is an important area for all those involved in criminal justice. The detection and prosecution of criminals without victims takes up an unwarranted amount of the time of skilled law enforcement personnel.

Crime is whatever a society defines as criminal. If we wished, we could define running as a criminal activity. Obviously, that would be patent nonsense, but it does make the point that actions in themselves are neither criminal nor noncriminal until labeled as such.

However, aren't some actions always immoral and criminal? For example, murder? While murder is usually criminal, is killing in time of war criminal? What about a police officer shooting an offender?

All such actions are defined by the function they serve in society. Killing during wartime eliminates enemies. It is defined as good.

Killing citizens during peacetime makes it difficult for a society to function; such killings are defined as criminal. Entering your neighbor's house to spy on him is defined as wrong. Entering an enemy official's house to spy on him may be defined as counterintelligence, therefore good. One action (spying on the neighbor) disrupts the business of society; the other is defined as helping society defend itself against its enemies.

Society's definition of crime works well as long as everyone in the society has the same opinion. However, when some people think one thing, some another, problems arise. For example, many people think prostitution could be better regulated if it were legal; many others feel that prostitution should remain a crime. Because so many people feel that prostitution should be legalized, the laws against prostitution are hard to enforce. There is little community backing.

Laws against Victimless Crime

Do we have on the books too many laws concerning actions that either cause no trouble or could be better regulated if legalized? Do these laws interfere with controlling crimes *with* victims? Shouldn't we spend our scarce criminal justice resources on the latter kind of crime? Why don't we?

Many laws against victimless crime exist for two reasons: (1) as historical remnants of a time when people were more puritanical and (2) because people have the conviction or hope that they can legislate morality.

Americans are "can-do" people. From our pioneer days, we learned that we couldn't sit around and think about things; we had to go out and *do*. We had to be effective. Frontier law was rough and ready.

Even today, it would seem natural to take the same approach to law enforcement. Enforce the law rigorously. Do something drastic to those who won't measure up.

Unfortunately, this kind of action is *not* effective in our complex society, and it is debatable whether it was desirable in pioneer days. Getting more and better guns, more sophisticated hardware to eliminate crime, was tried and found wanting in the early days of the Law Enforcement Assistance Administration. Attempts must be made to think about which actions should be forcefully prosecuted, which regulated, which ignored.

Realistically, we must resign ourselves to the fact that vice will always be with us. All cultures throughout history have had their mood- and consciousness-altering substances. Sexual activity similarly and even more obviously has always been and will always be with us. But sexuality is rarely confined to one type of behavior. Humans as well as animals engage in sexual activity with same-sex individuals, or in a wide variety of ways, when normal outlets are unavailable.

Does the fact that immorality and perhaps evil have always been with us mean that we should make no attempt at regulating such behavior?

In order to stop something through the force of law, it is necessary to do one of two things: (1) use such widespread and pervasive force that the public will be terrorized into conformity, such as in a police state, or (2) have the support of the people and enforce the law with their help.

This immediately shows the difficulty of regulating such behavior as drinking alcoholic beverages. People will not support regulation of such activities. Prohibition was, of course, a striking example of the inability to prevent behavior that almost everyone engaged in.

Enforceability of Laws

What makes a law enforceable? In order to answer this question, let us consider an area of law enforcement that does work reasonably well, that of laws against mugging.

When a mugging is committed, people usually are willing to (1) report the crime, (2) help find the mugger, and (3) testify against him.

In other words, people are willing to cooperate in detecting and prosecuting this crime.

Why?

People believe that mugging does definite injury to themselves and others. Muggers should, therefore, be arrested and deterred. The public expresses no doubt.

This illustrates the first principle of enforcement: In order for laws to be enforceable, the public must support them. The criminal behavior must be *regarded* as criminal. It must not only be considered wrong, but *sufficiently* wrong to require criminal sanctions. Second, the crime must be *visible.* Even if everyone in a society believed certain thoughts should be punished through the criminal justice system, laws against such thoughts would not be enforceable. How would one get evidence? Third, the criminal behavior must be of a nature that can realistically be changed. For example, if a person can survive only by stealing, he cannot realistically change that behavior. Suppose we were to pass a law against eating food with starch in it. Though it would be possible to survive without bread, spaghetti, beans, and so on, the attempt would not be realistic for those with low incomes. Such a regulation would be unreasonable and unworkable. People would always "find a way."

Many victimless crimes are either (1) not considered wrong by the general population, or not believed to be so wrong as to justify criminal sanctions, or (2) not visible enough to be easily identified, or (3) not controllable by the persons committing the crimes.

Drunkenness and gambling are considered by most people in our country today either to be not wrong at all or to be understandable, noncriminal vices.

Addiction is difficult to control; therefore, the addict is not usually deterred by the threat of punishment.

Prostitution is considered acceptable by many people in our society.

Homosexuality between consenting adults is not visible and is considered to be acceptable by a large and increasingly vocal minority.

Enforceability of Laws against Victimless Crimes

Is it possible to enforce laws against criminals without victims? The answer is both yes and no. Obviously, these laws are enforced, though at great cost.

What are the problems relating to this type of law enforcement?

One of the most striking characteristics of detecting and prosecuting criminals without victims is that there is no complainant. The gambler who loses money does not complain against his bookie. The "john" (customer) does not complain against the prostitute. The consenting homosexual most certainly does not complain against his or her lover.

If there is no complainant, how do you detect the crime? To do so, you must use marginally acceptable detection techniques, such as wiretapping, entrapment, use of underworld informants, and often search-and-seizure procedures of questionable legality.

Each of these deserves discussion in itself.

Many cases have been thrown out of court because of the illegal use of wiretapping or other electronic recording devices. While bugging is an extremely common device in spying, it is a potentially dangerous infringement on individual rights when used against persons in a democracy.

Entrapment, which involves setting up a situation in which a person is induced to do something against the law, is illegal. Being on the scene and approached is different from approaching; however, many situations may be hard to interpret. For example, while "sting operations" are legal, a recent ad for "hostesses," which led to the arrest of a number of prostitutes, was declared to be entrapment and the arrests were thrown out of court. Entrapment leads to infringement of individual rights—something law enforcement is fighting against, not for. In other words, in order to control victimless crime effectively, it is sometimes necessary to behave in a criminal fashion yourself. In a democracy this may be considered unacceptable.

Use of underworld informants poses another interesting problem. To use these informants it is sometimes necessary for an officer to pretend to engage in criminal behavior himself—for example, becoming a gambler in order to find out who is involved. Further, the officer may have to negotiate for immunity for an addict in order to get information about other addicts or pushers. This puts him in a position of protecting a criminal against the law.

Search and seizure procedures have sometimes been used in situations where they have been illegal, immoral, and subject to the exclusionary rule which mandates that illegally acquired evidence is not admissible.[1] Suits have been won against some law enforcement officials who broke into homes, destroyed furniture, terrorized the occupants—all on the mistaken assumption that drugs would be found in the homes. A notorious case of the early

1970s was that of Daniel Ellsberg, whose psychiatrist was burglarized by national administration personnel, a clear violation of the law. Similarly, the Watergate Democratic National Committee offices were burglarized by overzealous officials who felt they needed political information. It is clear from these examples that seizing personal property must be a carefully regulated law enforcement function if we are to continue to have a democracy. We need protective rather than terroristic law enforcement apparatus, which will nevertheless allow us to effectively investigate crime.

Enforcing the Laws

Trying to enforce laws against victimless crimes has several consequences—all negative.

1. An increased disrespect for the law. Formerly law-abiding citizens who would never have thought about breaking the law do so. The "law" becomes diminished as a result; people consider breaking other laws as well.

2. An increase in organized criminal activity. Because of support for the forbidden activity, people look for a way to continue it. If they can't find it legally, they will find it illegally. Unscrupulous persons will take advantage of this fact. Money that could go into the hands of the state goes into criminals' pockets. Then the state must spend even more money trying to restrict these activities.

3. Victimization of persons who consume forbidden products because the manufacture of these products is no longer regulated. Some of the liquor sold during Prohibition was practically a poison that could blind or kill those who drank it.

4. Further victimization of consumers because prices are not subject to usual marketplace regulation. Prices are much higher because the goods are sold illegally. Money going to organized crime comes from consumers' pockets.

5. Increased lawlessness because many persons labeled as criminals are forced into a criminal environment, partly because they must engage in crime in order to maintain their life-styles—notably true of the addict. The homosexual may become involved in blackmail to prevent revelation of his sexual activity, and he may then have to engage in illegal activities to pay the blackmailer.

If he is forced to deal with a loan shark, he may find himself in the debt of organized crime. Many such debts are collected by making the debtor participate in illegal activity to avoid prosecution. Often such individuals feel they have no choice, since their lives or the lives of their families have been threatened.

Some criminals may become part of a criminal environment in order to have companionship. Again, drug addicts would find it difficult to have friends if they did not associate with others in a similar situation. Such association supports and reinforces undesirable behavior.

Victimless criminals cannot use the law because of their own fear of discovery. They thus become likely targets for exploitation—and such crimes of exploitation can never be detected. In order to protect themselves they must then take the law into their hands—further criminal behavior. Prostitutes are a good example of such easy targets for exploitation, often by pimps. Their customers may be rolled, without complaints to the police.

Prohibition was a highly successful attempt to regulate private behavior—from the standpoint of organized crime, owners of speak-easies, makers of moonshine, and anyone else who enjoyed breaking the law. Prohibition led to many consequences its supporters had never foreseen.

Leftovers from the Past

One might then ask, Why have such prohibitions at all?

Some of them seem to be historical remnants—aspects of our past that we should probably have left behind many years ago. For example, the early settlers of New England severely punished any sexual activity except between husband and wife. Today we still punish homosexuals or individuals who want extramarital sex through prostitution.

Drug prohibition is somewhat different. Here again, however, even though we permit some drugs and not others, a conservative force is at work. Only drugs that we know well and have long used are legal.

Gambling seems a similar "leftover" from Puritan days, and it too is handled in a confused fashion. Some gambling is all right—

bingo games at the church, for example. Gambling in certain areas (Reno) is fine too. If a state supports it, it is all right (off-track betting, state lotteries). If it is private, in somebody's home, it is all right. If it is public, in back of a bar, it may not be.

Suicide presents a somewhat different problem. Sanctions against suicide stem from the disruption that occurs when members of a society do not stay alive to play their assigned roles. Killing oneself also implies that conditions of life are unbearable—an insult to a society. Certain kinds of suicides (Japanese kamikaze pilots who gave their lives in World War II by crashing planes into warships) are, however, encouraged by states.

Psychological Reasons for Obsolete Laws

It would seem quite clear that many of these laws make very little sense, since they do not accomplish the purpose of eliminating the behavior legislated against. So why are they still maintained?

There is a fairly simple psychological explanation for such behavior, irrational though it sometimes seems. All people have impulses to do the kinds of things we are talking about—gamble, enjoy sexual relations, drink, or take other substances to "feel good." Some people are able to engage in these activities to a moderate degree and live happy, comfortable lives. Other people, however, have been taught that they must not enjoy any of these things.

We laugh at the censor who carefully watches and reads all the pornographic movies and books that come out. We know that he is having his fun without having to admit that he enjoys his job.

He suffers from the same malady as do other people who condemn moderate self-indulgence in sex or alcohol. Since they prevent themselves from indulging themselves, they get upset if others enjoy sex, drink, and so on. Why should others enjoy what they have learned with difficulty to do without? The harder the lesson they have learned, the stricter they will be with others. The ex-alcoholic is more of a fanatic than the person who has never had to struggle to refuse a drink. However, even he will probably be more tolerant of others than the boy who was severely beaten for his first experiments with whiskey.

If children are prevented from satisfying their natural curiosity, they will try as adults to keep others from enjoying some of these same "forbidden" activities. This does not mean that people have to be gamblers, addicts, or sex fanatics to be tolerant. In fact, the reverse is true. The child who is allowed to try a few sips of wine at the table will learn how to drink moderately. Only the forbidden will tempt him to wild orgies and immoderation. If sex, alcohol, and/or gambling is available, people will satisfy their needs, but they will find that such activities do not solve all their problems. They usually acquire a reasonable attitude toward these pleasures and lead a balanced life.

Of course, the kind of business interests mentioned previously will not want to see laws against frequently desired activity repealed. These laws make too much money for them.

We must also remember that there are good reasons to try to regulate major abuses such as drug distribution, the spread of venereal disease, and so forth. Criminals involved in widespread drug distribution, for example, cannot be considered to have no victims.

Overview of Criminals without Victims

Let us review in somewhat more detail the groups who comprise the majority of criminals without victims.

Alcoholics

The alcoholic who stumbles along the street, especially if he is a member of a skid row community, represents a large proportion of criminals without victims. Such alcoholics have lost their family and community connections, live in deteriorating areas, spend most of their time on the streets. They are regularly and frequently booked, processed, jailed, and freed in a "revolving door" cycle.

Drug Addicts

The drug addict is a prime target for some very sophisticated and sometimes questionable law enforcement techniques. Thousands of law enforcement hours can be spent arresting and convicting addicts, while persons higher in the pyramid of drug distribution may continue their activities without interference. Is it worthwhile? Do addicts have to be criminals? Many users (some physicians, for example) continue to live normally in society.

Gamblers

Law enforcement personnel frequently spend months planning and executing gambling raids, which net small operators while the organized crime officials who support the gambling simply move their operations to another location.

Prostitutes

In many areas, prostitutes and police are good friends, because prostitutes are arrested regularly in a revolving door cycle similar to that of alcoholics. The prostitute gives the officer no problems, and he in turn may be careful to time her arrest so that she will still be able to see most of her clients. When I worked at a mental health reception center, prostitutes regularly admitted themselves, since they preferred the center to jail. In either case, valuable time and resources were spent on essentially futile efforts.

Suicides

Unsuccessful suicides, too, are subject to the law. Usually, however, law enforcement personnel are called upon to provide help for the potential suicide—for example, in some states the law provides that the attempted suicide must obtain psychiatric help. Frequently, officers are called when it is known that an individual is attempting suicide.

Consenting Homosexuals

The homosexual is subject to a number of problems stemming from his being defined as a criminal. He can be harassed or arrested by vice squad personnel, who may resort to elaborate systems of detection. He can be blackmailed if he is in a sensitive job. He may be eliminated from consideration for many jobs because of the blackmailing potential. He frequently will lead a "double life" and may worry constantly that his "straight world" of employment and sometimes family and friends will meet his "gay life" of after-hours sociability.

Other Sex Offenders

Laws of many states forbid such other sexual conduct as particular kinds of sex acts between consenting adults. However, fornication and other such laws are rarely enforced.

A Detailed Example: The Gambler

What is it like to be a criminal without a victim? Who are the people who engage in some of these crimes? How do these crimes affect their families? The answers to these questions are as varied as the groups just discussed. However, let us look at one kind of offender for a more detailed picture.

Compulsive gamblers devote their lives to gambling. They may be forced to patronize loan sharks or make illegal bets. They also do untold damage to themselves and their families.

What are their motivations?

Like many others, they gamble for sociability and excitement. But why does their gambling become compulsive—something they have to do?

Part of the answer to this question lies in the fact that compulsive gamblers are unable to find other satisfactions in life. Gambling makes up for this lack.

What is the lack for which gambling substitutes?

1. Gamblers feel inferior and unable to cope with life. They can daydream about the "big score." When they do have some winnings, they can buy expensive clothes or cars, treat everyone to drinks, and act out the daydream of being wealthy and important. Occupationally, gamblers are concentrated in the sales field, where again they can hope for big winnings. These dreams compensate for their feelings of inferiority, and offer a consolation for the unhappiness most of them experience.

2. Gamblers have just enough confidence in themselves to believe in these dreams. In this respect, the behavior of gamblers is very similar to the behavior of four-year-olds. They boast, swag-

ger, don't have much notion of the truth, and act as if they believe their lies.

"I can run a bulldozer," "I saw a tiger on the way home," "I'm going to marry Mommy." All of these statements are typical of four-year-olds trying to be impressive, to act like daddy, to control their worlds in unrealistic ways. The same little fellow who boasts that he can beat up anyone on the block will probably run when someone calls his bluff. Most children grow out of this stage; they are just trying to see how it feels to be grown up. Soon they enter school, feel some sense of achievement, and stop boasting.

Gamblers never grow out of this stage. They are unable to wait for satisfaction, to work on something for a while, to know that eventually they will have a reward. They must have their satisfactions immediately.[2] They may be able to wait only the sixty seconds it takes for the race to be run. Many are unwilling to wait a whole day to find out whether a bet they have made has come through.

3. Gamblers are losers. They want to lose. In all the literature that I have been able to find, not one gambler—except "business" gamblers who may cheat to win consistently—has come out ahead. The gambler, even if he has become the hero of the typical story of the guy who scored, will have lost in the end, even if he was riding high for many years. In retelling these stories, however, the gamblers do not talk about the fact that the "hero" was broke and died in a flophouse—or killed himself at the end.

Why is this so?

The primary reason is that the gambler, like many other self-destructive persons, is unable to deal with his unhappiness and frustration constructively. Instead, he is angry and expresses this anger by making other people—his family—uncomfortable, losing money needed for other purposes. Therefore, while the gambler says he wants to make his family rich, he would have to find other ways to deal with his frustration if he allowed himself to win. A further dynamic is the tendency of gamblers to marry domineering wives with whom they deal only indirectly through losing family money.

4. Gamblers are unable to have satisfying relationships with others. A striking conclusion of most people who have studied gamblers is that gamblers are loners. They may be married and

have a social life with other gamblers, but basically they do not receive real satisfaction from other persons. Their daydreams about others involve being admired—a typical four-year-old development—but not loving and being loved, getting satisfaction from seeing children develop, or enjoying activities with others—all adult goals.

Gamblers' marriages, while seemingly important to them—they seek help when wives seriously threaten divorce—have little substance. Gamblers spend little time with their wives and children and may boast about having been off at the track when their children were born. They do not include their wives in their drinking and gambling, and they become extremely angry if their wives attempt to get them home from a bar. Most of the wives accept this.

This difficulty with relationships makes it clear that the successful gambler would not know what to do with his time. He would not know how to enjoy his wife and family; he has no social life outside of his gambling circle. He does not even know how to talk with other gamblers except in the limited terms of gambling and women. He would be lost in an occupation that involved planning and waiting. He does not have any interest or expertise in organizing others, but wants to be able to be on his own.

Dealing with the Gambler

It is quite obvious that putting the gambler in jail would have little effect on gambling. Even the arrest of bookies leads only to their replacement by other bookies. In fact, the police officer will have little to do with the individual gambler, unless a community decides sporadically to raid local gambling houses. Most gamblers are not violent and pose little problem to a law enforcement officer.

Treatment for the gambler is difficult, but it is a better solution than arresting him.

Perhaps the most suitable treatment for the gambler is that provided by self-help groups called Gamblers Anonymous.[3] These groups have a religious tone and are modeled on Alcoholics Anonymous. They also have programs for spouses and are based on confessions and mutual support.

These groups provide solutions to some of the problems of an ex-gambler. They are a way for him to spend his time. They do not necessitate doing anything *with* his family, but provide an excuse for him to be away from his family. They provide a social life that is still built on gambling and woman-chasing—but this time discussing rather than doing.

Most new members are surprised at how readily they are accepted. Members boast a lot about how terrible their losses were before joining. This can serve two purposes: (1) Talking about problems helps the new member feel he is not alone—others have had even worse problems—and (2) such confessions give the older members the same chance to boast as they had when they were gambling: they can now boast about their progress. No one in the group seems very interested in back-sliders, so staying clean provides more of a chance for attention than slipping.

Gamblers Anonymous chapters are listed in phone books in major cities. Local chapters may also be found by writing to Gamblers Anonymous, National Service Office, P.O. Box 17173, Los Angeles, California 90017.

Recently, other groups such as the Johns Hopkins Compulsive Gambling Counseling Center (Baltimore, Md.) have been successful in adapting traditional psychotherapeutic methods to help compulsive gamblers.

The Gambler and the Loan Shark

Credit laws have made borrowing money relatively simple for most people. The usual credit rates are based on the assumption that most borrowers will pay back their debts.

What about the borrower whose credit rating is poor or nonexistent? What does he do in an emergency? If he is a gambler, or a drug addict, or a businessman engaged in marginal practices, he may turn to a loan shark.

Most loan sharking is in the hands of organized crime. The debtor borrows the money, obtaining it immediately and without collateral—except for his body. If he cannot come up with interest—which often amounts to 200 or 300 percent—*and* pay back the principal, he continues to make payments to the loan shark until he is bled dry, or goes to the police. If he is unable to make the interest payments, the loan shark sends a hit man—not to kill him, but to show him that he has to pay. He does this by hurting him, often by such bizarre acts as hanging him by the heels out a window, or hitting him over the head with a blackjack. Hit men known by such names as "leg-breaker Jack" get their names from their performances. This incredible mutilation sends the message.

If mutilation doesn't work, threats are made against loved ones. Sometimes this threat is the initial tactic. A gambler might be asked pointedly about routes that children or wife take in going to and from school or work. Girlfriends are called and threatened.

When the loan shark feels that he can get no more money out of a debtor, he may generously reduce the debt. The loan shark is realistic. He just makes sure that he gets what can easily amount to *1,000 percent* of the original debt before his generosity comes into play.

Another route taken by the loan shark when the debtor can't make good is to allow him to become a front man for the loan shark. The loan shark puts in his own people to run the debtor's business and collect most of the profits. In this way, organized crime has taken over many legitimate businesses. This takeover has been invisible.

If the debtor doesn't have business assets, he may be asked to perform illegal services, such as running dice games, or distributing drugs. Many employees of the Mafia become part of organized crime in this way.

Without illegal gambling, the loan shark would lose most of his business. Legalized gambling would make it easier to identify and prosecute loan sharks, since a victim would not be afraid to disclose his gambling.

Summary

The compulsive gambler can be characterized by his attempt to cope with the world through unrealistic dreams and desires. He is unable to live a satisfying life in a family and uses his gambling to isolate himself. He is a "loser" who cannot tolerate winning for keeps, since part of his losing is an expression of his anger at the world and specifically his family.

Problems for law enforcement are related to the connection between gambling and organized crime. If gambling were legalized, organized crime would lose a major source of revenue and recruitment. Some of this recruitment comes via loan sharks, who can use gamblers who are indebted to them. Gambling raids usually only scratch the surface of the organization. They are costly in both detection and planning. Prosecution is ineffective as well. It does not change the compulsive gambler's attitude.

Changes in compulsive gamblers' behavior have been brought about by Gamblers Anonymous groups, which seem to provide a substitute for gambling for some gamblers.

However, noncompulsive gambling has always been with us and probably always will be.

Conclusions

Since criminal behavior is defined as what a society *says* is criminal, that society must agree on what it considers wrong. No such unanimity exists in regard to crimes without victims. Therefore, alcoholism, addiction, gambling, prostitution, homosexuality, and similar offenses are prosecuted only at great cost in terms of manpower, illegal detection procedures, personal suffering of those considered to be criminals, and a high crime rate. The higher crime rate is due not only to the criminalization of these persons but also to their need to commit further crimes—to meet the cost of a habit (as in the case of addicts) or because they have become part of a criminal subsociety (as with prostitutes).

A high percentage of burglaries in urban areas is committed by drug addicts who may need to steal large sums to feed their habits. Many other crimes are linked—gambling, loan sharking, and organized crime recruitment, for example.

If the resources of our criminal justice system could be focused on crimes *with* victims, we might be able to gain some control over street crime, get a start on white-collar crime, and provide less support for organized crime. We would not need as much illegal surveillance of individuals. We could offer protection to those who need it but are denied protection because they are afraid to confess their own "crimes." We could prevent organized crime from growing richer—especially from gambling and drug trade. We could prevent organized crime from recruiting many people who feel they have no choice because they live on the fringe of respectable society. We could increase respect for law because its role would be more clearly defined. Law enforcement officials would not need to deal in shady practices and criminal associations.

Discussion Questions

1. What are the consequences of making private acts criminal?
2. If you were a legislator, what laws would you propose to deal with gambling, homosexuality, prostitution?
3. If you were a legislator, would you want to retain any laws against crimes without victims? What crimes would you include?
4. What are your personal experiences with gambling? Do you feel that you needed regulatory laws?

Suggested Reading

Bergler, E. *Psychology of Gambling.* N.Y.: International University Press, 1970.
Bruns, B. P. *Compulsive Gambler.* Secaucus, N.J.: Lyle Stuart, 1973.
Gamblers Anonymous. 3d ed. Los Angeles: G. A. Publishing, n.d.
Livingston, J. *Compulsive Gamblers.* New York: Harper and Row, 1974.
Packer, H. *The Limits of the Criminal Sanction.* Stanford, Calif.: Stanford University Press, 1968.
Rich, R. M. *Crimes Without Victims: Deviance and the Criminal Law.* Washington, D.C.: University Press of America, 1978.
Schur, E. M. *Our Criminal Society.* Englewood Cliffs, N.J.: Prentice-Hall, 1969.
Schur, E. M. *Victimless Crimes.* Englewood Cliffs, N.J. Prentice-Hall, 1974.
Smith, W. E. *Victimless Crime: A Selected Bibliography.* Washington, D.C., National Criminal Justice Reference Service, Department of Justice, Law Enforcement Assistance Administration, National Institute of Law Enforcement and Criminal Justice, 1977.

CHAPTER 11

Suicide

Suicide is both a crisis and a crime. As such, it is the responsibility of the police to take prompt action when suicide is threatened.

There are several ways of viewing suicide, each leading to different types of action. There are also several types of suicidal behavior, corresponding to different circumstances.

One way of viewing suicide is to regard individual life as something belonging to society. Each group member contributes, and he therefore has no right to take his own life. This view leads to the perception of suicide as criminal behavior.

Another way of looking at suicide is to assume that society has an obligation to the individual, rather than that the individual owes something to the society. In this view, the suicidal person is someone who needs help.

A third view is that the society should neither demand help from the individual nor offer help to him. If he wishes to kill himself, society should let him.

The discussion in this chapter is based on the assumption that society *does* have an obligation to help the individual, except under exceptional circumstances.

Types of Suicide

Suicidal behavior can be classified as a response to differing circumstances. These include the following:

1. Situations in which society prescribes suicide. This leads to a *traditional* suicide. For example, some societies have decreed that when a husband dies, his wife must kill herself. In some societies, when a person is dishonored, he is expected to commit suicide. Under conditions of war, soldiers may be expected to perform suicidal missions. Traditional suicide is, however, extremely rare in the United States, an approximation being the suicide of an official to escape the shame of prosecution.
2. Situations in which death is inescapable. For example, a prisoner who is to be tortured and executed might realistically kill himself. *Rational* suicide may also occur when a person suffers a terminal illness and prefers to end his life quickly rather than experience prolonged suffering, or subject his family to catastrophic medical expenses. This type of suicide may be increasing. According to the *Statistical Abstract of the United States 1979,* the aged population shows the highest rate of suicide.[1] This may reflect "rational" conditions or the low status of the aged in our society.

In these two circumstances, society would be unlikely to intervene.

3. Situations in which a person feels disconnected, unable to lead a fruitful, satisfying life. This situation leads to the kind of suicide with which this chapter is most concerned—*anomic* suicide. More suicides of this kind occur in unstable communities, such as inner cities; or places of transition, such as colleges. Anomic suicides are more frequent among the single or divorced.

Aspects of Suicide Important for Criminal Justice

Suicide is frightening. Although the suicide rate in 1977 was only 11.4 per 100,000 population, it ranks eleventh in the United States as a cause of death. Among young people (ages fifteen to twenty-four) it ranks fourth.[2] Because suicide seems unnatural as well as frightening, we find it hard to understand why any relatively normal person would want to end his own life.

People working in criminal justice need to be aware of several aspects of suicidal behavior. The following questions deal with some important aspects of suicidal behavior.

1. Are suicide threats that are not followed by serious attempts meaningless? No! Most people who successfully commit suicide have made other, less serious attempts. Any threat of suicide should be taken seriously.

2. Do people who try to kill themselves really want to die? No! With some exceptions, people who try to kill themselves feel ambivalent about dying. They want to kill themselves, but they also want to live. Often they allow fate to "decide." For example, a person might turn on the gas, knowing that a relative will be home shortly. If the relative returns on schedule, the person is saved. But if the relative decides to stop off for an errand, a life is lost.

3. Are people who try to kill themselves "crazy"? Not usually. Although some would-be or successful suicides are *psychotic* (what we think of as "crazy"), most people who try to kill themselves appear to be normal. In fact, they often are unusually "nice" people. Many are depressed and have serious problems, but they are certainly not "crazy."

4. Do people commit suicide without giving any warning? Not usually. While the "message" may not have been clear, almost every suicide has given some warning to those close to him. He has talked about wanting to die, said that life was meaningless, and so on. While psychotics appear to be an exception, they are not. These people give warnings, too, but their communications are difficult or impossible to understand. Their "messages" are given in what might be thought of as a code. For example, a psychotic young man who intended to jump off the roof of a six-story building felt he was letting the elevator operator know his intentions simply by looking at him. The elevator operator took him to the floor he requested. The young man took this as a sign that the operator wanted him to die.

5. Do would-be suicides want to be saved? With a few exceptions, yes! For most people who attempt suicide, the act is a way of

saying: "Does anyone want to help me? Does anyone want me to continue to exist?"

6. Do people who attempt suicide feel completely hopeless about life? No! While they do not feel sufficiently hopeful to *do something* about the situations that are making them miserable, would-be suicides are not without hope.

Do you remember the story of Tom Sawyer? In one episode Tom is missing. Everyone assumes he is dead, and a funeral is held for him. He arrives back in town, sneaks into the balcony of the church, and listens with feeling to the eulogies. This is a fantasy of many suicides. They cannot imagine themselves as no longer really existing. They think about the mourning of their survivors. "How bad they will feel! How sorry they will be for the shabby way they treated me. What sweet revenge!"

This fantasy is similar to another even more common one. Did you ever, as a young child, think of running away? "How my parents will miss me! *Then* they will be sorry. *Then* they will realize they should treat me better!"

7. Are people who want to kill themselves usually concerned about the welfare of others close to them? No! Usually the suicide is very angry with intimates and wants to force others to behave differently. Or, if this is not possible, the suicide wants to make them suffer as he has suffered. People who say they are killing themselves because of the welfare of others are setting the stage for those others to feel guilty: "I only considered your welfare, but look what you have done to me!"

8. Is it possible to predict which persons will try to kill themselves? Yes! A number of clues can help pinpoint potential suicides (see Figure 11.1). Some of these clues can be derived from psychological testing. Danger signs include depression, hopelessness, social isolation, and recent separation from loved ones. The most important clue, however, may be detected without a psychologist. It is a history of suicide in the family. For example, Ernest Hemingway killed himself in the same way as did his father. Another warning sign is the death of a father or mother while a person was growing up.

9. Does the danger of suicide decrease when a person who has been very sad and depressed suddenly becomes more active? No!

Figure 11.1
Signals of suicide

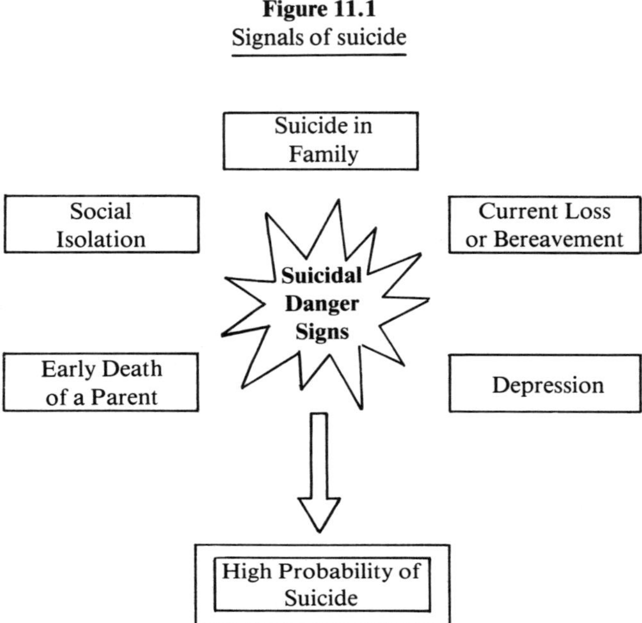

Many suicides occur just at this point, when family, friends, and even professional persons feel that the individual is getting better. This seems curious, but it may be explained rather simply. A person who is deeply depressed has little energy, not even the energy to plan and execute his own death. However, as he begins to feel better, he becomes capable of doing something about his unhappy situation. If that situation remains unchanged, his solution may be to plan his own death.

Persons who show some energy after being in deep depression need to be watched carefully. It is especially important that their families ensure that they are cared for at this point. If they are hospitalized, they should remain in the hospital. If they are under treatment by a mental health professional outside the hospital, they should continue their treatment.

10. Are the families of potential suicides doing all they can to prevent the suicide? Do they feel loving and caring toward the depressed person? The answer to both questions is usually no. This does not mean that a wife has no feeling for her suicidal husband. What it does mean is that usually those threatening suicide are

behaving in ways that are extremely irritating to the people who live with them.

Usually such a family has problems that no one knows how to solve—neither the would-be suicide nor the potential survivor. Each gets more and more angry with the other. Finally they reach the point at which the wife, for example, says of her depressed husband, "If he wants to kill himself, let him go ahead!" She does not do this consciously but unconsciously, which is even more dangerous. She cares, but she is so angry and hopeless that she becomes inattentive to her husband's warnings.

For example, the wife of a suicidal person took her husband to a rifle range for some target practice. Quite predictably, he shot himself. Similarly, a husband may insist on taking his wife out of the hospital against medical advice.

11. Can the motivations for suicide be specified? Yes. The category of suicide that includes most of the *exceptions* to the characteristics mentioned is *rational* or *realistic* suicide. As suggested above, if a man is dying of cancer, he may realistically want to end his life rather than suffer, accumulate large medical bills, and become helpless.

In cases of traditional or "cultural" suicide, a society prescribes that people should kill themselves for the sake of their honor or their country. Many such suicides occur in Japan. If a student fails an examination, it is considered reasonable for him to save his honor by killing himself. Japanese kamikaze pilots in World War II killed themselves by crashing their planes into American warships to help their country.

However, most suicides in America—especially among young and middle-aged persons—are of the usual type, called *anomic,* and they fall mainly into three categories: (1) cries for help, (2) attempts to coerce others into caring, and (3) expressions of anger turned inward against themselves.

Suicide seems a strange way to solve problems. However, suicides feel that they will hurt others by killing themselves, without realizing that revenge does not help a corpse.

12. Are there any agencies specifically set up to help suicidal individuals? Yes. Some large cities have suicide prevention centers that handle calls from would-be suicides on an emergency basis. Such centers are helpful to people who are willing to make the phone call. Interested counselors hold the individual in conversa-

Figure 11.2
Motives for suicide

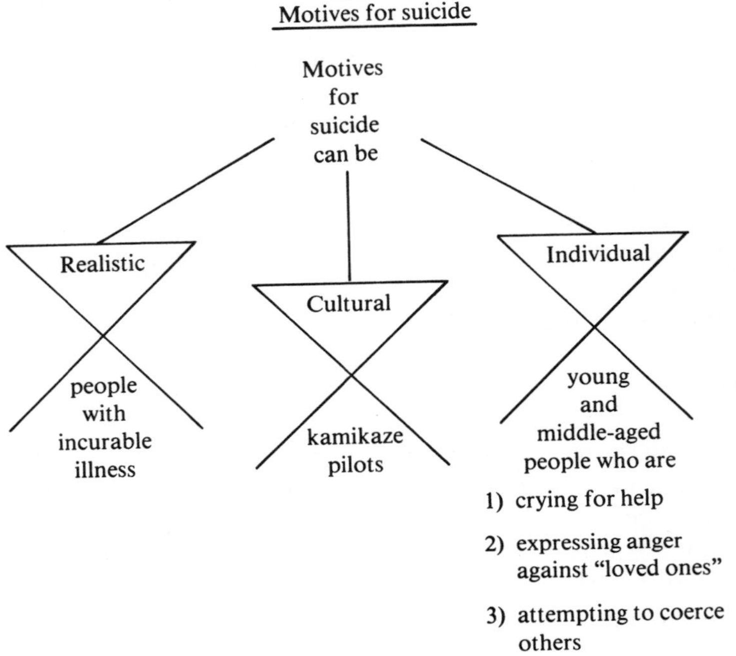

tion until he feels ready to reconsider his suicidal decision. They try to help him find an agency that can provide long-term support. If your community has a suicide prevention center, it should be widely publicized. But if no such center exists, setting one up would be a good police-community project.

Four Ways of Viewing Anomic Suicidal Behavior

Anomic suicidal behavior may be viewed in terms of the person's past history, the present situation, the suicide's relationships with others, and social pressures.

The Past

What sort of past history may have led up to the attempt at suicide? One very important factor is the way these individuals deal with their own anger. Do they express anger directly? Or are

Figure 11.3
Characteristics of suicidal persons

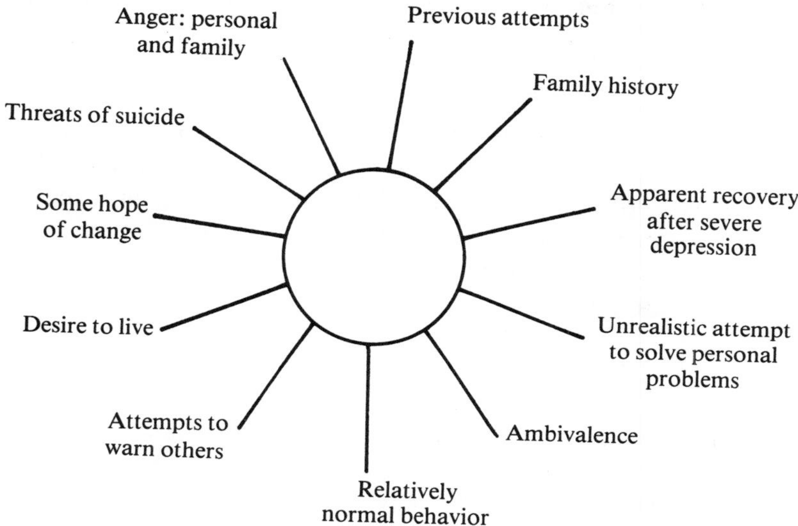

they polite but seething? Suicidal persons usually tell themselves they shouldn't be angry. They feel that they are not good enough to assert themselves, to demand their own rights. They have probably been depressed periodically for most of their lives. The final result of such a way of dealing with anger is a suicide attempt.

It is interesting to note in this regard that countries in which people express themselves freely have more homicide and less suicide. Countries in which people do not express anger directly have less homicide and more suicide. They turn anger inward, feeling guilt that leads to suicidal thoughts. This is true in the Scandinavian countries. The United States holds an intermediate position, ranking second highest in homicides and at about the middle of the distribution in suicide.[3]

The Present

Before a suicide attempt, something has usually happened to make the individual feel even more lost and alone. Frequently this event is a breakup of an important relationship, loss of a husband or wife through death or divorce, or of a girlfriend or boyfriend. Sometimes work problems cause a person to give up. There has usually been some type of rejection just before the suicide attempt.

Relationships with Others

The suicide attempt is a desperate communication to others. It is usually undertaken after other types of communication have failed. Would-be suicides have left notes saying such things as, "Since you decided not to stop going out with other women, I think it would be better for me to take my leave"—clearly a final plea for attention and love.

Social Pressures

Group pressures are usually not as important as other factors in an anomic suicide. Indirectly, a person may feel shamed and humiliated by his personal problems. He may feel diminished in the eyes of the community in which he lives.

More frequently, suicidal persons are isolated. A warm, helping group of friends could help the suicidal person to feel that there *is* a point in living. In this way, the group, by its absence, contributes to suicidal behavior.

Dealing with a Suicidal Emergency

Ideally, a suicide prevention center should be available for police referrals twenty-four hours a day, but this is not always the case. It may be possible to enlist the aid of a mental health professional (usually a social worker) in responding to suicide calls. Some states have laws requiring that all would-be suicides must have the care of a psychiatrist for a brief time. The period is often too brief to prevent further attempts, but requiring the help of a mental health professional is a step in the right direction.

In many communities, however, the police alone initially are responsible for dealing with would-be suicides. How can a police officer best handle this situation?

We know that the would-be suicide feels a great deal of anger and frustration. We also know that he derives some satisfaction from having other people get upset. Therefore the best approach is to show him that suicide will accomplish none of his goals. How can one do this?

First, although you know that this is a serious situation, do not act upset. One hospital instructed its telephone operators in the following way: "First, ask for the name and address. The individual will probably ask you why you want to know, feeling that he must foil your attempt to help. Tell him that you need to know where to send the hearse!"

I have heard many similar and effective ploys: "Well, if you're going to jump out the window, better take your key, because I'm not coming down to let you back in" (from a college roommate). "Well, if you decide to kill yourself, please do it on Sunday so I can give your Monday appointment to someone else" (from a minister).

Therapists usually try to find out at whom the patient is angry and respond something like this: "Well, your husband is certainly going to be relieved! He'll have a clear field to chase all those chicks he's been eyeing." Or "Your mother will certainly be glad to be rid of you. She'll probably throw a big party."[4]

Does this sound unfeeling? Or unbelievable? Neither is true. You can show your concern for a person, "I like you and I want to help you—but only if you stay alive," without being upset by his symptoms. Convincing the suicide that a relative will be happy to be rid of him is not as hard as you might think. After all, the relative has usually become extremely irritated with the depressed person.

Simple, matter-of-fact responses are appropriate. "Well, that blood from your wrist is getting pretty messy. Let's take you over to the hospital where it won't mess up your apartment." Or "You're going to be mighty uncomfortable from that poison. We'd better get you some help." These would be better responses than, "We don't want you to die. We must take you to the hospital immediately."

Such calm, matter-of-fact concern works best. Above all, do not abandon the individual on the mistaken notion that the crisis is over. This will only reinforce his feelings that no one really cares what happens to him. If possible, personally see that he receives appropriate professional counseling.

Further, more specific discussions of dealing with suicidal emergencies in several settings will be found in Appendix A.

Summary

Suicide is an important and serious problem in our society, and criminal justice personnel must frequently handle it.

Suicidal threats are almost always repeated. Whether or not someone "hears" the would-be suicide is extremely important. Suicide threats and attempts have at their root both despair and the need to hurt others. Danger signs include a history of suicide in the family or death of a parent when the person was young, the current loss of a loved one, and the beginning of recovery from a serious depression.

Individuals develop suicidal behavior in our society as a result of a long-standing pattern of turning anger against themselves. Social isolation is also an important factor.

Suicidal behavior should be viewed in reference to the victim's past, his present situation, his relationships with others, and any group pressures he may feel.

Dealing with a suicidal emergency requires a calm, matter-of-fact show of concern and insistence that some help be obtained. Asking other professional mental health workers (social workers, psychologists, psychiatrists) to help is frequently possible and desirable.

The application section (Appendix A) offers specific examples of how the suicidal person may be helped.

However, the helping individual must realize that he is not responsible for situations in which a suicide is successful. He can only do his best within the limits of time and opportunity.

Discussion Questions

1. Should threats of suicide be taken seriously? Why?
2. What factors are important in predicting a suicide?
3. What is the best way to handle a potential suicide? Role-play a would-be suicide situation. What helps? What doesn't?

Suggested Reading

Alvarez, A. *The Savage God: A Study of Suicide.* New York: Bantam, 1972.

Atkinson, J. M. *Discovering Suicide.* Pittsburgh: University of Pittsburgh Press, 1978.

Durkheim, E. *Suicide.* Glencoe, Ill.: Free Press of Glencoe, 1951.

Farberow, N. L., Schneidman, E. S. *Cry for Help.* New York: McGraw-Hill, 1961.

Farmer, R. E. *Law Enforcement and Community Relations.* Reston, Va.: Reston Publishing, 1976. (Crisis intervention.)

Grollman, E. A. *Suicide Prevention, Intervention, Postvention.* Boston: Beacon Press, 1971.

Karon, B. P. "Suicidal Tendency as the Wish to Hurt Someone Else, and Resulting Treatment Technique." *Journal of Individual Psychology* 20 (1964): 206–12.

Kiev, Ari. *The Courage to Live.* New York: T. Y. Crowell, 1979.

Miller, M. *Suicide after Sixty: The Final Alternative.* New York: Springer, 1979.

Reynolds, D. K., and Farberow, N. L. *Suicide: Inside and Out.* Berkeley and Los Angeles: University of California Press, 1976.

Stengel, E. *Suicide and Attempted Suicide.* Baltimore: Penguin, 1964.

CHAPTER 12

Drug Dependence

Concern over drugs abated in the late 1970s, but only briefly. Drug arrests still account for a major segment of criminal justice work, especially with youth. In fact, it almost appears that one type of problem emerges as another recedes. Older drugs such as marijuana are receiving less public attention. New drugs such as angel dust (PCP) and "T's and blues," have appeared on the scene, and cocaine has emerged as a widely used drug.

To what extent is drug use drug abuse? How do we deal with the use of alcohol, a common drug not often considered in discussions of drug abuse?

Let us start with the question of how we can differentiate drug use from drug abuse. Every society has used drugs of some type to ease the pains of life. Many of these drugs have been used by whole societies. In American society, alcohol is common at social gatherings of the more mature, while marijuana is frequently found in younger groups. Use of drugs to make life more pleasant thus seems an almost universal custom. It is, therefore, not drug *use* that we are concerned with in this chapter but drug *abuse.* Abuse involves excessive dependence on drugs to the exclusion of other sources of satisfaction.

Drug Addiction

First, what do we mean by drug abuse or addiction? There are two types of drug addiction—one psychological, the other physiological. Psychological drug addiction means that people are dependent on drugs in the same way that someone else may depend on watching TV every night. If the TV set breaks down and the TV repairman doesn't arrive for two weeks, the "TV-dependent" person will become extremely upset. This is because he has organized his time and style of life around watching TV.

Physiological addiction is similar but stronger and involves more of the body's functioning. Not only does the person physically addicted crave the substance, he craves it with all his being. While the psychologically addicted may substitute sandwiches for TV and feel better, a physical addiction does not allow the substitution of something else. It is more like the feeling of thirst on a hot day. The thirsty person *needs* water. In addition, however, large elements of psychological addiction accompany physical addiction.

Physical addiction is a complicated state. The human body is a complex system. The person who eats a big dinner and then has a drink is minimally affected by the liquor, because alcohol is not absorbed into the bloodstream as quickly when a person has eaten. Similarly, factors such as fatigue, stress, types of food eaten, and particular tensions change a drug's effect.

Further physical complications arise when the drugs taken are illegal and therefore are not regulated by the Food and Drug Administration. It is impossible to know how much pure drug is present in a drug purchased illicitly. The buyer may think he is receiving a dosage that will make him slightly "high" and instead receive a lethal dosage five times as great. Periodically, distribution of unusually pure concentrates of heroin are said to cause multiple deaths. In addition, the amount and kind of additives may cause dangerous side effects. Quinine in particular has been identified as dangerous. However, many doctors studying overdoses believe that these are most frequently caused by combinations of alcohol or barbiturates with heroin, and that *none* of the so-called overdose deaths is attributable to too much heroin alone. They feel that talking about overdose deaths perpetuates a dangerous myth, that such discussions make addicts feel safe when taking lethal combinations of alcohol and heroin, or barbiturates and heroin.

The psychological state of a person also dramatically changes the effect of drugs. For example, with drugs such as LSD, a person expecting to have a pleasurable but not significant "trip" will probably have just that. A person expecting to have a religious experience will usually *have* a religious experience. A person who is already upset may jump the border of sanity.

Becoming Drug Dependent

There are many horror stories about the young person who tries heroin on a lark—and becomes addicted for life. There are also horror stories about the youngster who takes some marijuana, is soon dissatisfied, and then graduates to hard drugs. Are these stories true?

First, does physiological dependence begin with the initial introduction of the drug into the system? Fortunately, the answer is no. While habituation to a drug such as heroin is rapid, many people have tried heroin once, twice, three times—without habituation. This is because individuals' psychological and physical states, their basic personality types, all vary.

What of the "progressive" theory of drug dependence—that persons who begin with a mild drug graduate to harder drugs and higher dosages? This theory is based primarily on studies showing that people taking hard drugs have taken soft drugs previously. However, these studies do not show how many people have taken soft drugs and *not* graduated to stronger fare.

Using the reasoning of such studies, one could also "prove" that smoking cigarettes—or even taking showers—leads to coffee drinking.

The Alcohol, Drug Abuse and Mental Health Administration has published data indicating that drug usage in teenagers depends on fads more than on a process of increasing usage. For example, teenage marijuana use increased from 1975 to 1978 (6 percent to 11 percent) but remained stable in 1979. On the other hand, cocaine usage increased from 6 percent in 1975 to 12 percent in 1979, reflecting its popularity.[1]

Of course, people who live in a drug culture, as in poverty-stricken areas, are very likely to go through the gamut of all drugs. Similarly, those who are impulsive or alienated frequently try a variety of drugs.

Drugs Defined

You may think you know the answer to the following question; however, try to answer it: What is the most dangerous drug in America today? Did you answer alcohol? There are more alcoholics in our society than any other type of drug addict. Many people forget that drugs are not just something exchanged illegally on a street corner. Drugs are also sold in respectable establishments called liquor stores, as well as in pharmacies, which dispense tranquilizers and antidepressants. Many respectable citizens are alcoholics, or are addicted to tranquilizing or antidepressant pills.

Amphetamines are another source of addiction. I recall a fellow student who, when studying for doctoral exams, took amphetamines to stay awake, then barbiturates to go to sleep. By the time of the exam, she was totally unable to function. This is a dramatic example of what happens to many housewives, businessmen, and others. They become depressed and their doctor prescribes an amphetamine. Then they can't sleep; so they use barbiturates—and the cycle continues. They take antidepressants, feel good, and work very hard. They exhaust themselves and get so depressed that they must increase the dosage.

Drug Categories

The most common drugs used today are of three types—hard drugs, soft drugs, and pharmaceutical drugs—with some overlap. In addition, a relatively new psychoactive drug, phencyclidine (PCP or angel dust), is both different and dangerous enough to constitute a fourth category.

Hard Drugs

Hard drugs include the narcotics—opium, the opium derivatives (morphine, codeine, heroin), and the synthetic drugs Demerol and methadone. Methadone has been used to help heroin addicts. These drugs are physically addictive and produce a deadening of sensitivity and feelings of euphoria. They are illegal. Individuals trying to obtain such drugs are responsible for a major portion of drug-related crimes.

"T's and blues" are two pharmaceutical drugs that have been combined to form a street substitute for heroin. Talwin (pentazocine) and Pyribenzamine (tripelennanine) are both legitimate drugs, but may cause psychological and/or physical dependence when combined. They can cause death if mixed with depressants. See Figure 12.1.

Figure 12.1
Types of Drugs, Excluding Alcohol

Narcotics (hard drugs)
Cause sleep or stupor and a feeling of euphoria; used for relief of pain; physiologically addictive

Opium

Opium derivatives
Morphine

Codeine
Heroin
Demerol (meperidine hydrochloride)
Methadone

Soft Drugs
Hallucinogens. Produce mild euphoria, visual distortions, and hallucinations

LSD 25 (lysergic acid)
Diethylamide 0
Peyote
Mescal
Mescaline
Psilocybin
DMT
STP (DOM)
MDA

Not Usually Hallucinogenic. Produce mild euphoria and visual distortions

Cannabis substances
  Marijuana
  Hashish

Pharmaceuticals

Amphetamines. Produce restlessness and appetite reduction

Methadrine (speed)
Dexedrine
Benzedrine
Cocaine

Antidepressants. Relieve depression and act as a stimulant

Dibenzapines
  Ritalin
  Elavil
  Tofranil
Lithium
MAO inhibitors
  Nardil
  Parnate

Tranquilizers. Decrease anxiety; sometimes produce dryness of the mouth, blurring of vision, drowsiness, ataxia, and nausea

Phenothiazines
  Thorazine
  Compazine
  Stelazine
Librium
Valium
Reserpine (rauwolfia)

Sedatives. Induce sleep and decrease anxiety

Barbiturates
  Nembutal
  Seconal
  Phenobarbital
Doriden
Chloral hydrate
Meprobamates
  Miltown
  Equanil

Soft Drugs

The most common soft drugs are marijuana and LSD. Other drugs in this category include peyote and its derivatives (mescal and mescaline); the synthetic drug similar to the peyote drugs (psilocybin), and the synthetic drugs DMT, STP (DOM), and MDA. All these drugs produce mild euphoria. Visual distortions and hallucinations may also occur.

Although all of these soft drugs are hallucinogens, marijuana usually produces only a mild state of euphoria or contentment (a high) in the dosages normal in the United States. In other countries, however, marijuana is consumed in much higher dosages and can produce effects similar to the effects of LSD. The other soft drugs all change perceptions and cause hallucinations. Alice of *Alice in Wonderland*[2] describes the kinds of visual distortions commonly noted by LSD users.

Other names for marijuana are grass, pot, hash, tea, and marijane. Hash or hashish is a strong form of marijuana.

Unlike heroin, marijuana and LSD are not physically addictive. In fact, with prolonged use, smaller quantities of marijuana are needed to cause a high. There may be a repeater effect with LSD; individuals may suffer the effects of the drug long after taking it.

Psychological addiction to both marijuana and LSD is possible, but those who are psychologically addicted probably constitute a small minority of users. Such persons are known as "potheads" (marijuana users) and "acidheads" (LSD users).

None of these drugs is dispensed legally, except for experimental purposes with many restrictions.[3] LSD may be easily, if illegally, synthesized in the laboratory.

Pharmaceutical Drugs

The third type of problem drug can be legally dispensed in drugstores, although some are available only by prescription. These "pharmaceuticals" include the amphetamines, the antidepressants, the tranquilizers, and the sedatives.

Some of the amphetamines—Methedrine, Dexedrine, Benzedrine, and even cocaine—may be prescribed for dieters. They are taken by people who feel down and/or want more energy. They are also used as antidepressants. They are quite dangerous physically because the body cannot maintain a heightened pace without damage.

Of these stimulants, cocaine has become a very popular "in" drug for the affluent.

The specific antidepressants—such as Ritalin, Elavil, Tofranil, Nardil, and Parnate—are prescribed by doctors for depressed patients. Lithium also has come into wide use in the treatment of depression. Even so, the use of these drugs poses dangers. Sometimes they do not produce the desired effect, illustrating again that the effect of drugs on specific individuals is not totally predictable.

Tranquilizers are prescribed by doctors to relieve anxiety. They, more than any other drugs, are responsible for the peaceful functioning of mental hospital wards. The most popular of the tranquilizers are the phenothiazines (Thorazine, Compazine, Stelazine). Side effects of the phenothiazines are common and, unless the dosage is very small, patients may become dulled and apathetic. Those who take these drugs for a long time must run the risk of other physiological damage—for example, lens damage and coordination problems are frequently observed in long-term phenothiazine users. Other popular mild tranquilizers include Librium (chlordiazepoxide) and Valium (diazepam).

Sedatives—the barbiturates—include Nembutal, Seconal, and phenobarbital; Doriden, chloral hydrate, and the meprobamates, which you probably know by the trade names of Miltown and Equanil. These too can be used to reduce anxiety and of course to induce sleep. You will notice their names in reports of suicides.

Phencyclidine (PCP)

Our fourth category includes only the drug PCP. It is put in a category of its own, not only because it does not fit into any of the other categories, but because of its potential as *the* most dangerous illicit drug. It can produce agitation or, in greater amounts, stupor or coma. Not only can it produce a state similar to schizophrenia, but its repeater effects are unpredictable. As if this were not enough, the drug may make a person homicidal or suicidal, violent or confused. Its street name is angel dust, but it is sold under more than seventy other names as well. Some of these are crystal, peace pill, tack, sheets. It is sold as a powder, tablet, leaf mixture, liquid, and crystal. One of the problems is the ease with which it can be synthesized in the lab, thus making it an extremely profitable drug to merchandise.

Alcohol

A major drug we have not discussed is alcohol. Although it provides initial stimulation, it is essentially a depressant, with many dangers in its use. Like soft drugs and pharmaceuticals, however, its dangers depend on how it is used.

The Attraction of Drugs

Tune in to the commercials on your television set at almost any hour and you will see that ours is a drug culture. Have a headache? Take a drug. Feel tense? Take a drug. Trouble with your mother-in-law? Take a drug. Trouble sleeping? Take another kind of drug. The list could be continued, but the point is that our society has become accustomed to seeking a drug as a solution to almost any problem. The drugs that are advertised on television are legal, but they form the basis and support for our children also to "take a drug." The drugs they take are often illegal, or self-destructive, or both.

What is the alternative to taking a drug for any and every ill? Obviously, drugs do not really solve the problems. Do you overeat? Why not cut down? Do you get tense? Why not develop releases for your tension, or think through the problems so that you can find solutions instead of always being tense? It is sometimes even *good* to be tense. If you face a serious problem, tension can help you be alert to all its aspects in order to find a solution. The next time a similar problem comes up, you will have a backlog of success to draw upon—instead of a large bill, growing larger, from the drugstore.

The reason that we have developed such a drug-taking pattern is perhaps more difficult to specify. After all, if nobody bought the sleeping pills, the headache pills, the uppers, and the downers, the TV commercials would go off the air. The reason may be related to our mechanized, technological society, in which we believe there must be some scientific way of finding a quick solution to every problem (see Figure 12.2). Pills seem to be such a quick solution, but in using them we tend to forget we are human beings! Our impatience, however, is the most general reason why these commercials are on the air, why people turn to drugs, and why we have a tremendous problem with drug use by increasingly younger children.

Figure 12.2
Are people the same as machines?

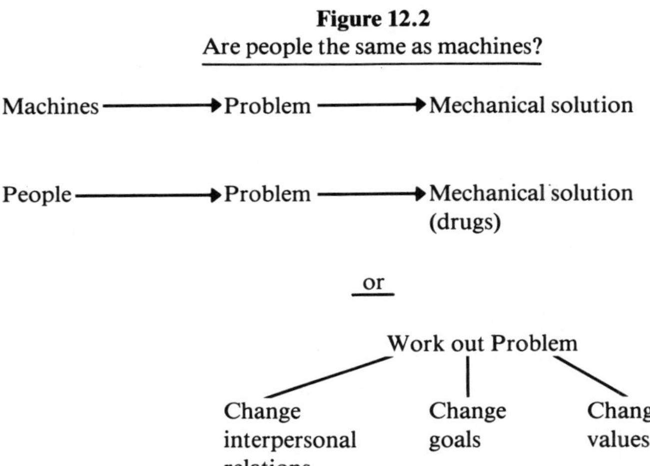

The use of drugs in limited quantity is much different. Almost every society studied has some type of ritual that includes drugs. Many are ceremonial occasions in which people have a chance to get away from their routines to experience exhilaration and excitement. For example, among the American Indians, the Indian Church of Oklahoma during the 1930s used peyote in the manner of a sacrament. Peyote and water were passed around, and in some ceremonies it was "eaten for four nights, with four days given up to the excitation."[4]

Effects of Drugs

Now let us turn to the effects of the various types of drugs.

Effects of Hard Drugs

Hard drugs are dangerous, and have given rise to a serious social problem. Hard drug addicts account for a large proportion of street crime and burglary. Addicts must steal thousands of dollars' worth of goods to support their habits, partly because, unlike marijuana, such drugs as heroin require increasing quantities for the same effect.

Further, while the body requires a "fix" in order for the individual to feel physically right, concomitants of continued use include loss of appetite, constipation, and temporary impotence. Children born of addicts may be (and all too often are) also addicted.

The dangers are both individual and social. The drug addict will not be able to do much besides attend to his habit. He frequently does not take proper physical care of himself. Malnutrition is widespread among hard drug addicts. Infection from improperly sterilized needles is also common. The social danger also affects the individual. If he must steal to support his habit, he will find it impossible to lead a normal life.

It must also be remembered that many addicts are able to live socially acceptable lives. This occurs when they are able to obtain their drugs without illegal activities. Doctors, for example, sometimes become addicts; but since they have ready, legal access to drugs, their addiction is frequently unknown.

It is premature to say that addiction causes destruction of the individual. We would have to say again, however, that addiction to hard drugs, under certain circumstances, does cause such destruction. What are these circumstances?

We do not know what percentage of hard drug addicts suffer ill consequences. It appears to be high. However, the addicts who are unaffected are not known. This is similar to the situation with homosexuals. Homosexuals who are doing well in society do not become known to social agencies or police. It is hard to research these questions because we do not know the extent to which addicts could function normally if they didn't have the problem of illegality. Problems for addicts which come from malnutrition, lack of sterility of needles, and so on might be easier to solve if the substance were legal.

A related question is the effect of withdrawal, which has been described as ranging from extreme torture to death. However, some people who have worked with addicts feel that the descriptions are melodramatic and are used as rationalizations for continuing the addiction. Major physical effects of withdrawal include vomiting, chills, perspiration, and cramps. The individual is definitely uncomfortable and needs medical supervision; however, he is probably no more tortured than a person suffering from a bad attack of intestinal flu.

Effects of Soft Drugs

In the 1960s, many people became frightened of hallucinogens, especially LSD. There were indeed isolated cases of persons going crazy and not returning to sanity. However, the danger was neither as widespread nor as mysterious as rumored. Those who became psychotic after taking LSD usually were able to return to normalcy. The few who did not were already close to insanity.

The immediate effects of the soft drugs are dependent on a number of circumstances. Whether someone is available to help can make a great difference to a person whose perceptions have suddenly become distorted. Anticipation that the experience will be exciting and pleasant will lead to a very different experience from anticipating a terrifying time. If one knows that one's perceptions will be distorted, one will have more ability to handle the experience than if someone has slipped a sugar cube containing LSD in the punch. For this reason it is very important to let people know what effect drugs they are taking will have. One reason many people can "handle their liquor" is because they know what to expect. They know they will get a little silly after one drink, so they don't take it if they have to write a report; they get somewhat aggressive after two drinks; and they are pretty fuzzy after four or five, so they don't try to walk on the edge of a wall or drive a car. See Figure 12.3.

In general, LSD appears to affect productivity negatively. There also may be chromosomal damage in users. Damage may also occur if the drug is taken during pregnancy. More positively, LSD has an opening-up effect that can be useful during psychotherapy. Some users report that extremely pleasurable and valuable ideas were developed through hallucinogens.[5] Unlike LSD, DMT appears to be hallucinogenic without increasing anxiety.

Among the nonhallucinogens, the effect of marijuana is distin-

Figure 12.3
Effect of hallucinogens

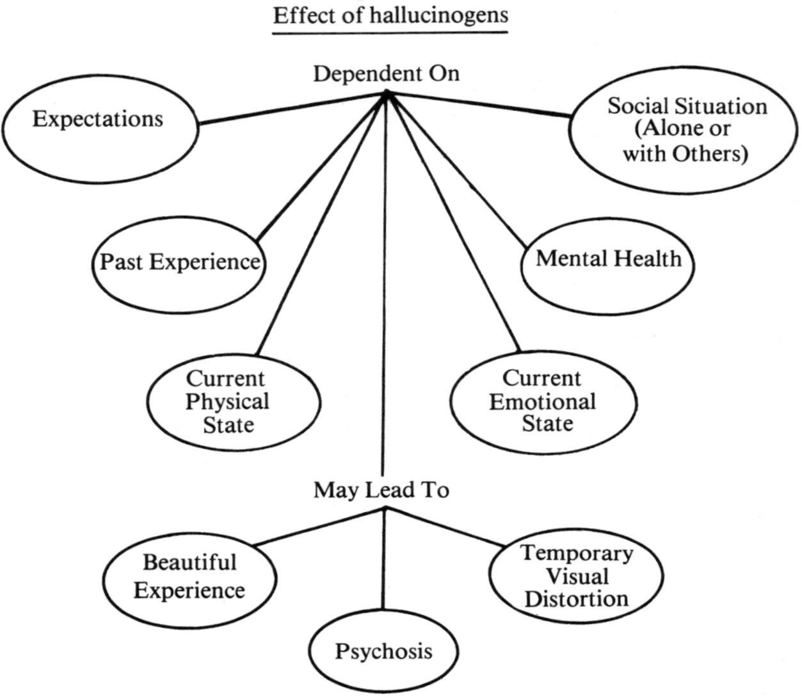

guishable from the effect of other soft drugs. It produces a pleasant, often giggly, state in the user. It decreases both aggression and sexual drive. It also lessens efficiency, quite clearly in motor tasks such as typing. Long-term effects of marijuana use are not completely clear. There is continued controversy, for example, about whether chromosomal defects occur in users. Some believe there are; other studies suggest that the defects are similar to chromosomal defects in the general population. There may be more spontaneous abortions in smokers, but the possible damage to the unborn child is unclear. A study of heavy users (ten years) showed little damage, though some organs were affected negatively in the same way as nicotine would affect them (notably the lungs).[6]

Effects of Pharmaceuticals

Amphetamines. Amphetamines (speed, etc.) are frequently prescribed for persons wishing to lose weight, or as an aid in battling depression. Amphetamines speed up mental processes and activity level. Unlike marijuana, amphetamines must be taken in larger and larger doses to produce "highs." The "highs" come quickly, followed by exhaustion and depression. There is danger of heart failure in the "rush" following injection of the drug, although this is a rare outcome. The major problem, however, is the physical and emotional strain produced by the unnaturally prolonged high level of activity. Deaths from "speed" are a major source of concern.

Tranquilizers. The danger of tranquilizers is the dulling of the mental processes. People who are tranquilized may be unconcerned about their real problems and live in a permanently foggy state. Although tranquilizers are not usually thought of as addictive, there are indications that people do become physiologically, as well as psychologically, dependent on the drugs. Long-term side effects can also be damaging.

Another danger with tranquilizers and other drugs, both prescription and over-the-counter, is that they can combine dangerously with other drugs. The combination of alcohol and barbiturates, for example, can be fatal. Many people believe that most overdose deaths are really due to a combination of drugs.

Barbiturates. Barbiturates (sleeping pills) are, of course, frequently used in suicide attempts. The unregulated prescription of large quantities of this drug can be fatal to someone who suffers from depression.

Phencyclidine. Our final drug, PCP, can cause death or a state resembling schizophrenia. In fact, it is often difficult to know whether a young patient who appears to be suffering from schizophrenia is really suffering from PCP ingestion. Violence frequently results from repeated use, but it can occur with a single dose.

Problems of Addicts

Before we can begin to treat addicts, we must consider the personality of those who turn to drugs.

Drug abuse, as contrasted to drug use, stems not only from an atmosphere in which drugs are readily available and/or in which the norm is frequent drug use, but also from a personality type characterized by one or both of the following: (1) impulsivity and (2) alienation.

Impulsivity

People who look for pleasure without working for it need specific kinds of help. They need to learn the satisfaction of working for what they want. They need goals to work for. They need hope. They need controls. They do *not* need sympathy. They do *not* need understanding of the "I know it is impossible for you to tolerate your kind of life" variety. They do *not* need someone who will believe their lies. They do *not* need someone who can be manipulated by them.

This prescription is similar to that for children who cannot control themselves.

Alienation

People who take drugs are alienated. There are two types of alienation: (1) failure to see oneself as an important member of society—any society—whether the larger community, a family group, or a group of friends; a feeling that life is pointless, without goals, hopeless; (2) a sense of separation from one's feelings. Persons suffering this kind of alienation do not know how they feel. They are somewhat like machines who function more or less effectively, but without emotion. The drugs help them to feel again.

Many housewives and students suffer the first kind of alienation—failure to see themselves as important members of society. Housewives may feel this way for a number of reasons: (1) They are lonely and isolated. Most of their chores do not bring them into contact with others. Contrast the modern housewife putting her clothes in her basement washing machine with the group of women all washing their clothes together in a stream. Or the housewife mending in front of the TV, contrasted with women gathered together for quilting bees in earlier days. (2) They do not feel their jobs are useful. Taking care of a home may not give the same degree of satisfaction as it did in the past. Housewives in the eighteenth century probably went to bed too exhausted to worry about whether their goals were fulfilled. Their goals were simple—

to cook, wash, sew, mend, and take care of the children. These chores were viewed as important.

This feeling of not being useful can affect many men as well. Those whose jobs in factories seem meaningless and futile may feel similarly alienated.

While students feel alienated for many reasons, the most frequent seems to be disenchantment with the material society provided by their parents. Material things have given them no sense of achievement and meaning in life, other than "getting more." They must look for other goals. Often they do not find them.

In contrast, lower-class addicts often feel alienated from society because they truly *are* alienated. They are cut off from the material rewards of our society. It is much harder for them to find jobs, to feel a sense of worth, and to succeed in school.

It may be that all addicts suffer from the second type of alienation—separation from the self. What, for example, is the mild depression that many people feel? It comes from learning to deny their feelings. If they do this enough they find they no longer know how they feel. This suppression of feeling makes people lose both the joy and the pain of living.

Why? First, people "know" they should not be (*a*) angry, (*b*) sad, (*c*) pained. If they feel any of these things, they put a lid on the feeling. The energy they must use to keep these feelings from showing makes it impossible to get over the feelings. It is as though they are always standing with a finger in a dike. If the dike has just a small leak, they may find energy for other things. If it is large, they cannot. There is also a spiral effect: the more they are busy with internal shutting off of feelings, the less successful they are, and the less they have to feel good about.

Treatment of Drug Dependence

Drug addicts may be treated in four basic ways: (1) imprisonment or hospitalization; (2) psychological treatment; (3) physical methods; and (4) legal means.

Imprisonment or Hospitalization

Imprisonment is frequent for drug addicts and alcoholics. Some federal prisons, such as Lexington, are set up to deal exclusively with drug addicts. While confinement is an effective way of *getting* people off drugs temporarily, it is not effective in *keeping* them off. This may be because the treatment, like any "escape," does not change the person's life-style. He goes back to the same conditions that caused him to take drugs initially. For example, alcoholics may be picked up on skid row, put in jail for a few days, and then turned out again (the revolving door effect).

Some people feel this rather peculiar custom should be abolished. Obviously, it does not prevent crime. It costs the taxpayers money, and it doesn't cure anyone. Why arrest these people at all? Strangely enough, the reason is humanitarian. Allowing alcoholics three days in a warm jail, with food and medical care, can make the difference between survival and nonsurvival. Of course, this is a waste of money in that it never changes the condition. Withdrawing this source of help, however, would cause more human suffering. A better solution would be the use of institutions along with psychological means of help.

Psychological Treatment

Psychotherapy has been found to be ineffective in treating drug addicts. Addicts usually can successfully manipulate the largely middle-class, non-drug-sophisticated psychotherapist. In this way, they make him or her ineffective.

Group methods, however, can be effective. Groups are usually composed of people who are successfully fighting the addiction and have been leading normal lives, as well as people who would like to be cured but are still addicted. This approach has the advantage of contact with people very familiar with the dangers and dodges that keep people from changing. Such people also provide a great deal of psychological support and help. Alcoholics Anonymous has provided help on a twenty-four-hour basis for those who want to give up alcohol addiction. It works because the people involved understand the problem and care. Very few professionals would be willing to get up at two in the morning to help a drunk. What sort of person would? A fellow sufferer! He both reinforces his own cure and helps another by participating in such groups as Alcoholics Anonymous. Common problems can be sorted out; aid and succor given to the alcoholic's family. Many spouses of alcoholics follow a personality pattern that seems to make them psychologically dependent on the alcoholism. Such spouses are "martyrs." Therefore, they need help themselves so they will not unconsciously undermine the alcoholic's attempt to cure himself.

Synanon is an example of an encounter method. Members of Synanon groups "tell it like it is." They do not put up with any excuses from members but insist that each one take responsibility for his own actions. Since members live in resident groups in a controlled environment, with everyone having work and responsibility, the requirement of showing a person how to attain self-respect through work seems to be met by this method. While this may seem similar to unsuccessful institutional treatments, there are a number of differences. The focus is directly on the problems in the outside world, not on adjusting to an authoritarian institution.

Synanon is called an encounter group because members "encounter" one another with "the way it is"—no polite, but false, niceties are allowed. Such directness seems to help the addict fight the problem of alienation from the self.

A variant of the encounter groups stresses the release of feelings. Members are encouraged to "let loose" their emotions. When the angry, sad, or painful feelings are expressed, feelings of warmth and closeness arise. People care for one another. They get "high" without drugs.

Other techniques of getting "high" without drugs include learning to control brain waves. It has been found that when the brain emits alpha waves, pleasant feelings result. People can be trained to emit alpha waves through conditioning. People also emit alpha waves when following a variety of Eastern meditation methods (Transcendental Meditation, Yoga, etc.).

Other types of activity methods may also prove useful. In one program for delinquents, participants take on high-pressure physical assignments—mountain climbing, survival in the wilderness, and so on—with, of course, the kind of supervision necessary to make these assignments successful. The resulting self-esteem has helped delinquents cope with the frustrations to which they will return. This kind of method could be used for addicts.

Physical Methods

Distribution of methadone as a substitute for heroin has been the most successful wide-scale treatment for heroin addiction to be used in America. Although some feel that methadone substitutes one drug for another and does nothing to change the addict's life-style, it does enable addicts to function in society, relieved of the burden of stealing to support an illegal heroin habit. Results of methadone treatment centers have varied. Failures appear related to interpersonal difficulties, police infiltration, or unrealistic standards of behavior for an addict's continuance in a program. Using centers as political footballs can also be highly destructive. Nevertheless, overall results of such programs have been promising.

Antabuse for alcoholics works somewhat differently from methadone. Antabuse makes an addict ill if he drinks alcohol. He therefore is conditioned to feel negatively about alcohol. However, it provides no substitute for the positive attraction of alcohol.

Legal Means

If major problems result from the illegality of addiction, another method would be to change the laws to make some drugs legal. In Great Britain, drugs have been legalized. In the period following World War I, our country similarly legalized heroin. Both experiments were highly successful, and it is unfortunate that the United States did not continue the program. While some problems attended both the U.S. and British programs, these problems were minor compared to the problems we face today with the maintenance of a black market in drugs.

In regard to alcohol addiction, most of the problems are interpersonal or relate to traffic fatalities. Countries with stiff drunken-driving laws have cut down on traffic fatalities.

Problems Related to Current Drug Laws

For individuals in the criminal justice community, drugs produce a very complex problem. Drug laws reflect neither current research findings nor accepted practices among large minorities.

Current research has shown that cigarette smoking is definitely related to cancer and heart disease. Research on alcohol shows that, if it is used over a long period of time, extensive physical damage occurs. In addition, a high proportion of traffic accidents is caused by drivers who have been drinking.

How do the laws reflect these findings? No laws penalize users of tobacco, although there are laws regulating advertisement and sale to minors. Laws do not penalize users of alcohol at all, unless such users are also doing something else against the law (speeding, for example).

The laws against users or sellers of drugs are confusing and differ in different administrative units—local versus state, state versus federal. Such laws confuse hard and soft drugs and ignore the danger of pharmaceutical drugs.

Large areas of the population (youth, college students, some high school students, and middle-class urban adults) accept the use of certain drugs, primarily marijuana. Yet laws may be harsh. Such discrepancies produce particular problems for law enforcement.

How can the problem be dealt with rationally by the criminal justice community?

One approach is to "go hard"—especially in the area of hard drugs. New York State, for example, enacted a law making sentences as harsh for selling narcotics as for killing a policeman. This led to two unanticipated consequences. Initially, there was more gun-carrying among drug users and pushers; they talked of killing policemen, if caught, since the penalty was no greater. There also arose a group of underage "pushers" who were not affected by the new law, since it applied only to adult offenders. On a longer-term basis, it was found that cases were less likely to proceed to conviction, since all concerned were aware of the severity of the sentences.

Another approach has been to attempt to prevent importation of drugs. This is difficult and seems similar to trying to stem an ocean tide, though it has met with some success.

It seems likely that some type of legalizing and regulating of drug traffic and use would be a more successful approach. This appears to be occurring with marijuana; however, until this occurs, it is unlikely that the widespread crime surrounding the acquisition, sale, and use of drugs will diminish. In fact, drug traffic appears to be replacing gambling, which is becoming legalized, as the new domain of organized crime.

Alcoholism

Although alcoholism has been discussed only briefly, most of the causes of drug abuse apply to alcoholism as well. The general climate and specific personality problems of drug addicts are frequently found in alcoholics.

A particular criminal justice problem raised by alcoholism is, however, the large groups of "skid row" alcoholics who are periodically picked up and "dried out." A major problem of these and other alcoholics is general physical neglect, especially malnutrition.

While skid row alcoholics cause damage primarily to themselves, many alcoholics who are still part of the community cause untold damage to their families.

Dealing with Drug Emergencies

The most serious drug emergency is the overdose. When an overdose of drugs has been taken, or some combination of drugs is causing serious effects, immediate care is vital. A person may die within fifteen to thirty minutes of an overdose. An unconscious person must have immediate help to survive. Drug crisis centers are frequently equipped for immediate administration of drugs that can reverse the toxic process. Otherwise, first-aid teams or emergency rooms at hospitals should be used.

If a person is conscious but has taken hard drugs or hallucinogenic drugs such as LSD, he should be taken to a hospital emergency room and watched. Hallucinogenic drugs can cause him to do irrational and dangerous things to himself. Hard drugs can cause death in a variety of ways: a combination of drugs (strychnine has been used in small quantities with other drugs) may prove lethal; unregulated street drugs have unknown quantities of the pure drug. The previous physical condition of the taker may affect his reaction. All these conditions can prove dangerous and often lead to fatalities. PCP users need to be watched because they often do aggressive things and act as though they were psychotic.

Dealing with the Family

Dealing with the families of drug addicts or drug fatalities poses a variety of problems, ranging from an upset family whose son has just been charged with marijuana possession, to the shocked family of a hard-drug addict, to the bereaved family of a child who has died of an overdose. Families may be upper-class, middle-class, or lower-class.

In the case of an arrest, families may be concerned about the drug use, the arrest, or both. Frequently marijuana usage is accepted by families—the parents may even be using marijuana themselves. In these cases, empathy with their feeling that the arrest is unfair can be combined with a clear statement of the situation and procedure to be followed.

Other families may be concerned about the addiction. They may evidence shock, disbelief, or guilt about their child's behavior. Or they may feel that they can do nothing about the addiction, that they have tried, that they are now helpless. It is important that information about rehabilitative treatment be given to the family. Drug and alcohol centers may be available; family social work agencies are almost always within reach and can help directly or serve as referral resources.

Families who have had a member die of a drug-related cause are in a very different situation. They can have no hope of the victim's return. Such families initially will be in a state of shock. It is important that help be mobilized for them. A police officer can make a difference in their later reactions to bereavement by getting immediate, concrete help. Ministers, relatives, and doctors can be called. Having someone there to help during the initial adjustment to shock is important. Such concrete help is a better indication of concern than any statements that might be made. Nonverbal communication of concern for the survivors is also important. A hand squeeze or a touch on the shoulder can make the survivor feel that someone cares. It is equally important to accept outbursts of rage, to let the survivor know that, even though he is angry, you are still available to help in such matters as contacting relatives or providing transportation. While police officers cannot provide extended help, they can see to it that some other persons or agencies are available to provide such help.

Summary

Drug addiction may be legal or illegal, psychological or physical, sudden or gradual. Drugs affect different people in many varying ways.

The most dangerous and widely used drug in the United States today is a legal one: alcohol. Other common drugs in use today are (1) the hard drugs, including codeine and heroin, (2) the soft drugs, including LSD and marijuana, and (3) the pharmaceutical drugs, including amphetamines and tranquilizers.

The use of hard drugs has given rise to serious problems both for society and for the individual. The dangers of soft drugs are less clear. The pharmaceutical drugs are especially dangerous in combination with each other or with alcohol.

The addict is frequently characterized by impulsivity and alienation from society. His problems are compounded by current cultural pressures to "take a pill" when one has a difficulty.

Drug dependence may be treated in four basic ways: imprisonment, psychological treatment, physical methods, and legal means. Most promising are group psychological methods, such as Alcoholics Anonymous and groups providing an outlet for feelings; and physical aids, such as Antabuse and methadone. Of equal importance is an ongoing review of drug laws to be sure they reflect current professional and popular opinion.

Users of soft drugs should be treated tactfully, with special concern for physical and overdose problems. With hard-core addicts, caution is necessary; some are harmless, some desperate and dangerous.

In dealing with both addicts and their families, be sure all avenues of help and referral are explored.

Discussion Questions

1. What is the feeling of alienation? Have you experienced it yourself? Try sharing some important feelings with your group. How does this change your feelings?
2. What do you think are the best solutions to the drug problem? Long-term solutions? Solutions that can work through changes in the legal system?

3. Try to arrange a visit to a drug treatment center. Can you pick out what is helpful, not helpful in dealing with addicts?
4. Watch television for two or three evenings. Identify the drug-suggesting commercials. What kind of pitch do they make? How do they treat feelings of discomfort, lack of energy, tension, pain?

Suggested Reading

Aaronson, B., and Osmond, H. *Psychedelics.* Garden City, N.Y.: Doubleday, Anchor Books, 1970.

Bourne, P. G., ed. *Addiction.* New York: Academic Press, 1974.

Brecker, E. M., and the editors of *Consumer Reports. Licit and Illicit Drugs.* Boston: Little, Brown, 1972.

Brown, B. S., ed. *Addicts and Aftercare: Community Integration of the Former Drug User.* Sage Annual Reviews of Drug and Alcohol Abuse, vol. 3. Beverly Hills, Calif.: Sage Publications, 1979.

Casriel, D. *A Scream Away from Happiness.* New York: Grosset and Dunlap, 1972.

Coles, R.; Brenner, J.; and Meagher, D. *Drugs and Youth: Medical, Psychiatric and Legal Facts.* New York: Avon, 1970.

Cortina, F. M. *Stroke a Slain Warrior.* New York: Columbia University Press, 1970.

De Ropp, R. S. *Drugs and the Mind.* Rev. ed. New York: Delacorte Press, 1976.

Dornbush, R. L.; Freedman, A. M.; and Fink, M. *Chronic Cannabis Use.* New York: New York Academy of Sciences, 1976.

Ferguson, R. W. *Drug Abuse Control.* Boston: Holbrook Press, 1975.

Goldstein, P. J. *Prostitution and Drugs.* Lexington, Mass.: Lexington Books, 1979.

Grinspoon, L. *The Speed Culture: Amphetamine Use and Abuse in America.* Cambridge, Mass.: Harvard University Press, 1975.

Grinspoon, L., and Hedbloom, P. *Marijuana Reconsidered.* 2d ed. Cambridge, Mass.: Harvard University Press, 1977.

Lindesmith, A. R. *The Addict and the Law.* Bloomington: Indiana University Press, 1965.

Madden, J. S. *A Guide to Alcohol and Drug Dependence.* Bristol, England: Wright & Sons, 1979.

Scarpitti, F. R., and Datesman, S. K. *Drugs and the Youth Culture.* Sage Annual Review of Drug and Alcohol Abuse, Vol. 4. Beverly Hills, Calif.: Sage Publications, 1980.

Sobell, L. C., ed. *Evaluating Alcohol and Drug Abuse Treatment Effectiveness.* Elmsford, N.Y.: Pergamon Press, 1979.

Yablonsky, L. *Synanon: The Tunnel Back.* New York: Macmillan, 1964.

Part Three

Criminals with Victims: Sex Crime and White-Collar Crime

CHAPTER 13

Sex Crimes

Sex crimes are an important problem area for the criminal justice community for two reasons: (1) Violent sex crimes, such as rape or rape-murder, are the kind of crime most feared by the public, and (2) sex crimes that are not serious, such as homosexuality between consenting adults, appear to be associated in the public mind with the violent crimes, producing strong reactions. Sex crimes that are intermediate in seriousness, such as exhibitionism, also produce reactions out of proportion to their importance. It is therefore essential that criminal justice personnel understand the meaning and degree of seriousness of various sexual behaviors.

How Prevalent Are Sex Crimes?

Some sex crimes receive wide press coverage. Such crimes are so abhorrent that we expect outcries and urgent cries for prevention.

Fortunately, however, most sex crimes are victimless, consisting of such acts as fornication, prostitution, statutory rape, masturbation, and homosexuality between consenting adults. All of these crimes constitute from 2 to 6 percent of indictable offenses and felonies in most jurisdictions.

Somewhat more serious are such sex crimes as exhibitionism (displaying the genitals), scoptophilia (peeking), coprolalia (using obscene language), frotteurism (rubbing), pedophilia (sex with children), incest (voluntary sex within a family). Although nonviolent, they can cause psychological damage.

Some sex crimes, of course, have victims in the usual sense. These would include rape, sadism, and rape-murder.

It is easy to understand the feeling of the public against violent sex crimes. However, it is less understandable that the public should be as concerned with pornography or homosexuality.

Part of the answer lies in American attitudes toward sexuality. For Americans, sex is particularly tempting because it is so often forbidden, especially for the adolescent. Attitudes learned during adolescence are not easily forgotten. While extramarital sex is frequent, it is still the cause of much guilt among Americans.

In addition to being forbidden, sex is emphasized in the mass media. Being sexually attractive, for example, is touted in most commercials. If one believes the message of the commercials, being sexually attractive must be one of the major goals of life (being clean—and having a clean house—seems to be another). Magazines such as *Playboy* are devoted primarily to the glories of sex, while cities are overrun by "massage parlors" (centers for prostitution), pornographic bookstores, and X-rated movies. These businesses are so successful that they can frequently pay double or triple the rent of legitimate businesses.

Another example of our attitude toward sex is our movie rating system. Much of the system has been devised to make it clear to the public that some films have sexual content unsuitable for youth. That the public is concerned about the issue is evident. An announcement that a major TV network was going to show X-rated movies brought thousands of letters of protest from parents concerned that their children would see these films.

Another example of our problem about sex is that dirty jokes are frequently sex jokes, considered improper for the ears of women or children.

In our society sex seems to be considered "dirty," attractive, and not to be discussed publicly except in relation to sexual attractiveness.

Psychologically, this leads many people to try to prevent sexual expression in others since they themselves have such conflict about sexuality.

Psychosocial Reasons for Sex Variations or Crimes

Why would anyone need to satisfy a desire for sexual gratification by stabbing and killing a woman? Why would someone find sexual satisfaction from setting a fire? How does a perfectly normal need become perverted so that an individual can fulfill it only by behavior that ranges from the unusual to the gruesome?

There are three causes of sexual variation or crime: (1) The individual has not been allowed to accept and direct his sexual desires because his parents or others have taught him that sexual impulses are horrible and frightening; (2) The individual has been exposed to unusual or disturbing sexual behavior, such as growing up with a mother who is a prostitute and openly allows her son to see her sexual behavior; (3) The individual has grown up in a subculture, usually a ghetto, where violent expression of impulses is acceptable behavior. Such an individual would grow up to believe that gang-rape is acceptable behavior.

Suppression of Sexual Impulses

When children cannot accept their sexual impulses because they have been taught that they are wrong, the children learn to hide these impulses, even from themselves. This leads to erratic behavior, since they do not know what is making them uncomfortable, restless, or angry. Thus a "good boy" who has never engaged in the usual childish sex play may, as an adult, become an exhibitionist.

Exposure to Disturbing Sexual Behavior

In the case of the individual who has been exposed to unusual sex behavior on the part of adults around him, the resulting overstimulation may make it difficult for him to be aware of his impulses. Overstimulation is just as frightening to a child as being told that masturbation will cause his penis to fall off. He may be overstimulated by constant sexual activity, such as a child of a prostitute might witness; or by occasional but dramatic experiences, such as a child being stimulated by an adult; or by associating peculiar circumstances with sexual arousal—seeing a mother undressing and putting on fuzzy slippers could lead to a fetishistic attachment to slippers, or fuzzy articles. Such experiences lead to unusual sexual behavior in some cases, and in rare cases to sex crimes.

Acceptability of Behavior to the Subculture

The third condition leads to the separation of sexual impulses from more civilized behavior. The child growing up in an environment where people grab what they want and have no concern for the feelings of others will learn to grab sexually. Sexual customs in ghettos frequently dictate that violent sex is manly. Sex criminals, influenced by such conditions, are likely to act with others, or for personal gain. The sexuality of individuals exposed to the first two conditions is more likely to be expressed in *individual* acts, or in acts that bring no conceivable gain.

The following section will indicate that, while a person's behavior may constitute an act that is punishable by law, it may be a simple variation that is not harmful and may be helpful. Criminal justice is concerned primarily with the individual whose unusual experiences lead him to violent acts.

What Are Sex Crimes?

As suggested above, there are several different kinds of sex crime. It is possible to define the areas of sex crime in a variety of ways. We shall, however, consider six types:

1. Crimes involving sexual intercourse of a sort defined legally as unusual. These would include cunnilingus (male oral contact with the female genitals), annalingus (oral-anal contact), and fellatio (female oral contact with the male genitals). Many people today consider such types of intercourse pleasurable and harmless.
2. Crimes involving sex for profit, chiefly prostitution.
3. Crimes involving sexual intercourse with an unusual object.

These would include bestiality (sex with animals), homosexuality (sex with a member of the same sex), incest, pedophilia (sex with children), necrophilia (sex with corpses). These crimes may be committed by those who are frightened of seeking adults of the opposite sex as partners.

4. Crimes involving an unusual means of sexual arousal. These would include fetishism (arousal through a symbolic article), kleptomania (arousal through stealing certain items), frotteurism (arousal through rubbing), pyromania (arousal through setting fires).
5. Crimes that assure men of their potency. These include exhibitionism (displaying the genitals), scoptophilia (peeking), coprolalia (as in obscene phone calls).
6. Crimes involving sex combined with violence or hostility—sadomasochism (arousal through inflicting or receiving pain), flagellation (arousal through beatings), piquerism (arousal through stabbing), rape, rape-murder.)

Crimes Involving Unusual Types of Intercourse

Obviously, we need not be particularly concerned with this first type of crime. Freud defines any sexual behavior short of sexual intercourse as perverse—but only if it did not lead to sexual intercourse; therefore, even in his terms such behavior is not abnormal if followed by sexual intercourse. Varied types of intercourse are now common in our society, and it is hard to believe that they are still considered criminal in rare cases.

Crimes Involving Sex for Profit

The second group of sex crimes is of more concern—though it can be said to involve a victim in only an indirect manner.

The existence of prostitution as a flourishing enterprise depends chiefly, of course, on social conditions that do not permit sexual relations to everyone wishing them.

Prostitution also is closely related to a double standard of viewing sex as natural for men, unnatural for women. A segment of public opinion still suggests that sex for women is an obligation rather than a pleasure. Unmarried men, therefore, may have difficulty finding sexual partners, and even married men may find that their wives are not sufficiently interested in sex, especially of unusual types. Men then seek a prostitute. Prostitutes on a higher level—call girls—are also hired by businesses to entertain clients who find it inconvenient to look for sexually interested young women. Prostitution is also a means of satisfying perverse sexual tendencies such as masochism.

What problems does prostitution present to society? The first is prostitution-related crime. This involves using prostitution as a way of robbing clients, or luring them into areas where they may be more seriously assaulted. It also involves drug-related crimes, since hard drug use and prostitution are closely related.

A second major area of difficulty is that of disease. In some countries prostitution is legal and medically supervised, but where it is illegal it is very difficult to ensure that venereal disease does not spread as a result. Regulation rather than prohibition would be a partial solution. However, it should be noted that only a very small percentage of venereal disease is communicated through prostitutes.

The third area of difficulty is the prostitute herself. Whether solely because of the nature of the business, or because of the circumstances surrounding the work (social disapproval, illegality), most prostitutes studied have been found to be extremely maladjusted and unhappy people. In a study by Harold Greenwald,[1] almost all the call girls interviewed had attempted suicide. Further, girls have been illegally lured into prostitution in ways reminiscent of the "white slave trade." In this country—and in other countries—prostitution is forced upon thousands of young girls simply because they are destitute.

It would seem then that even though prostitution performs an important service, a much better answer would be a more permissive attitude toward fulfilling sexual needs for both men and women. If people are comfortable with their sexual desires, they will be able to find suitable partners without making the process a commercial enterprise.

Crimes Involving Sex with an Unusual Object

Crimes involving sex with an unusual object can be more serious; however, some of the crimes falling within this category are of little concern to society.

Bestiality. Bestiality, or sexual acts with animals, is regarded as of little consequence in the country court, though a city judge less familiar with its incidence would consider it more serious.

Necrophilia. This crime involving sexual attraction to the dead is extremely rare and therefore, though horrifying, merits little criminal justice attention.

Incest. Sexual acts between close relatives are probably more frequent than most of us want to acknowledge. Among families that are isolated physically and/or socially, sexual relationships between fathers and daughters, brothers and sisters, and, more rarely, mothers and sons may occur as a result of the combination of a disturbed marriage, physical accessibility, sexual urges, and lack of ability to find appropriate partners outside the family. Frequently wives know about and tolerate relationships between their husbands and daughters. Sometimes it is years before they feel able to report such problems. Sometimes they do so out of desperation. Children frequently do not report the problem, adding further difficulty to identifying and correcting the situation.

The primary psychological problem within incestuous relationships between a parent and child is the unequal power situation. The child becomes a pawn of the adult's sexual needs.

Homosexuality. Homosexual activity between consenting adults seems of little real concern for the protection of our citizens. Many homosexuals feel that theirs is a satisfactory life-style. Recent research suggests that they are correct, finding no difference in adjustment between a group of homosexuals and a group of individuals similar to the homosexuals who were heterosexual.[2] Homosexuals are, through such movements as Gay Liberation, increasingly asserting their right to live as they wish. They must, however, still face legal penalties in thirty-one states (1978). Often homosexuals are barred from sensitive positions because of their vulnerability to blackmail. This deprives both the homosexual and society of valuable opportunities.

In the past, psychiatrists and psychologists usually disagreed with homosexuals who felt that their life-style was as mature as that of heterosexuals. It is only now becoming possible to investigate homosexuals who are leading satisfying lives. These studies show that homosexuals have as many different life-styles as others.[3] Some are healthy, some immature, some just all right. The same is true of heterosexuals.

Another type of homosexuality frequently develops in prisons and other places where no members of the opposite sex are available. It is natural for individuals to seek sexual satisfaction in whatever way possible. Individuals who have turned to homosexuality under such circumstances return to heterosexuality when the opportunity permits. In reform schools and other penal institutions, however, homosexuality often is combined with violence and becomes a major problem. Stronger inmates may intimidate others. Homosexuality also occurs with greater frequency in the armed services.

When homosexuality is combined with pedophilia, the act and the person committing it must be scrutinized. Usually pedophiliacs are not dangerous. The harm they inflict on a child by their seductive activities causes less psychological damage than one would expect, especially if adults react matter-of-factly.

If a young person finds homosexual contact to be pleasurable, he may seek further homosexual activity. However, if his experience also includes heterosexual activity, it is most likely that he will develop in a heterosexual fashion. In fact, a large proportion of males do have homosexual experiences, many while growing up. They still turn to heterosexuality.

It has recently been noted that sexual contacts with older men may be initiated by teenagers, who find homosexual solicitation to be a safer and easier way of obtaining money than by stealing or other types of nonsexual crime. For such youths, solicitation is a business similar to prostitution. Sometimes the older men are victimized by theft, more frequently not. These boys do not become homosexual, suggesting that the social context (a good way to make money) rather than the act itself is important in determining how sex experience affects adjustment. It is, therefore, erroneous to consider these boys to be victims of older men, a position one would have to take according to vice laws, in which the minor is always the victim.

Men or women who become permanent homosexuals sometimes have had very frightening experiences with the parent of the opposite sex. The parent may have been overly seductive or overly severe, or may in some way have made the child feel that he or she could not safely have sexual relations with someone of the opposite sex. Sometimes the child feels he cannot identify with the parent of his sex and seeks to act like the other sex. At other times, parents have wanted a child of the opposite sex, have dressed the boy in girls' clothing (or vice versa), and in numerous ways trained the child to identify with the opposite sex. However, the majority of homosexuals have had some heterosexual experience. Similarly, many heterosexuals have had homosexual experiences.

The concern of society seems to be more reasonably directed toward child victims of homosexual attack. Psychologists have found, however, that parents' reactions often make the situation more negative than necessary. If children are treated kindly during homosexual contacts and are not particularly bothered by them, adults should refrain from communicating their feelings of horror. No serious consequences would be expected if such contacts were infrequent and reacted to matter-of-factly by adults.[4]

If experiences are frequent, however, they could cause children to develop mature sexual interests while they are still young. Such premature arousal can cause further problems. If the adult attacks with violence, the experience becomes very difficult to deal with. The actual experience the child had must be evaluated as well as his reaction to it.

Why do men become pedophiliacs and how dangerous are they? Pedophiliacs are usually men who are frightened of adult women. They turn, therefore, to young girls, or boys, to relieve sexual tensions and sometimes loneliness. They are dangerous only if they have had a history of violence or if their record of offenses indicates increasing violence.

Crimes Involving an Unusual Means of Arousal

Fetishism, kleptomania, and frotteurism do not pose serious problems. Fetishists sometimes steal objects of sexual interest to them. A fetish arises from early experiences that cannot be accepted and that have been sexually arousing.

Kleptomania. This condition is related to fetishism in that the true kleptomaniac steals particular, and arousing, garments, such as women's underwear. True kleptomania seems to be extremely rare. Most shoplifting has little to do with this kind of sexual problem.

Frotteurism. Frotteurism, or rubbing against others for sexual pleasure, is similarly harmless, though it can be annoying. It usually occurs in crowded areas, such as subway trains.

Pyromania. The love of setting fires, known as pyromania, seems to be a symbolic means of sexual gratification. In fact, police have often noted that the pyromaniac can be spotted because he masturbates while watching the fire. For example, a young man whose mother was promiscuous set fires as an indirect way of dealing with his sexual arousal. This arousal started when he watched his mother entertain a series of men sexually.

Crimes That Assure Men of Their Potency

Crimes that assure men of their potency are of some concern to society, though the damage they do is minor.

Exhibitionism. This crime is a way of assuring oneself of potency. If the viewer reacts with horror, the exhibitionist knows he must have a powerful penis. Exhibitionism does no real harm, and there have been cases of persons with high status in their communities who have had to use exhibitionism to achieve orgasm.

However, one aspect of exhibitionism is worthy of comment and concern: exhibitionists frequently show their penises to children. If one realizes that children look at such behavior as they would look at animals copulating ("Isn't that interesting?" or "What are they doing?"), one need not become excessively alarmed.

Another aspect of exhibitionism is its occasional relationship to serious sex crimes. Exhibitionism usually simply repeats itself. In some cases, however, individuals move from one type of sex crime to another. In cases that eventually lead to murder, it is usually possible to see slowly increasing elements of violence. It is, therefore, wise to look carefully at the records of any sex criminals and the details of their search for orgasms. If there appears to be no element of violence, or if the level of violence remains the same, they probably present little danger to society.

Scoptophilia. "Peeping Toms" may be even more annoying than exhibitionists. Scoptophilia, too, is an immature way of seeking sexual satisfaction. It is indulged in by men who are frightened of actual intercourse. If repeated without violence, there is probably little danger; however, the caution mentioned in the discussion of exhibitionism applies.

Coprolalia. This practice is similarly annoying, but presents little danger. If recipients respond neutrally to obscene phone calls, they are unlikely to be repeated.

Crimes Involving Sex Combined with Violence or Hostility

Crimes in which sex is combined with violence or hostility are of more serious concern to society. *Sadomasochism* may be no more than a reflection of a culture that says one should be punished—or punish others—for sexual desire. If its outlet is confined to acts with consenting partners, there is no problem; however, the sadist who imposes his desires on others *is* a problem for society.

Flagellation. Receiving sexual pleasure from being beaten has its history in religious movements. It is of little concern in modern society, although it is frequent in accounts of activities of prostitutes. It has two psychological meanings—one is the alleviation of guilt for sexual pleasure, and the other is that the buttocks, the most common site of spankings and whippings, are an erotic zone, causing sexual arousal. The importance of this connection is demonstrated in the frequency of sadomasochism, involving beating of the buttocks, in pornographic literature. Children who have been beaten sometimes develop an interest in continued beating for sexual arousal.

Rape. This crime increased rapidly from 1966 to 1972.[5] However, from that time to 1977, the incidence remained the same.[6] Forcible rape appears to be little understood by either the criminal justice community or the larger society. While a potential for injustice to a man accused of rape is present, the justice system seems to have tipped its scales to favor the accused rapist. Rape is the only crime in which many states require a "cautionary instruction" warning the jurors to examine the testimony of the complainant with caution. While the victim can be and usually is questioned closely about her sexual morality and behavior, the accused rapist usually cannot be asked any questions about his past. This leads to situations in which the accused may have a history of sex crimes but is acquitted because the jury believes that "such a nice-looking young man could not possibly have committed rape." There is a general attitude that most if not all women who are raped have "asked for it." This attitude persists even in cases where women have been terrorized, have tried to get help, and have been injured.

The attitude is similar to that of telling a person who was mugged that he "asked for it" because he was carrying a wallet or was walking down a city street without a companion. Another inequity exists in the advice given women not to resist—after which the presumption is that, because she did not resist, she wished to be attacked. To return to the analogy with mugging, the person who is mugged is not told he was a willing victim because he chose not to fight back for fear of being killed.

The manner in which rape victims are often handled also suggests an attitude of contempt on the part of the police, hospital personnel, and attorneys. There is an assumption among many males that women enjoy being raped. The assumption has its basis in the passivity of the female sex role. Many women do prefer to have men initiate a sex act, and many do admire active, aggressive men. However, the brutal rapist who terrifies and mutilates is a grotesque caricature of the active, aggressive male who initiates mutually pleasurable sexual activity. Even for those who may have fantasies of rape (and there is very little information about women's sexual fantasies) there is a marked difference between being raped—a violent act out of one's control—and thinking about rape—which can be stopped at any time.

At any rate, either because women do have fantasies of rape, or because women are told they should or do have such fantasies, many women feel responsible for their own victimization. The findings of the National Commission on the Causes and Prevention of Violence indicate otherwise.[7] In a review of victim precipitation—the contribution of the victim to the crime—the commission found that 4.4 percent of rape victims had contributed, as contrasted to 22 percent of homicide victims and 14.4 percent of assault victims. A special New York City crimes analysis squad found only 2 percent of rape reports to be unfounded, a striking contrast to the assumption of some forces that *most* such reports are unfounded. Instead, rape is grossly *underreported,* according to the FBI. The 2 percent figure gains added credibility since it corresponds with figures for false reports of other violent crimes.

In the light of such evidence, as well as case reports, it seems strange that men—and some women—continue to believe that rape is a consensual crime. The answer may lie in reviewing the treatment of other groups that are subject to discrimination. The larger society tends to label them as enjoying their oppression (the "happy, singing Negroes" of the nineteenth and early twentieth centuries), or as being not really human (the "gooks" of the Vietnamese War). This enables those who discriminate or persecute to be more comfortable and less guilty about their behavior.

Who are the rapists? Rapists have been categorized in a number of ways, but there seem to be two major groups—a psychiatrically disturbed group who have grown up with a distorted view of sex, hampering their ability to achieve normal sexual gratification, and a group who are asocial in their orientation, who view anyone weaker as "fair game" and feel no remorse for their crimes.

1. The psychiatric group can be illustrated by a man who was married, had children, was well respected by his business associates—but slipped away repeatedly to rape women. Such men, because of unfortunate early experiences, are unable to establish satisfying relationships that include sex with women. Sex is often isolated from other parts of life. Women may be seen as either pure or promiscuous. Although this attitude is fairly general in our society, it does not prevent most people from normal sexual gratification. For deviants the attitude may prevent normal gratification. Because of the buildup of unsatisfied sexual need, needs for affection or expression of anger, the needs become uncontrollable and are expressed in acts in which the rapist feels he cannot stop himself.

2. The nonpsychiatric, asocial group may be similar in believing that women are either pure or promiscuous. However, this group feels that there is nothing wrong with exploiting women, participating in gang-rapes, or simply raping a woman because she looks appealing. Among this group, there appear to be three subgroups: (*a*) those who direct deep anger at women, even though the anger may have originated in nonrelated experiences, (*b*) those who feel a strong need to control women, and (*c*) those who wish to appear manly and distortedly see rape as a way to prove masculinity. Pornographic images may contribute to this view. In practice, many rapists would not fall clearly into just one of these groups.

Of these nonpsychiatric rapists, some are unable to get sexual satisfaction from their attacks, often attacking because they feel forced into it by friends. Some do get sexual satisfaction and rationalize their behavior by saying that the women enjoy it. Many will kill their victims if they feel they will otherwise be discovered, or if they become angry enough. These rapists are more likely to be lower class than are the psychiatric group, who come from all social classes. Lower-class rapists frequently steal as an incidental crime or, conversely, commit rape incidental to burglary.

What can be done? Detection and deterrence are of obvious importance. Treatment is possible, though difficult. However, a larger problem is involved. The emphasis on sexuality divorced from caring, violence as a way of proving manhood, cannot but contribute to the problem. Less directly, problems of unemployment among youth provide a pool of restless, insecure individuals with the energy, time, desires, low self-esteem, and poor self-control that characterize many rapists. These social problems may be with us for longer than we wish. In the interim, women must be educated to deal with rapists; the criminal justice system must provide fairer treatment to their victims; and the general attitude toward the rapist must become one of outrage rather than tolerance.

Piquerism. Piquerism appears frequently in connection with rape-murder and appears to be a way of substituting an object (knife) for the penis. The normal thrust of the penis is translated into attacks with a knife, causing hideous destruction. It is a perversion of the normal aggressive function of the male. While the origins of such behavior are not clear, some case studies suggest extreme hatred and desire toward the mother. The murderer is unaware of this hatred. The hatred becomes propelled by sexual desire, and the murderer may perform the act in a trance state. In such cases a background of having a butcher as father seems to appear more frequently than one would expect in murders; however, the relationship is suggestive rather than causal. Seeing a father "butcher" animals may get connected with pleasure or manhood for such children, but many other elements need to be present as well.

Rape-Murder. Whether rape-murder occurs with or without piquerism, it is of course the most serious of sex crimes. Rapists may murder because they become frightened, because they become caught up in the excitement of their own violence, because they become angry at their victim. The psychiatric group who commit rape-murder, often in bizarre ways, are frequently found to be schizophrenic, though the vast majority of schizophrenics are harmless. Many would-be victims have escaped death by treating their assailants firmly, calmly, and matter-of-factly.

A major question for the criminal justice system is whether individuals who are exhibitionists or pedophiliacs or who have committed other sex crimes will later become murderers. While most sex criminals repeat a particular kind of deviance, a small but dangerous minority do not. Therefore, it is important that all sex criminals be supervised to the extent that the law permits, and that any signs of increasing violence serve as warning that the individual may be more dangerous than his earlier history suggests.

Dissemination of Pornography

Another sex-related crime, the dissemination of pornography, is a repeated issue in our society. It has been thought by some to be a major cause of sex crimes and perversion. In 1970, a government report on obscenity and pornography could find no evidence linking pornography with sex crime.[8] The report cited the Danish experience in free access to pornographic materials. Denmark's sex crimes *decreased* in the period when pornography became more available. A reasonable explanation would be that men were better able to express their sexual impulses with free access to pornography. However, the commission cautioned that it is dangerous to make generalizations from one society to another, that our access to pornography *and* the occurrence of violent crimes had increased.

This is because other influences may be present. For example, in Sweden, government officials have been unable to find any evidence connecting pornography with sex crimes. However, Sweden bans the depiction of violence in pornography, and it is possible that such a combined depiction is more likely to incite criminals than sex alone. This possibility seems to be ignored by many censors, who look at the overt content of pornography rather than the message, which may be one of violence, exploitation, or tenderness—with consequently different effects.

The commission did not recommend censorship for adult sexual material, but it did recommend censorship for juvenile and youthful audiences, declaring that although no real evidence existed, most people did feel pornography has a negative effect on youth. Other studies have shown an increased *interest* but no change in usual sexual activities.

If one is to judge from studies of behavior change after watching movies, it appears that viewing movies has some effect on behavior, that the effect is greater for violence than for sexuality, and that those who are already suggestible may be influenced, though the majority of the population would not be. This means that if someone is already a rapist, seeing pornographic material will not incite him further; if a person is healthy sexually, pornographic material will similarly have no effect. If he is somewhat unstable or young, he may well be affected. It may be that we should consider a different type of censorship—outlawing materials that would tend to incite individuals to criminal rather than noncriminal sexual activity. This could include the large body of sadomasochistic pornographic material and material romanticizing rape.

Treatment of Sex Criminals

Those who have worked with sex criminals have tried a variety of methods, ranging from psychotherapy, through hormone treatments, to castration. Some methods have succeeded.

Criteria for sending sex criminals to treatment centers have not been consistent or rational. Most of those working with sex criminals have stressed the offender's shock at being institutionalized. Many such persons do indeed feel their acts have been essentially private (consenting homosexuals, for example) and should not be of social concern. They are probably correct. One solution to the problem of treatment would be to arrest only those who present a genuine threat to the community.

Many sex criminals are passive. Treatment, therefore, must be active. One successful approach has involved intensive group experiences, during which persons expressed many feelings they had never known they had, let alone confessed. Others have stressed awareness of the wrongness of the actions and the immediate conditions that led to the crime. The person could then control his behavior before it started. Much supervision must be available in this process.

Conclusions

Sex "crimes" cover a wide variety of sexual behavior. The area of sex crime produces unnecessary terror, since many acts are essentially victimless. Only a small percentage of sex crimes are of the type that most people would think of when they read sex crime statistics.

A more accepting attitude toward sex in our society would lead to a decriminalization of many sex acts, such as homosexuality, and to a decrease in offenses. Sexual offenses are committed by persons who have not learned to accept their own sexuality. Many feel inferior and use sex to try to gain self-esteem.

Nonviolent sex criminals pose little problem to law enforcement officers. The officer must remember that these are people with extremely low self-esteem and can be treated courteously without danger to the officer.

Violent sex criminals may be psychiatrically disturbed or normal. Rapists are dangerous and claim many victims, although many people in our society do not take the crime or their victims seriously. Rape sometimes leads to murder. Psychiatrically disturbed rape-murderers may be schizophrenic. They need to be calmed down in a firm but quiet manner.

Treatment in group therapy situations appears to be most useful for offenders with real problems (as opposed to private acts that are essentially noncriminal). The expression of strong feelings (as in primal therapy) has been helpful. Treatment for sex criminals is essential if they are not to be released to commit further criminal acts.

Discussion Questions

1. What could be done to help children develop a healthier attitude toward sex?
2. What could cause Americans to be less preoccupied with sex?
3. What would be a more reasonable definition of sex crime? What should be included? Excluded?

Suggested Reading

Bell, Alan P., and Weinberg, Martin. *Homosexualities: A Study of Human Diversity.* New York: Simon & Schuster, 1977.

Brownmiller, Susan. *Against Our Will: Men, Women and Rape.* New York: Simon & Schuster, 1975.

Burg, K. K. *Womanly Art of Self-Defense: A Commonsense Approach.* New York: A & W Publishers, 1979.

Csida, June Bundy, and Csida, Joseph. *Rape: How to Avoid It and What to Do about It If You Can't.* Chatsworth, Calif.: Books for Better Living, 1974.

Delin, Bart. *Sex Offenders.* Boston, Mass.: Beacon Press, 1979.

Ellis, Albert, and Abarbanel, Albert, ed. *The Encyclopedia of Sexual Behavior.* New York: Jason Aronson, 1973.

Ellis, Albert, and Brancale, Ralph. *The Psychology of Sex Offenders.* Springfield, Ill.: C. C. Thomas, 1956.

Greenwald, Harold. *The Elegant Prostitute: A Social and Psychoanalytic Study.* New York: Ballantine, 1973.

Groth, A. Nicholas, with Birnbaum, H. Jean. *Men Who Rape: The Psychology of the Offender.* New York: Plenum, 1979.

Hughes, Donald A., ed. *Perspectives on Pornography.* New York: St. Martin's Press, 1970.

Justice, B., and Justice, R. *The Broken Taboo: Sex in the Family.* New York: Human Sciences Press, 1979.

Masters, William, and Johnson, Virginia. *Human Sexual Response.* Boston: Little, Brown, 1966.

Mueller, G. O. *Sexual Conduct and the Law,* 2nd ed. Sloan, Irving V., ed. Dobbs Ferry, N.Y.: Oceana Publications, 1980.

Simons, G. L. *Pornography without Prejudice: A Reply to Objectors.* London: Abelard-Schuman, 1972.

Storaska, Frederic. *How to Say No to a Rapist—and Survive.* New York: Random House, 1975.

CHAPTER 14

White-Collar Crime

White-collar crime is an intriguing and significant, though difficult, area of criminology. It is a paradoxical area—invisible, yet so pervasive that some authors have called our society a "criminal society."[1]

For criminal justice professionals, white-collar crime is significant in three ways: (1) Some white-collar crimes—con games, shoplifting—are dealt with in the criminal justice system as are other, ordinary, crimes and need to be understood for this reason; (2) white-collar crime has a significant impact on the public's attitudes toward the law; and (3) white-collar crime offers an insight into criminal behavior quite different from that offered by regular crime.

White-Collar Crime Defined

White-collar crime is any crime that is both "respectable" and nonviolent. The term was coined by Sutherland.[2] You will notice that the term, like "juvenile crime," refers to those who commit the crimes rather than the crimes themselves.

White-collar crime contradicts many theories about why people become criminals. These include the poverty theory (people commit crimes because they are poor), the lack of opportunity theory (people commit crimes because this is the only way they can get anything they want in society), the broken home theory (people commit crimes because they have not had a mother and father to care for them). None of these theories accounts for white-collar crime.

The list of white-collar crimes is long and can be divided into three categories: business crimes, crimes committed by individuals, and corruption.

Business Crimes

Business crimes include antitrust violations and crimes involving regulatory agencies such as the Food and Drug Administration, the Civil Aeronautics Board, the Internal Revenue Service, and the Federal Communications Commission. These are basically crimes against consumers—monopolistic price-setting through antitrust violations; marketing of drugs that are overpriced or unsafe; use of airplanes without appropriate safety measures; underpayment to the IRS so that other taxpayers must take the burden; promotion through advertising that misleads consumers and overprices products.

Crimes Committed by Individuals

Crimes committed by individuals can include con games and swindles, cheating on taxes, cheating employers (including embezzlement), and shoplifting—a major criminal activity sometimes undertaken by seemingly respectable housewives and young people. Confidence games may be started by professionals. They are maintained because citizens cooperate. "You can't cheat an honest man" is true of many swindles. Swindles include questionable as well as obviously illegal practices—salesmen sell aluminum siding for exorbitant prices; small businesses (usually in ghettos) charge too much and extend too much credit, making a profit by repossessing furniture and appliances when payments are not made; and realtors sell Florida land that is misrepresented, overpriced, and sometimes unusable. Many of these practices are simply big business practices taken over on a small scale by small operators. Obviously illegal practices, such as forgery, cashing checks with no bank balance, or failure by landlords to meet safety or other requirements also fall in this category.

Cheating on taxes is widespread although it is no less a crime than stealing in other ways. Cheating employers is also usually accepted and can range from taking home pencils and paper, through padding expense accounts, to the ultimate crime against an employer—the stealing of millions of dollars' worth of inventory through computer processes. A better-known crime is the embezzlement of thousands to millions from banks or other businesses.

Corruption

Corruption is the third type of white-collar crime. While it is often not included in discussions of this kind, corruption is respectable, nonviolent, widespread, and just as destructive to public morality as other kinds of white-collar crime. Political corruption includes acceptance of bribes by public officials, violation of election laws, and use of the power of public office for illegal activities. For example, the awarding of contracts is a common method used by public officials to get money and support. Bidding for contracts makes it easy for corrupt officials to award the contracts, often involving millions of dollars, to firms who offer support to the officials. In an example of more direct bribery, the milk industry allegedly "paid off" Nixon administration officials in order to gain price advantages. Campaign contributions may be "channeled" or "laundered" to avoid the law.

Society's View of White-Collar Crime

All areas of "respectable" crime share a common characteristic: the crimes are tolerated by society at large. For example, if someone steals some TV sets from a warehouse, people ask, "What's wrong with the police? Why can't they catch and punish those thieves?" or "Don't coddle criminals; punish them! Let's get tough!" In contrast, when politicians take bribes, many people shake their heads and say, "That's the way it goes." Similarly, if a business executive goes to jail for embezzlement, people again shake their heads and say, "What a shame! He seemed like such a fine person."

One reason for this difference in tolerance is that people view nonviolent crimes as crimes they themselves could have committed. Unfortunately, people are not always honest. There seems to be a little larceny in everyone. If each of us stops and thinks, he will probably remember more than one dishonest act. Therefore, we tend to try to forgive and forget dishonesty when it is not too obvious.

There is another major difference between nonviolent and violent crime. Since many people who make the laws are the very same people who commit white-collar crimes, it is not surprising that these laws allow some dishonest, harmful practices to become legal.

A third major difference between nonviolent and violent crime is its invisibility. Even if it is visible, sometimes it is difficult to know who prosecutes whom and how.

A fourth major difference is that *violent* crime is usually committed by powerless persons against more powerful ones. It is then forcefully prosecuted, since those with power have the ability to punish. *Nonviolent* crime is usually committed by powerful persons against less powerful ones. It is then almost impossible for the victims to receive redress for their injuries.

This is perhaps the most important reason why it is essential that nonviolent crime be attacked forcefully. Without such an attack, less powerful persons do not see why they should obey the law, since they believe that people with power don't. This makes a mockery of our entire criminal justice system.

Differential Law Enforcement

How prevalent is white-collar crime? Is it only a minor part of the crime problem of our society? This *appears* to be true. In all types of statistics on crime, white-collar workers and their families are underrepresented.

Yet our discussion has suggested that white-collar crime is much more common than one would think—that what we see is merely the tip of the iceberg. While part of the lower white-collar crime statistics is due to differences in public attitude and visibility, part is due to differential law enforcement.

Because decisions about people are made individually, such factors as status in the community are importantly related to every stage of the law enforcement process. For example, the businessman who is drunk and creating a nuisance is more likely to be taken home than the unemployed laborer, who is more likely to be taken to the station house and booked. If arrested, the "respectable" criminal is likely to be freed on bail, either because he is given low bail or because he is able to make whatever bail is set. If he is brought to trial, the judge is likely to consider the "disgrace" of arrest sufficient punishment, or to set a low fine. Prison sentences for executives or public officials are rare, although they have occurred—for example, in connection with the events surrounding the Watergate break-in during the Nixon administration and the Washington ABSCAM cases, in which members of Congress were sent to jail for accepting bribes.

Many "respectable" crimes are never reported, particularly such crimes as embezzlement. Often a business is reluctant to let people know it has had financial leaks, or that its employees are dishonest. This is frequently true of banks. Businesses often prefer to handle such problems internally.

We will now consider various types of nonviolent crime and why middle- and upper-class people commit such crimes.

Business Crimes

Let us first discuss the area of business crimes, those involving regulatory agencies such as the Federal Communications Commission, Food and Drug Administration, Civil Aeronautics Board, Internal Revenue Service. Crimes by regulatory agencies are difficult to identify or prosecute. For example, almost every day someone discloses crimes against consumers—us—by industry or government. Such offenses include misleading advertising of products that do little or nothing of what they are supposed to do; putting on the market dangerous products such as many toys, plastic products that cause allergic reactions, insecticides that leave dangerous residues in food, or drugs that have been inadequately tested (an example is thalidomide, a sedative that later produced deformities in babies of women who took the drug while pregnant).[2]

Such crimes also include operation of public carriers in violation of regulations. Airplanes may be produced and used even after engineers have pronounced them to be dangerous. Inadequate or improperly tested equipment has been used in airports. An excessive number of airplanes may be allowed to use an airport. Such crimes are difficult to identify. Such suits or other actions are initiated only when employees who know about abuses in the manufacture or service of the product come forward, or when major disasters occur.

Antitrust and other such business violations are difficult to identify. Many companies walk a fine line between legality and illegality in regard to antitrust violations. Relying on the letter of the law, the complexity of the law, and the invisibility of their operations, companies may proliferate under different names, but with the same persons serving on the boards and controlling stocks. Corporations diversify in order not to be accused of antitrust violations. For example, ITT (International Telephone and Telegraph) rose from the eighty-ninth largest corporation in 1955 to the eighth largest in 1970 by diversification. ITT has absorbed Sheraton (hotels), Avis (car rentals), Bobbs-Merrill (publishers), Levitt and Sons (builders), Continental (bakeries), and Smithfield (hams) among others. Such vast corporations are often able to control legislators through bribery or other types of pressure. They can force competitors out by reducing prices temporarily, or they can force the price of commodities to extremely high levels (the high price of sugar in the mid-seventies may have been an example).

The Psychology of Business Crime

It is not difficult to understand the psychology behind such crime. Folk wisdom has it that "power corrupts." Our society applauds those who succeed, even if by marginally legal methods.

Although business titans do not need more money or more business, they do need to define themselves as successful. They do this by trying to become bigger and bigger, more and more powerful.

They rationalize many of their actions in the name of efficiency, or normal business practice. Others do it, why not they? Business criminals are no different from other criminals in this respect. They also contribute enough money for community projects, welfare, education, research, or other charitable activities to see themselves as benefactors rather than predators.

Stopping Business Crime

What can be done about business crime? Because there are laws regulating business activities, it is possible for such white-collar crime to be checked. It is important that regulatory agencies be independent enough to prosecute a corporation. Sometimes it is necessary to have a congressional investigation before action is initiated.

Consumers can also file class action suits in which all consumers affected by a certain business practice take action against the offending industry. In the mid-seventies consumers began to win such suits.[3] Consumer-advocate organizations employ lobbyists and exert political pressure on behalf of consumers. Common Cause, founded by John Gardner, formerly secretary of health, education, and welfare, is such a group. This organization has been successful in helping pass legislation favorable to consumers, especially in the political sphere.

An informed citizenry could make business crime much more difficult by complaining of violations *en masse* to governmental regulatory or legislative bodies.

Crimes Committed by Individuals

Three categories of crime committed by individuals will be discussed: (1) con games and swindles, (2) cheating on taxes, cheating employers, and shoplifting, and (3) embezzlement.

Con Games and Swindles

Con games, swindles, and other forms of deceit become important to police in their role of protecting individuals in their communities. While these crimes usually do not involve violence, they range in destructiveness from causing minimal damage to ruining lives and businesses.

Examples of Cons. An example of a con game that is not usually destructive is pretending to be something that one is not. Most such imposters have performed their pretended jobs adequately, some brilliantly. Injury to society has been minimal or nonexistent. Even though such criminals steal other people's records to pretend they have attended certain schools, they usually do not injure anyone in the process (although they may embarrass those whose records are stolen, as well as those who think that ability and understanding can be acquired only through organized training institutions).

On the other hand, many con games rob people of their entire life savings. Frequently the victims are elderly persons who have no opportunity to recoup their losses. In a familiar con game of this nature, an individual calls the "mark" (or victim), usually an elderly lady, and tells her he is a bank officer checking on fraud. According to her records, he asks, how much does she have in her account? He then asks for her cooperation in finding out whether someone in the bank is swindling. She can do so by withdrawing the entire sum. Then the con man tells her he will see whether the withdrawal is recorded accurately. He will then pick up the money at her house to redeposit it for her; except, of course, the deposit is into his own pocket.

Many swindles affect businesses. Banks are particularly vulnerable to clever swindlers who persuade busy tellers to cash rubber checks. A frequently used method is to forge bank officers' signatures or initials on checks. Swindlers do this after cashing valid checks and thus obtaining legitimate samples of officers' signatures.

Other con games, such as the "Spanish prisoner swindle," have become notorious. This con is quite complex, but the main point is that the "mark," sometimes called the "vic," is told that a man is in prison in Mexico and his entire fortune is locked in a chest in America. He can get the keys to the chest from the prisoner and then return to America to pick up the chest. All he need do is bring money to the prisoner, who will give him the keys. Of course, the trunk with the fortune does not exist, and the mark is out the money given to the prisoner.

Many swindles rely on people's desire for a bargain. Con artists on the street sell watches that somewhat dishonest customers think may be stolen. The watches look good but are worth less than the few dollars asked for them. Other such street cons include selling perfumes made to look like expensive brands for more than they are worth.

Somewhat more complicated versions of cons relying on the desire for a bargain are such ploys as the aluminum-siding game, in which salesmen do indeed sell aluminum siding but for much higher prices than are charged by legitimate businesses. Another version is the cheap rug con, in which salesmen pretend to sell wall-to-wall carpeting for wholesale prices; these prices turn out to be about three times the usual price of carpeting.

These are simple cons, but stock swindles can reach worldwide proportions. Such swindles involve selling stock for nonexistent or relatively worthless companies and holdings. Dividends are paid from the stock purchase money until the fraud is discovered, at which time all stockholders lose money.

Another fraud of very serious proportions is the use of computers for swindles. These swindles can include stealing computerized mail order lists, and then selling them; stealing secret industrial processes and other information; and even subverting processes of government through changing computer instructions.[4] The difference between computer swindles and more simple cons is one of magnitude. Computers can provide access to millions of dollars. Millions of lives can be affected.

The Psychology of Con Men and Their Victims

Authorities have only a little to say about the psychology of either con men or their victims.

However, some studies have shown that con men are indeed similar to our description of the sociopath (see Chapter 9 on mental illness). They are close to being schizophrenic, with grossly inaccurate reality perception. Their perception of their behavior differs radically from their actual behavior. They tell themselves and others that they are successful most of the time, but, according to some studies, they are successful roughly 10 percent of the time.[5] They have no concern about right or wrong, or any type of sustained relationship. They can therefore be super-pleasant to anyone and everyone, in contrast to most people, who are warm only when they mean it. Con men have no sense of conscious guilt and justify themselves by believing that "everyone is like that." If everyone does it, why should they be any different?

The psychology of the victim is frequently similar to that of the con man—except that he is involved part-time, nonprofessionally, and he *always* loses. The con game has been described as a drama in which everyone knows his role except the mark. Like the con man, however, he wants to "beat the system," get something for nothing, and emerge a winner.

Con men get a charge out of manipulating others. This seems to be more important than the financial reward. Con men will drop money through gambling, wild spending sprees, and falling for other con games. An investigator who studied con men offered them money for their participation. The con men did not ask for any of this money, although it was legitimately theirs.[6] A similar situation occurred with an impostor who was discovered to be teaching at a university without benefit of formal degrees. He was offered the opportunity to read for the degrees and get them quickly so that he might legitimately continue his work. Instead, he preferred to leave and resume his deception elsewhere.

Part of the swindler's problem appears to be anger. The con man "kills" his mark (without actual violence, of course) and feels better, having expressed his anger. Sometimes the anger of the con man is quite obvious, as in the case of a man who made it his business to swindle banks: during the Depression his mother had lost her life savings in a bank. He was consciously "getting even." Another con man, an embezzler, said he would never have embezzled if he felt that the company he worked for had treated him fairly. It was a good way to get revenge.

Cheating on Taxes, Cheating Employers, and Shoplifting

Now let us turn to the second category of individual white-collar crime.

Cheating on Taxes. Much white-collar crime involves tax fraud, whether by multinational corporations, big or small businesses, or individual taxpayers like ourselves. The seriousness of this criminal problem, however, is reflected in the statisticians' estimate that the tax burden of the nation would be decreased by 40 percent if everyone paid his taxes honestly.[7]

Those with salaried jobs have less chance to cheat on taxes than those who are self-employed. Those with higher incomes can find more loopholes than those with low incomes. The wealthy find loopholes through their businesses and through access to skilled tax professionals. Persons in lower-level salaried jobs, therefore, pay a higher proportion of the tax burden than is mandated by law. They are literally "ripped off" by the system. Senator George McGovern, in his campaign for the presidency in 1972, discussed the "welfare payments" our system allows for the very wealthy, some of whom pay no personal income taxes whatsoever. The argument was reiterated by Jimmy Carter in his campaign for the presidency in 1976.

Cheating Employers. Cheating employers is an area of crime less frequently discussed.[8] However, millions of dollars' worth of inventory are stolen by employees each year, the cost being passed on to the consumer. Usually the amount stolen by individual employees is small, though occasionally someone steals millions through computer manipulation, or through embezzlement by falsification of company records.

While no business would willingly allow an employee to steal such sums, many businesses assume that a certain percentage of their inventory will be stolen. Employers take action against only employees who exceed this somewhat unclear limit. They overlook pilfering because they believe that employee job satisfaction may depend on the worker's feeling that he has gotten something for nothing, something extra, an illegal "fringe benefit." This is surely a symbol of our society's belief that stealing can be moral.

Shoplifting. Because it is an individual crime with an easy-to-spot perpetrator, police can do something about shoplifting much more easily than about business and government crimes. Shoplifting is a widespread crime, a major expense passed along by retail businesses to the consumer.

At one time, shoplifting was regarded as a sexual perversion and called kleptomania. Shoplifters were thought to steal articles or garments that were sexually arousing. It seemed like a senseless crime, since many of the people who shoplifted could easily have purchased the items stolen. Today, however, shoplifting is so common that it would be meaningless to call such offenders perverts. Instead, we can say that many factors in present-day society contribute to shoplifting.

Perhaps we could relate shoplifting to going for a walk through the woods and picking some berries to eat—or apples from an apple tree. What could be more natural? We see something we want; we take it; we enjoy it; nobody minds.

In our more complicated society, however, rules related to private property are extremely important. Protection of property is part of the territorial instinct found in most species. It is perfectly natural not to allow people to take your things. Burglary, however, in which someone comes into someone else's house to steal, is much rarer than shoplifting. It is committed for different reasons and in very different circumstances.

This is because goods in stores are in a special "never-never" land. They do not seem to be property in the same sense as belongings in a home. The public is welcome in a store and the goods are displayed so as to make them attractive to pick up. The owner is not visible; in fact he seems nonexistent, an abstract corporation with no personal interest in these belongings. It seems as though the attractive goods are reaching out to say, "Take me!" There is only one catch—he who takes commits a crime.

Deterrents also are not as visible as they are in a locked house with a barking dog and a known owner. Practically speaking, it appears to be easy to pick up something in a store and not be detected, and in many cases it is. No violence is necessary. Salespeople frequently do not attend to shoppers. We have probably all had the experience of looking for a salesperson in order to pay for an item. How much easier just to slip an item somewhere on one's person!

The lack of visible deterrents is compounded by the tremendous attraction of some items. We have mentioned that items are attractively displayed. Advertising practices increase their desirability. For example, ads suggest that, if you are dressed in the latest style, nothing will be unavailable to you. Sex partners, success in business or job, being treated with respect—all these will be yours if *only* you have the proper suit, dress, or accessory. Therefore, it does not seem strange that those with inadequate money would find stealing tempting. Looting, for example, has been described by some rioters as the only way they would ever have a chance to obtain furniture, appliances, and so on. Our mass media tell us that such possessions are essential to the American way of life. Therefore, we would expect people without possessions to steal. While our "poor" are not really poor by international standards, they are relatively poor—without the goods that they are constantly told others have and enjoy.

It is less understandable that people with money shoplift. Affluent teenagers and adults alike do so. This can be explained in two ways. One way is based on the idea that possessions bring happiness. If people believe this, what happens to them when they have possessions and are still unhappy? What should they do? What can they do?

People don't want to change their beliefs. Instead of changing their beliefs, they will try to act in such a way as to make their beliefs come true. They often will decide that, while they do own many things, they need other things. Let's get more, more, more. Compulsive eating, compulsive sex, compulsive gambling, all stem from trying to satisfy one need with another. The lonely young man who goes to the refrigerator because he doesn't have a date will not feel completely satisfied. He will feel slightly better, however, and therefore he will continue the eating, even though it never satisfies the original need.

In successful behavior needs are satisfied. A normal person has one or more orgasms and is satisfied. He or she becomes interested in other things. Only when sexual tension again builds up will one become interested in sexual relations. Similarly with hunger: an obese person with excessive food "hunger" eats when attractive food is around, not when his body signals that it needs food.

Similarly, the affluent shoplifter looks for goods when he is feeling dissatisfied about other things, rather than when he needs something to wear or use. Shopping becomes a recreation important in itself. Many suburban teenagers use shopping centers as places to go on dates. This emphasis on buying, and the frequently greater availability of shopping centers than of meaningful recreation, makes it easy for the compulsive buyer to continue his "habit" and to believe that it is a reasonable way to behave.

The second major reason for shoplifting is that it is a way of expressing anger or rebellion. This is most evident in teenagers who are insecure about themselves and their abilities. They tend to look outside themselves for help and become angry when others fail to solve their problems. What easier solution than to take goods, the symbols of adulthood and status in our society, and take them without paying.

For adults, the same motives can apply. Suburban housewives may be bored and frustrated. Stealing can lend excitement to their lives as well as express anger at their frustration. This anger may come from being unhappy, even though they have the material goods that are supposed to make people happy. Again, advertising and our general consumer economy contribute to the problem by making people believe that ownership is the equivalent of happiness.

Embezzlement

Embezzlers have been studied as a separate group because researchers have been curious about why respectable people would become criminals. It has been found that the embezzler usually started his criminal behavior when he had a "nonshareable problem," knew it was easy to get money to solve the problem through embezzling, and saw no other solution. The nonshareable problem might be something like gambling or a woman other than his wife.

Many embezzlers have been "super-respectable," so that even a minor slip-up would be regarded by the potential embezzler as too terrible to share with employer or relatives. Some have felt that embezzling was expected, that they would lose their jobs if they did not change things around a little. This might occur in a situation where everyone was doing it, or in a situation where an embezzler would be fired if he had a shortage. One embezzler was told directly that, if he did not falsify accounts, he would be out of a job. When a shortage occurred, he therefore falsified it. He continued to do so. He expected to and did pay back the difference for a while, but later became unable to do so. Other embezzlers describe situations in which they were unable to keep up a life-style appropriate to their jobs. Bank employees are often expected to be pillars of the community, to make contributions to worthy causes, to dress well, and to have expensive homes. This is impossible for tellers or minor bank officials with small salaries. Some are tempted to steal to make up the difference.

Crimes Involving Corruption

There has recently been much concern about corruption at all levels of government. Corruption involves not only money but misuse of power. While it has occurred in many previous administrations, such corruption became visible to all when Richard Nixon provided taped records of the practices of his administration. The vast quantity of illegal activity known as Watergate toppled an administration, sent many of its top lieutenants to jail, and shocked a nation. As a result, many other attempts to influence government illegally on a legislative and executive level were exposed. These exposés gave rise to the suspicion that all politicians were dishonest, a view no more accurate than that all politicians are honest, or all business people corrupt.

Corruption on the part of the police has also been widely discussed. The individual police officer who accepts bribes is more easily exposed than the politician. However, many police departments not only protect their officers but encourage them to become part of a well-established system of bribe-taking. Needless to say, the effects on law enforcement and attitudes about law enforcement are negative.

The Psychology of Corruption

Why do individuals engage in corruption? For one thing, it is part of human nature to do courtesies for others in exchange for favors. Often such corruption does not seem out of the ordinary. Would you refuse someone who wants to take you out for dinner—a simple act of friendship? Would you not give this same friend first crack at a job you knew about? Such simple acts of friendship and favor-exchange can become corruption when power is involved. However, it is easy for such persons to tell themselves they are doing nothing unusual, that it's the "smart" guys who win. This is not unlike the argument of con artists. There is need, the means are at hand, there is temptation and little chance of getting caught.

Another important motivation is the feeling that "everyone else is doing it." Many people in businesses and corporations as well as government are strongly influenced by their feeling that if they didn't participate in "shady" practices, they would lose their businesses, have problems with their corporations, or not have enough money to be reelected.

This belief in individual success and using any means to obtain it contrasts with beliefs in other societies. For example, in Zuni society, a man would be disgraced if he had more possessions than another Zuni. Few crimes occurred in Zuni society, a fact that might be worth further attention from criminologists. Stealing, homicide, suicide, and sex crimes were nonexistent. How did this happen? One clue is a value system that taught children and adults alike that participation as an equal in the group was the most highly desired accomplishment. Violence was almost nonexistent.[9]

What Can Be Done?

Unfortunately, many of the values that are intended to make our society "bigger and better" may also lead to criminal behavior. We emphasize that there are winners and losers. When we push someone else aside to become a winner, we make a lot of other people losers. We emphasize individualism—each one does "his own thing." But other people may be hurt in this process.

Our emphasis on competition—winners and losers, success and individualism—tends to develop a personality that values "coming out on top" without particular regard to how one gets there.

Con men, those who make fraudulent deals with them, or corporation executives who add (illegally) another company to the fold, all are living up to this ideal. The goal is to win—and we don't care how.

Personal control and power seem to result from getting more than the other fellow, not from sharing equally or according to need. Concern for others is a luxury to be indulged in only after the fruits of success have been obtained. Therefore, the "robber barons" of the early part of the century are said to have built their empires by stealing and even murdering. Only later did their names become associated with universities, churches, and foundations dedicated to the improvement of society.

We have seen many examples of this desire for power in discussing the different categories of white-collar crime. The "con man" doesn't seem very interested in the money he steals. He wants to be successful, to feel powerful. His victim has the same motivation. Corporation executives do not need an extra $20,000 a year. Such extra money at the income level of a top executive can go only for conspicuous consumption—the consuming of goods not because they are needed or enjoyed but to display power or status. Most shoplifters have the same motivations. They do not need the clothes or other items they steal. They simply enjoy the satisfaction of getting something for nothing.

Much time and effort are expended by people who try to show their personal effectiveness by "beating the game." Their motivation has much more to do with status than with need.

Our society as a whole and we as individuals need to reevaluate our goals—primarily in terms of means rather than ends. More participatory and individual sports, fewer spectator sports would make life more enjoyable for individuals and emphasize values such as physical well-being instead of winning at all costs. We need to work for goals that will benefit others instead of just ourselves.

Human service workers, including criminal justice professionals, receive much pleasure from providing help for others. By exemplifying values other than winning, they can provide a model with which others can identify.

Summary

White-collar crime is by definition "respectable" and nonviolent. It differs from violent crime in its invisibility and in the tolerance granted it by society. Because it is usually committed by the powerful against the vulnerable, white-collar crime frequently is dealt with leniently.

Law enforcement efforts are frequently complicated by the offender's status in the community and by the fact that much white-collar crime goes unreported.

The three types of white-collar crime are (1) business crime, (2) crimes committed by individuals, such as tax evasion, embezzlement, and shoplifting, and (3) corruption. In many cases, the offender is searching for power and the joy of manipulating others, not money or goods.

In the case of business crime and corruption, laws already on the books need to be enforced, and regulatory agencies must be independent of the groups they are regulating. Citizens must be vigilant and well-informed and should take advantage of class-action suits and consumer-advocate organizations.

Perhaps the biggest factor in white-collar crime is society's emphasis on competition and winning at all costs. Too often ends are used to justify unsavory means. Society must reexamine its values and consider goals that will benefit others.

Discussion Questions

1. Does everybody have a "little bit of larceny" in his soul? If so, what can be done about it?
2. Why are so few white-collar criminals behind bars?
3. What do you think of the idea that emphasis on winning leads to crime? Does that make sense to you? In what way?

Suggested Reading

Beigel, H., and Beigel, A. *Beneath the Badge: A Story of Police Corruption.* New York: Harper and Row, 1977.

Bequai, A. *White-Collar Crime: A 20th Century Crisis.* Lexington, Mass.: Lexington Books, 1978.

Blum, R. H. *Deceivers and Deceived.* Springfield, Ill.: Charles C. Thomas, 1972.

Bollens, J. C., and Schmandt, H. J. *Political Corruption: Power, Money, and Sex.* Pacific Palisades, Calif.: Palisades Publishers, 1979.

Cameron, M. O. *The Booster and the Snitch.* New York: Free Press, 1964.

Clarke, Thurston. *Dirty Money: Swiss Banks, the Mafia, Money Laundering, and White-Collar Crime.* New York: Simon & Schuster, 1975.

Clinard, M. B., et al. *Illegal Corporate Behavior.* Washington, D.C. Department of Justice, National Institute of Law Enforcement and Criminal Justice, Law Enforcement Assistance Administration, 1979.

Cressey, D. P. *Other People's Money.* New York: Free Press, 1953.

Edelhertz, H., and Rogovin, C., eds. *A National Strategy for White-Collar Crime Enforcement.* Lexington, Mass.: Lexington Books, 1980.

Geis, G. *White-Collar Crime: Offences in Business, Politics, and the Professions.* New York: Free Press, 1977.

Geis, G., and Stotland, E., eds. *White-Collar Crime: Theory and Research.* Beverly Hills, Calif.: Sage Publications, 1980.

Schur, E. M. *Our Criminal Society.* Englewood Cliffs, N.J.: Prentice-Hall, 1969.

Part Four

Family and Youth-Related Disturbances

CHAPTER 15

Family and Neighborhood Crises

Family and neighborhood crises account for a large proportion of police problems.[1] Such crises can constitute one of the most dangerous situations for the police. Yet with proper training, injuries and fatalities can be reduced dramatically. This chapter provides some of the basic concepts underlying conflict situations and suggests guidelines for handling them. Appendix B offers additional examples.

Major Reasons for Violence in the Family

Why is it that families cause so many problems? There are four major reasons why American families today are so often the center of difficulty and even violence (see Figure 15.1).

Figure 15.1
Major reasons for violence in the family

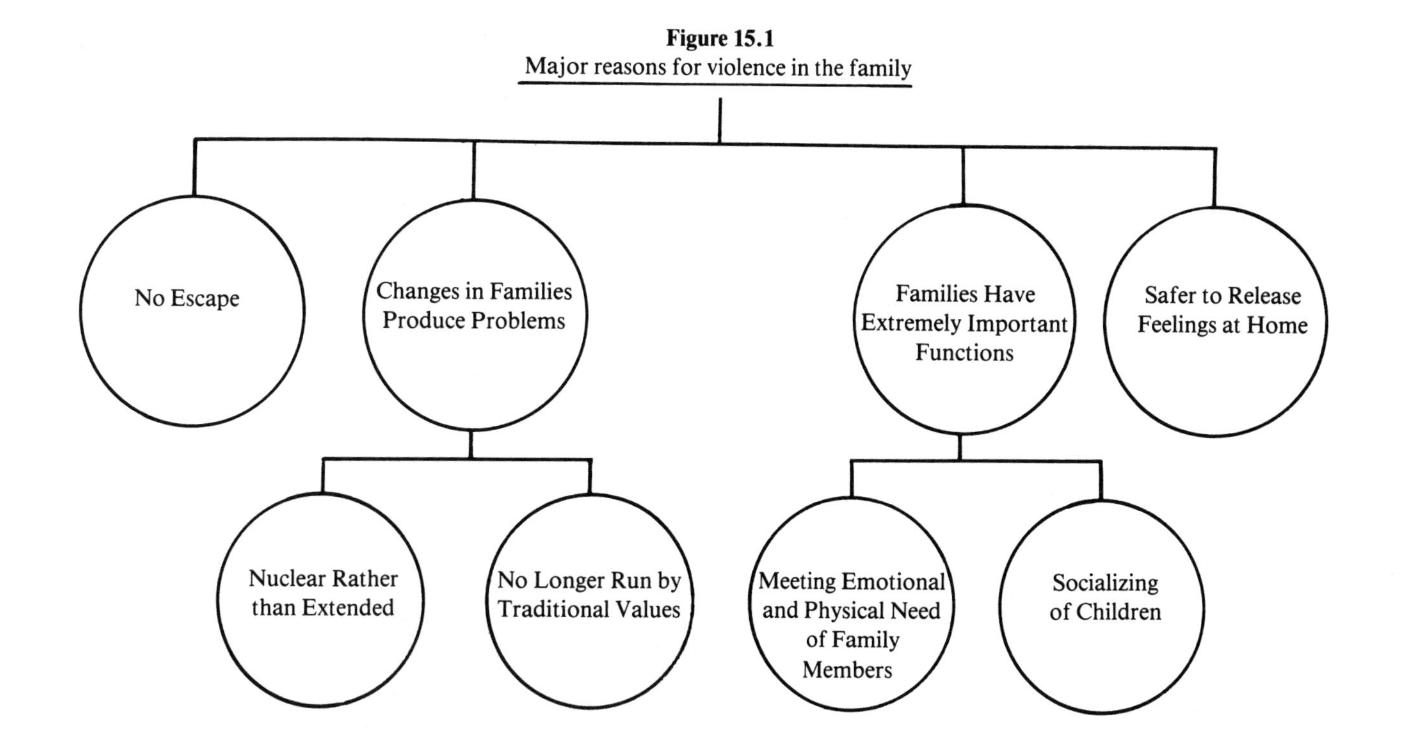

No Escape

It is hard to escape from other family members. If we are upset with a fellow worker, we can usually avoid him or her. If we are upset with a remark made by someone in a bar, we can go to another bar. But at home, it is difficult to escape.

Children cannot just walk out of the house—though some try. Fathers and mothers usually cannot send their children away—though some do. Nor can parents walk out on each other without paying a heavy emotional (and sometimes financial) price.

Feelings Released at Home

It is safer to release feelings at home. Most of us feel it is safer to release our feelings at home than at work or elsewhere. Often we build up tensions and bring them home to our spouses and children. This is called *displacement,* the familiar kick-the-dog phenomenon. We hold back our frustrations elsewhere and then let loose at home.

Changes in the Family

Changes that have taken place in families produce problems. The modern family has changed in two major ways: (1) The family is now small. Called a *nuclear* family, it consists of a mother, father, and one or more children. Most families used to be larger, including mother, father, grandfather, grandmother, an uncle or aunt, a hired man, and perhaps a cousin or two. This was called an *extended* family and was typical of agricultural America prior to the twentieth century. In urban America, families are split up. Grandmothers and grandfathers go to retirement homes or small apartments instead of living with their children. Aunts and uncles have their own apartments. Only in rural areas is it still possible for extended families to live together.

Because nuclear families are small, individual members are more important. When a mother is ill, the needs of the family may not be met. When a father leaves the family, the needs of the family may similarly remain unmet. According to the 1978 *Statistical Abstract of the United States,* in that year, 25.4 percent of all households had only a female head.[2] Temporary or permanent problems often affect children in a highly dramatic fashion.

2. Families no longer have traditional rules to live by. Each family is "on its own" to develop its own rules of living. This can be very difficult, even for mature persons. When people of sixteen or seventeen marry, they find it even more difficult.

Importance of Family Functions

The fourth major reason why families cause so much trouble is that they have such important functions, primarily (1) meeting one another's emotional needs, (2) meeting physical needs, and (3) socializing children (see Figure 15.2). When these functions are not fulfilled adequately, serious problems develop.

Figure 15.2
Family functions

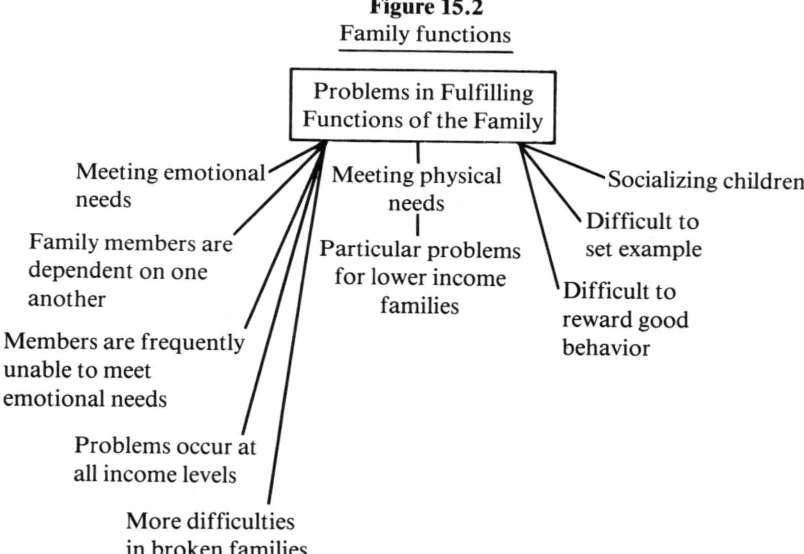

Meeting Emotional Needs. Every family member depends on every other. Many of you are familiar with the feelings that result when one family member is angry. Having a mother or father angry and silent can be devastating to a child. Knowing how important adult family members are to each other can help us to understand that family members are even more important to children. If neither a mother nor a father is able to help the child meet his emotional needs, the child will grow up emotionally crippled. A *very few* of these "cripples" kill their parents. A *great many* engage in family fights when they are old enough to do so. When families are broken, difficulties occur because a mother whose emotional needs are not met by her husband finds it hard to meet the needs of her children.

Meeting Physical Needs. For the family with adequate income and energy, meeting physical needs is not a problem. For many lower-income families, however, meeting physical needs is a daily struggle. Many mothers and fathers simply give up. They leave, or stay and neglect their children.

Figure 15.3

Maturity is learned from parents or others who act mature.

Source: Charles M. Schulz, *You're a Winner, Charlie Brown!* (Greenwich, Conn.: Fawcett, 1969). Copyright ©United Features Syndicate, Inc.

Socializing Children. Through socialization, parents teach children how to live good, productive lives in society. Parents do this by (1) setting an example to be followed and (2) rewarding or punishing their children's behavior. These are difficult tasks, especially in small, nuclear families, because the behavior of the parents is crucial. If the father is unable to hold a job, the child will not learn how to hold a job. If he gets angry and fights when problems arise, the child will learn to fight to deal with problems.

Rewarding and punishing children can also be difficult. Often parents have neither the time nor the energy to reward good behavior. As a result, they only punish. This is not very effective. The difficulty in meeting these family functions is related to the change from extended to nuclear families.

The Influence of Society on the Family

In order to understand families, one must be aware of the influence of the larger society on the family.

In our society, we teach children to compete, to set great store by success, to be clean and neat, to be obedient and conforming, to be aggressive. These teachings are neither good nor bad in themselves, though they do have good and bad consequences. For example, in a study of obedience, 50 percent of the people taking part were obedient to the point of inflicting severe shock on a man who begged for release as he supposedly suffered a heart attack.[3] The My Lai case, which involved the killing of innocent villagers in Viet Nam, may have resulted from similar obedience. However, in some situations obedience is helpful; in an emergency it can save lives.

Good and bad consequences also result from teaching children the value of competition and success. The good consequences are that children can work harder and become better producers. In less competitive societies, less is produced. A negative consequence is that people in our society tend to feel driven and angry. They are not very comfortable with themselves and not very pleasant to live with. Figure 15.4 suggests further advantages and disadvantages of the values our society teaches.

Social class also influences families. Middle-class families frequently have a more stable structure than those at either the bot-

Figure 15.4
Our Society's Values

Societal Value	*Advantages*	*Disadvantages*
Competitive, successful	Provides motivation. People/children work harder, try to achieve more.	Work is done not for its own sake but to get the better of someone else. Not everyone can win. Losers often give up.
Clean and neat	Better general hygiene; less disease; aesthetically preferable.	Can become an end in itself; not always related to hygiene. More important goals are sidestepped.
Obedient and conforming	Allows society to function smoothly with leaders and followers. Production and other functions more efficient.	Loss of individuality. Sometimes goals are destructive and people follow blindly.
Efficient	Allows a society to become productive, affluent.	Human values may be lost. Ecological problems arise. Means, not ends, become important.

tom or the top of the social ladder. More families in the lowest social class than in other social classes are without a father. The mother must provide for her family financially. She must also provide love and care. She has the certain knowledge that her chances of rearing her children to be successful are low. Even if she is able to maintain a stable home for her children, she must deal with street influences. In some neighborhoods, a law-abiding child becomes a social outcast. It is not surprising that few such mothers can succeed.

Many mothers without husbands understandably rely on casual or semipermanent relationships with men to satisfy their emotional needs; even emotionally mature adults need someone to lean on. However, taking on temporary "husbands" can cause problems. The man may feel little commitment to the family, even though the woman may want and expect involvement. Emotional needs are not satisfied, and fights result. Children—whom the man regards as *her* children—are a source of tension, sometimes even a target for abuse. Financial support is another source of conflict. A man in such a situation may want to keep his salary for himself.

Most of all, lower-lower-class family members have little hope for the future. The lower-class father does not have the sense of security that being a responsible family member will give. He feels freer than the middle-class father to "do his own thing".

The lower-middle-class family has different problems. They have more security, more hope of achieving a satisfying style of life, more stability. The wife and mother may, however, feel a sense of boredom, and the husband is likely to hold a dead-end job, which is also frustrating.

The Family As a Unit

Let us consider more specifically the family as a unit and how problems within the family may be resolved.

Defense against Outsiders

We are all familiar with the observation that when brothers or sisters are attacked by an outsider they stoutly defend each other, even if they are constant enemies within the family. Members of a family view themselves as a unit.

Balancing of Strengths and Weaknesses

But members of a family are a unit in another way. In a sick family, the personality strengths and weaknesses are divided up. One member is "the conscientious one." Another is "the one who gets into trouble." Another is careful, another a spendthrift. It is as though there are a predetermined variety of ways to be—sociologists call such behavior patterns *roles*—and each family member selects an available role when he arrives on the scene. This pattern can be seen most vividly in the case of alcoholics and their wives. Those who work with alcoholics have found that the alcoholic's spouse frequently does not want him to change. If he does change, the spouse may become alcoholic. In these families, there is a limited choice of roles—alcoholic and nonalcoholic. The spouse frequently assumes the alcoholic role when the husband or wife reforms.

Absorption of Blame

Another way in which the family functions as a unit is by providing a scapegoat for problems originating either outside the family or within an individual. If the housewife does not get enough of her work done, it is because her husband doesn't take her out enough, and this makes her unhappy and depressed. If the husband is unsuccessful, it is because his wife nags him all the time. From the outside, it is easy to see the effect of blaming: instead of giving support, the family members become enemies.

Handling Family Problems

The sequence of steps listed here suggests a way to work out family problems.[4] Because the family *is* a unit, one member will not change if other members remain the same. In fact, some members of the helping professions call together an entire *extended* family as well as neighbors and friends in order to try to solve an individual's problem.[5]

The model for dealing with family problems involves the following steps:

1. Narrow the issues. Do not discuss how totally rotten someone is. A rotten personality cannot be changed. But the number of times a spouse goes out alone, for example, *can* be changed.
2. Resolve one issue at a time. Do not discuss many, many issues. This will simply feel like a barrage of criticism and will do no good. Work on one small issue.
3. Encourage! Show a family member something good that he or she has done. This will make him feel more cooperative *and* give him a clear idea of what is wanted.
4. Show that you understand by paraphrasing the concerns of each individual. Be sure the individual agrees on what you believe he has said. For example, a woman might say, "All that no-good bum ever does is drink up his whole salary every Friday night." A response to this might be: "You feel he should be giving more money to the family." Sometimes you may want to show your understanding of something a person is not saying, but *is* acting out. For example, a man who is throwing things could be responded to by saying, "You must be goddamn mad about some-

thing." (Incidentally, swearing often has more impact than polite language.) Teaching family members to restate each other's feelings is important.

5. Insist that each individual take responsibility for his own feelings. Not "You are a rotten son-of-a-bitch," but "When you turn your back on me, I feel helpless and anxious." The individual must describe his *own* feelings and reactions and must not accuse others. He must both express the problem in personal terms and avoid being inflammatory. This takes practice, but it is extremely important.

People will find that they have much more control over their lives when they follow these rules and no longer directly try to control others.

Dealing with Emergency Conflict Situations

Those in the criminal justice area, particularly law enforcement officers, may find the following model helpful in dealing with family crises (see Figure 15.5).

Keep Your Cool

First, don't allow people to rattle you. Don't exchange insult for insult. Take a detached attitude. Look around. Try to understand what is happening. Several factors will tend to make it hard to maintain a detached attitude, however: (1) The family often doesn't know what it wants or what kind of help it needs. An officer has more important things to do than to go to a home and be told, "Everything is fine; we don't need you," or, "No, no problem here" – when the disturbance could be heard on the street and the children's faces give testimony to their fear; (2) one or more family members may curse and scream at you. On most such complaints people have low boiling points and a fine vocabulary of insults. It's hard not to get angry.

Should you keep your cool? To answer this question, it's important to look at the role an officer is playing. If you strip away some of the outer trappings of the situation, you'll see that a wife calling to complain about her husband is similar to a child saying, "Hey, Daddy, Johnny just hit me. Do something!" In other words, peo-

Figure 15.5

Seven steps to success in handling domestic disputes

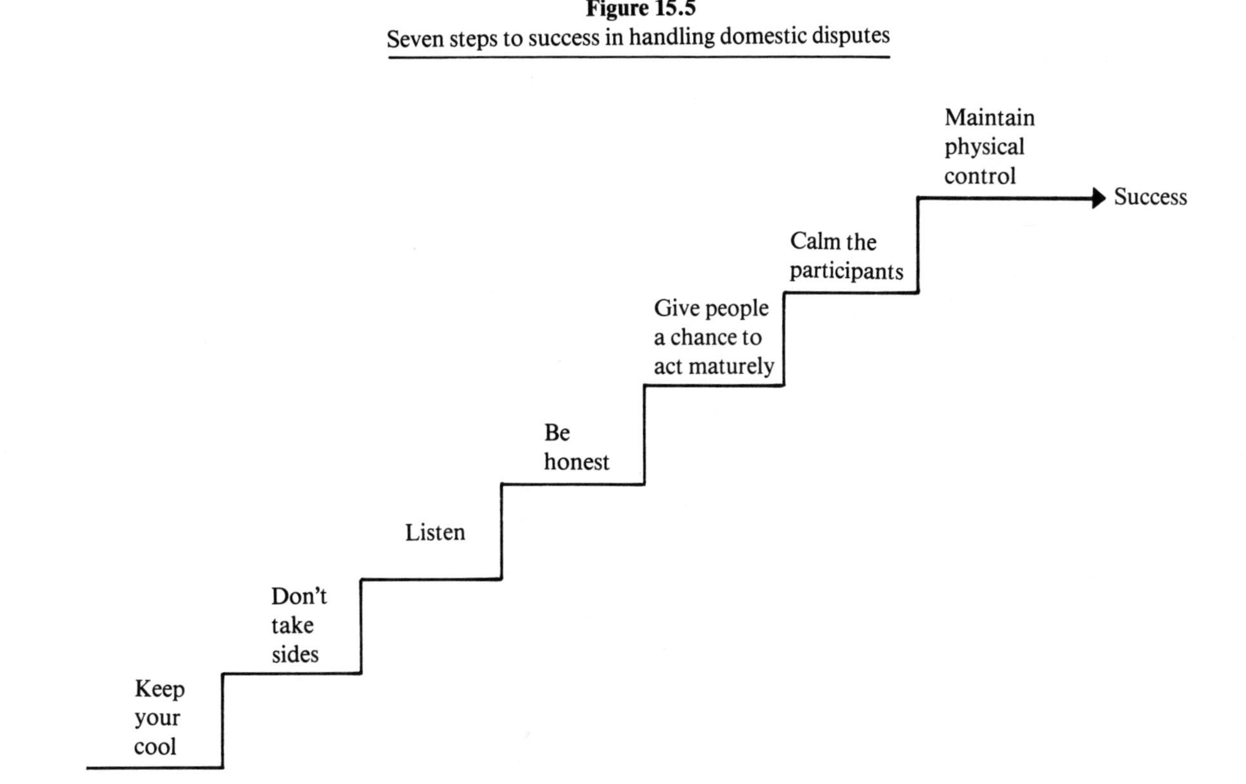

ple may see you as a parent, but their feelings are mixed up. Obviously, the husband is going to be angry and see you as the "bad" parent, since you are interfering. But because you also represent the "out group," the "bad world," the "establishment" that persecutes families—especially very poor families—you will also be rejected by the wife. This happens even though the family asked *you* for help.

If you come in and fight back, you will be playing a role very similar to that of the complainant's own parents. You will add fuel to the fire instead of representing firm but fair and concerned authority.

Don't Take Sides

In a family fight, you are very likely to be put in the middle. This is but one of many crossfires in which law enforcement and other authority figures frequently get caught. Each party will try to enlist the professional on his or her side. Don't let yourself get trapped. Being aware of your own professionalism and role will help. You are there to check out the situation; you will also try to help, within the limits of your legal and professional responsibilities.

Taking sides makes it difficult to be objective about a situation. Having a partner with you who can talk to one participant while you talk to another is a good solution. If this is not possible, let each person know that you will listen to him in turn. Repeating to him what he has said, or what you believe he *means,* allows a person to know he is understood. "I guess you feel, Mr. X, that there really is no problem, and your wife's call was unnecessary." If Mrs. X objects, ask her to wait, telling her you will also be interested in knowing how she looks at the problem in a few minutes.

Listen

Having only one person at a time speak offers another advantage. Each person must have a turn. This will allow you to listen carefully to each individual. Then you can repeat to him what you think you've heard. "I guess you feel that your wife is making a big fuss about nothing."

Be Honest

If you feel that the problem is not within your professional role, say so. If you can be firm but sympathetic, you will have helped the family begin to look for new solutions. A police officer responding to a neighbor reporting a family fight might say, "I understand that you have real concern about this, and it sounds like a bad situation. However, unless you are willing to file a complaint, I can't help. Would you like me to give you the name of an agency that could help with this sort of problem?"

Give People a Chance to Act Mature

You can give people a chance to act mature in two ways: (1) by giving them a chance to make a decision (this can be as simple as "Would you rather talk to me in the hall or here?" or "Would you rather come to the station house or calm down and talk here?") and (2) by understanding and respecting their feelings. "I know that you're really upset by having somebody else come in—I'd feel that way, too, but I'm here, and we might as well talk."

Try not to damage self-esteem. While you may have little reason to respect a man who is beating his wife, remember that only your respect can help him respect himself and others. Respecting means assuming that he doesn't like his behavior any more than you do. Respecting means assuming that he wants to change it. Respecting means giving him a chance to make a choice, even if it's only between talking to you in or out of handcuffs. Respecting means realizing that he has feelings, and that they are probably hurt feelings. This is true because he is in trouble—enough trouble for him or someone else to have called you.

Calm the Participants

You will not be able to accomplish anything in a situation where people are screaming and fighting. You can also reduce the chances of getting hurt yourself by immediately calming the participants. You can do this first by acting calm yourself—even if you don't feel that way! You may have to speak in a loud tone of voice, or hold someone, but make sure you do so in a firm, even, and nonbelligerent fashion. Second, look directly at the person you are speaking to. Try to let him know you are there to help. Many times people who have been confronted by a mentally ill person about to attack have been able to escape injury without using any force, simply by looking directly at the assailant and speaking to him reassuringly. Do *not* argue; do *not* become defensive; do *not* accuse. Third, as quickly as possible, indicate what steps the people involved must take to make a solution possible. Let them know the ground rules: "I'll talk to you—one at a time." "No more fighting!" "Your turn—come out in the hall. The rest of you can wait in here."

You can calm the parties by indicating your understanding and concern. Do this by repeating your understanding of what each one has said. People find it hard to fight if no one fights back. Try to get the participants to turn to you instead of fighting with each other. "I am here to help. Please be quiet until I can hear your side of the story." Separating the participants will often help them be able to listen to you. Ask husband or wife to come into the hall, "It's too noisy to hear you," or to come to your patrol car, "It would be more private in the car."

Surprise techniques may also help. One officer asks a brawling, beer-drinking couple to get *him* a beer. Another officer sometimes asks the wife to make some coffee. Your ingenuity may suggest other surprise tactics that redirect the flow of anger to a concrete task.

Maintain Physical Control of the Situation

Following the steps outlined so far should help you gain psychological control. However, remember that you must have physical control as soon as possible. This is not a psychological matter, but it has important psychological consequences. If you feel threatened by someone with a knife, you won't be able to carry out any of the earlier steps. Be prepared to combine psychological and physical methods, such as holding a person and then talking to him.

Appendix B will give you further ideas on how these principles can work in practice.

Other Neighborhood and Disturbance Calls

Many problems with which police must deal involve not families but people living close to one another: landlords and their tenants, neighbors, people whose children play with one another. Although the same principles apply, there are some additional considerations. For example, it helps to know that many neighborhood problems may be contributed to by crowded conditions.

Crowding produces abnormal behavior. Experiments with animals have shown that rats, when crowded, become sexually perverted and cannibalistic, and they desert their young.[6] Experiments with children have shown that they demonstrate increased aggression and decreased constructiveness in play when they are crowded. If you are working in a crowded inner-city area, it is likely that disturbances will occur more frequently. Even suburban housing developments seem to suffer from lack of adequate space. People often get in each other's way.

People need space to function effectively. Even animals defend "their" space. When an area is not clearly defined, as in a tenant-landlord situation, each person may feel it is *his* space, that he should be able to do as he wishes. He may be less willing to back off from the fight than in a domestic disturbance. In other ways, these disturbance calls are similar to those arising from domestic disturbances.

The general principles mentioned earlier are important here—keeping control by keeping your cool, not taking sides, listening, being honest, giving people a chance to act mature, calming the participants, and maintaining physical control.

Helping people maintain their self-esteem is also important. A complainant may have staked his pride on having the police back him. In many situations, you will decide that there is no reason for police action, even though there may be problems. If you say something like, "You have no case here—these people aren't doing anything against the law," it is difficult for him to retreat honorably. If you instead recognize the feelings involved, "I know you find it hard, Mr. Y, to see the X family neglecting their animals; I wish we could help directly, but we can't. We appreciate your interest and we hope our suggestion will help." Or say to those complained against, "I know you feel you have the right to take care of your pets the way you want. It must make you angry that your neighbor complained."

The important thing to remember is to let both parties know that you understand and accept their *feelings* though not necessarily their *actions*. A sincere statement like, "I can see how you would feel that way—it's really a shame we can't help directly" can make a real difference in how others react.

In more serious situations, two courses of action may be available. One would be arrest, which is necessary in most cases of child abuse or neglect, or when you have reason to believe that a crime *has been committed*. Another course of action, if a family is in considerable distress (for example, a husband may be alcoholic but committing no criminal offense), is to suggest sources of help. Predicting future problems may move families into action. "If you don't do something about this situation, here's what's likely to happen: . . ." Your prediction may not have immediate effect, but when the next problem arises, the family may react in a more mature way, especially if you have given specific suggestions on obtaining help.

In conflicts arising from children fighting with one another, families may *project*, or attribute to others, the negative qualities that are really in themselves or in their children. "Jimmy, not my child, is a bully." "Tommy is always grabbing my kid's things." You can let families know that you are aware that most such difficulties arise from the relationship between the *two* (or more) children.

Some difficulties arise, however, from inadequate supervision. Children who are allowed to play with knives or dangerous toys, who are never restrained when they hit other children, can be a menace to others their size or smaller. This calls for direct and authoritative action.

Experience shows, however, that parents frequently are still fighting long after the children are best friends.

Again, Appendix B gives examples of neighborhood disturbances and ways to deal with them.

Summary

Families are important units of society—units in which trouble for a law enforcement officer can easily start. The reason is that the family is extremely important to its members. Its modern-day characteristics of smallness, with little escape for members, not much support from the outside, and new social challenges, make it an easy place for fights to start. It also seems safer to fight in the family than outside—you don't lose your job.

American families typically teach their children to be competitive, successful, clean, obedient, and efficient. Some of these values can cause problems. Additional problems arise in social classes where families have little chance for adequate child-rearing.

Dealing with family and neighborhood crises involves a high degree of professionalism and a knowledge of basic principles of what to do and what not to do. These principles involve keeping one's cool, not taking sides, being honest, not damaging self-esteem, calming participants, and maintaining physical control.

If one understands and follows these principles, it is possible to decrease the danger involved in family disputes, to be more efficient, and to help families and neighbors deal with their problems constructively.

Discussion Questions

1. Why are domestic disturbances more dangerous for police officers than most other calls? How can the danger be minimized? Role-play a domestic disturbance. Change roles so that all participants know how (*a*) the officer feels, and (*b*) the family feels. What helped? What didn't help?
2. What principles help an officer keep control? How do *you* keep control?
3. Why do people engage in neighborhood disputes? What is the best way of handing them? Role-play a neighborhood dispute situation. Change roles and discuss feelings as above.

Suggested Reading

Aiello, J. R., and Baum, A., eds. *Residential Crowding and Design.* New York: Plenum, 1979.

Aldous, J. *Family Careers: Developmental Change in Families.* New York: Wiley, 1978.

Bach, G., and Wyden, P. *The Intimate Enemy.* New York: Avon, 1968.

Belnap, W. D. *Raising Families in Our Permissive Society*. Salt Lake City: Hawkes, 1978.

Bernard, J. *Marriage and Family among Negroes*. Englewood Cliffs, N.J.: Prentice-Hall, 1968.

Berne, E. *Games People Play*. New York: Grove Press, 1964.

Borland, M. *Violence in the Family*. Atlantic Highlands, N.J.: Humanities, 1976.

Burgess, E. W. *E. W. Burgess on Community, Family and Delinquency*. Edited by L. S. Cottrell, Jr., et al. Chicago: University of Chicago Press, 1977.

Cavan, R. *The American Family*. 3d ed. New York: Crowell, 1963.

Cope, J., and Goddard, K. *Weaponless Control for Law Enforcement and Security Personnel*. Springfield, Ill.: C. C. Thomas, 1979.

McMurrian, T. T. *Intervention in Human Crises: A Guide for Helping Families in Crisis*. Atlanta: Humanics Ltd., 1975.

Specter, G. A., and Claiborn, W. L. *Crisis Intervention*. New York: Behavioral Publications, 1973.

Steinmetz, S. K., and Straus, M. A., eds. *Violence in the Family*. New York: Dodd, Mead, 1974.

Wicks, R. J., and Fine, J., eds. *Crisis Intervention: A Practical Clinical Guide*. Thorofare, N.J.: C. B. Slack, 1978.

CHAPTER 16

Child Abuse and Neglect

Child abuse and neglect, particularly abuse, are serious problems in the United States today. They are being reported increasingly to law enforcement officials. An officer may become the only immediate protector of a child being physically abused by a parent. Other criminal justice personnel may become involved when a case is prosecuted.

What do we mean by child neglect? Every so often we are made aware, through newspaper headlines, of children who have been left alone and who perish in a fire. This is one type of "neglect." Other situations are frequently noticed by teachers. Children are sent to school hungry, with inadequate and poorly maintained clothing. These children also have been "neglected." Often they come from low-income homes where the mothers and fathers are too immature to care for their children.

Child abuse is quite a different matter. It involves families of all social classes, including the middle class, where children usually are tidy, well dressed, well fed. They are simply physically abused. The parents take an interest, but one or both parents—more frequently the father—takes the wrong *kind* of interest. He actively uses the child as a subject on whom to vent his own anger and frustration. He literally tortures the child. Such torture may include burning, severe beating, breaking bones. This abuse is to be clearly differentiated from the occasional slap or spanking that normal parents use to express anger. Frequently the parent will bring the child to the doctor or hospital, explaining the injury in some flimsy fashion, saying that the child had an "accident." However, such injuries as a burn that circles a child's leg cannot be the result of an accident.

Child Abuse

What can be done about child abuse? What is the meaning of behavior so shocking that, until the 1940s, no one really believed it could occur?

Prior to that time, children had been brought to hospitals with bruises and fractures that doctors could not explain. They looked like injuries from accidents, but the parent either reported no accident or described the situation so vaguely that it did not fit with the injuries. While these children made good recoveries in the hospital, they became strangely ill as soon as they were released. Improved X-ray techniques eventually led to the difficult conclusion that the parent himself had inflicted the injuries on the child.

Since then, the occurrence of child abuse has been amply demonstrated, though estimates of its extent vary widely. It is, at the least, a serious problem. If it is as widespread as even the less conservative figures indicate, it is of epidemic proportions. According to Douglas Besharov, Director of the National Center on Child Abuse and Neglect, 1.6 million cases of abuse and neglect occur annually, with 2,000 to 4,000 deaths.[1]

Why Child Abuse Is Not Reported. One of the difficulties in identifying child abuse is that cases are often not reported. Doctors, social workers, and teachers are reluctant to contact authorities. All states have laws requiring that people report cases of child abuse—either to child welfare agencies or to the police. However, these laws are frequently ignored. Why? Figure 16.1 summarizes the reasons.

Figure 16.1
Why child abuse has not been reported

Unclear laws

Fear of lawsuits

Fear of parents' anger

Unwillingness to interfere in family privileges

Tradition that parents may physically mistreat their children

Lack of conviction that something can be done

Fear that children will be mistreated further

Outcome

25% to 50% chance of permanent physical injury or death

↓

Children who survive will abuse next generation

Another problem is fear of the parents' anger. This fear is related to another fear—imposing on the privacy and prerogatives of the family. There is also the problem of distinguishing between child abuse and permissible discipline. Because parents are allowed and sometimes expected to beat their children, others find it difficult to decide when the parent is overstepping the bounds of discipline.

Another reason for not reporting child abuse is the belief that nothing can be done. If the child cannot be separated from the parent—either by removing the parent through a criminal action or by moving the child to a foster home—will more harm than good be done by reporting the abuse? If the child merely returns to the parent, the parent will be even angrier and more likely to abuse the child. The situation is complicated if provision cannot be made for immediate placement outside the home or treatment and supervision if the child is to remain.

The laws for mandatory reporting of child abuse now provide protection for those reporting, including teachers, physicians, and so forth. Not only severe but milder cases can now be reported. Many more parents are also voluntarily seeking help. All of this seems to be the result of more open discussion of child abuse.

Causes of Child Abuse

Before discussing the ways in which parents and children may be helped, some attention should be directed to the causes of child abuse.

Do abusing parents have no feeling for their children? Just the opposite is frequently the case. Child abusers often report feeling totally miserable as their children sob or scream.

Though there is some disagreement among authorities, several social and individual causes can be identified (see Figure 16.2).

Social Approval of Violence. Social causes of child abuse include our attitude toward violence as well as our family structure. It does not take much to realize that our society is "hung up" on violence. We watch murder mysteries avidly. Our streets are full of violence. When something goes wrong, many people suggest violence as a cure. We encourage people to "beat out" other people with our competitive interests.

Psychologists have proven that even such a harmless pastime as watching a football game on TV increases our tendency to act aggressively. It is easy therefore to see that our general emphasis on violence makes it more likely that people will actually behave violently. In cultures where people rarely resort to violence (such as that of the Zuni Indians), a person would not think of expressing frustrations by beating a child.[2]

Social Approval of Child Punishment. In addition to this general social approval of violence, there is specific approval of physical punishment of children. Parents are told, "Spare the rod; spoil the child," and they believe this, even though the theory works

Figure 16.2
Causes of child abuse

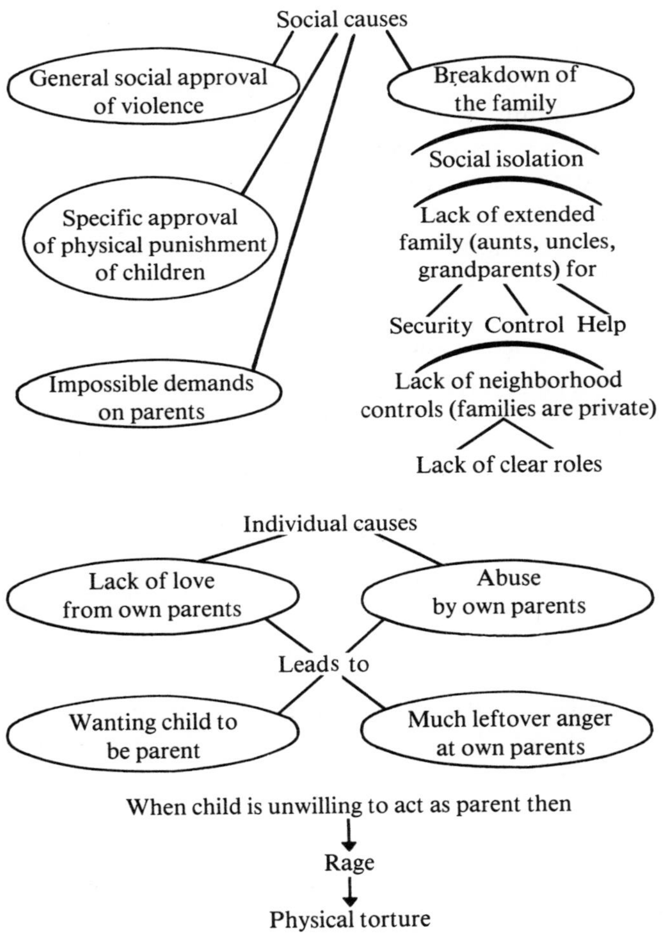

poorly. Physical punishment usually either makes the child more violent himself, or completely subdues him to mindless obedience. However, because physical punishment is generally accepted, parents who are angry are able to tell themselves that they are "doing the right thing." It is typical for abusive parents to say that the child deserves this severe punishment. In our society it is easier to agree than to assume that, if a child behaves that badly, something must be very wrong with the entire family. This would entail offering help.

Breakdown of the Family. Another social factor is the breakdown of the family. Picture a large rural family of the nineteenth century. Three generations were likely to live together—mother, father, children, and grandparents. Frequently, there was a widowed or unmarried aunt, an uncle, or a cousin.

Then picture a family of today in an urban ghetto area. Over a third of these families consist of a mother and children.[3] The father or boyfriend visits only occasionally. Even today's middle-class family, which is more likely to have a father (though the divorce rate is climbing to more than one in four in many areas), usually consists of only parents and children living together. While this family may have neighbors as close friends, frequently it does not. How extremely isolated the modern family is compared to the nineteenth-century rural family! Is it any wonder that things go awry in such lonely, friendless families?

The lack of an extended family of aunts, uncles, and grandparents makes people less emotionally secure, even though they have more freedom. They have less help with household chores and care of children. There is also less control of behavior. A person would not dare abuse a child with so many other relatives around. In fact, one of the problems in prosecuting cases of child abuse is the absence of witnesses. The child abuser is usually abusive only when alone.

In addition, modern families often lack clear role structure. The young mother or father often does not know what she or he is supposed to be doing! She does not know how she is supposed to care for her home or her children. The husband too is faced with a variety of possible ways of being a father. Should he go off and hang out with the boys? Should he come home right after work? Should he help with the children? With household chores? Should he approve if his wife goes to work? Little is clearly defined in today's changing society.

These social factors are a reality for almost everyone. Still, some people abuse their children; others do not. Why? We must look at individual, as well as social, factors.

Impossible Demands on Parents. Many child abusers suffer from demands they are unable to meet. They may have too many children, too little income, and inadequate housing.

Unrealistic Expectations of Child. The major individual cause of child abuse is an unrealistic emotional expectation. Abusive parents expect their children to take care of *them,* because the parents themselves never experienced tender, loving care from *their parents.* Parents of abused children hope that their children will be parent-substitutes. James and Jongeward quote a mother who had beaten her month-old child, who later died of the injury, as saying, "No one loved me all my life, and then I had my baby and thought he would. When he cried, I thought he didn't love me, so I hit him."[4] Of course, young children cannot provide this kind of love.

Parents' Own Abusive Upbringing. Another striking finding in the study of child abusers is their own sadistic upbringing. These parents, as children, were treated in much the same way they treat their own children. When these adults were children, they could do nothing about the rage they felt. Now, as adults, they strike back—at their own helpless children. The memory of how their own parents treated them, together with their own rage at the child's not providing love, produces the child abuse.

The parents, however, rationalize this abuse by saying that the child deserves it. The parent is completely unrealistic in his expectations of the child.

A most important rule in dealing with another person is to expect only as much as he can do. This is particularly important in dealing with children. Abusive parents expect their infants and toddlers to accomplish fantastic feats. They might, for example, expect a three-month-old child to be capable of toilet training or feeding himself. In reality, most abused children *are* extremely well behaved—because they have been terrorized into obedience. These unrealistic expectations are necessary to the parent's view of the child as parent-substitute. Some abused children follow the example of their parents, become violent, and are difficult to deal with even by normal parents.

Who Are Abusive Parents?

While the courts seem to see a disproportionate number of poverty families, as stated above, child abuse is not confined to any one social class. Children may be well dressed, clean, and otherwise well taken care of; their homes may be beautifully furnished, their parents well educated and financially comfortable. Or they may come from poor homes and bear the stigma of poverty-stricken as well as cruel parents. These are likely to be the families where impossible demands on the mothers occur. These demands are related to lack of resources. Many of the parents are alcoholic; many are not. Abusing parents may be overcontrolled or excessively impulsive.

Have abusive parents no understanding that they are doing something criminal? Because most of these parents have very high standards for themselves, or feel very inferior, they would not be able to bear it if they saw themselves realistically. However, it is quite clear that many do realize, unconsciously, that they are doing something very wrong. Because of this, it is sometimes possible to enlist the parents' cooperation in seeking help for themselves and their child. Parents in some areas are working together to help themselves through a group called Parents Anonymous. For parents whose problems stem from inadequate resources, the obvious solution is to provide concrete help.

Without some sort of help, these parents find it impossible to control their behavior, even though some of them are generally overcontrolled. For these parents, child abuse means "letting off steam." For some, the only hope seems to be intensive and careful treatment. For others, self-help groups can provide a climate in which the parent can learn greater control. However, parents cannot change simply on order from the court.

Are children really in danger from these parents? It is quite clear that any child who has been abused will be abused again. Many children, particularly those under the age of four, die as a result. It is extremely important that they be protected from their parents.

Why doesn't the spouse do something? In these families, the

spouse is usually in some ways too dependent to give up the security of the marriage in order to protect the child. While usually only one spouse hurts the child, the other typically does nothing whatever to prevent the abuse. She—or he—feels that to do so would be to lose the spouse's love.

What Can Be Done?

We have already discussed that the difficulties in reporting incidents of child abuse stem partly from the belief that nothing will be done.

Another problem is the reluctance to begin *criminal* proceedings against a parent. Some authorities believe that dependency proceedings, in which the child is a declared ward of the court without establishing any legal blame, are adequate to protect the child. Dependency proceedings have several advantages. No "crime" need be proven. If the parent has been treated honestly and his cooperation requested, he will be likely to agree to such proceedings. There is less damage to the parent, with equal protection for the child. Further, sending a parent to jail—sometimes a consequence of criminal procedures—will often deprive a family of needed income. Other children in the family need support, and they would lose this support if a parent were imprisoned.

Other authorities, however, feel that the only real safety for the child lies in criminal prosecution. They feel that a parent is unlikely to cooperate in giving up the child. Further, since child abuse is a crime, why should the parent not be punished by the law? Many law enforcement officials become horrified and angry and wish to prosecute someone committing such deeds.

Whether the procedure is a dependency petition or a criminal hearing, what may be done to protect the child after legal intervention? There are several possibilities:

1. Permanently remove the child. The result of this kind of action is to ensure the child's safety. This is the only way of knowing that the parent will not abuse him further. It does of course permanently separate him from his family and make it necessary for the community to care for him until he is grown. It may seem a small price, however, to save a child's life.

2. Punish the parent. If the child is not removed, any further

action will cause the parent to be more frustrated. This will increase rather than decrease the abusive behavior. Putting him in jail so that he cannot mistreat the child is a stopgap measure. He will return to abuse the child further.

3. Treat the parent. As mentioned above, some groups have successfully helped child-batterers become adequate parents who protect rather than abuse their children. Such treatment may be through self-help groups such as Parents Anonymous. For those who voluntarily seek help, this would appear to be a significant avenue of treatment. For those who do not seek help, professional support may be necessary. Such support can be expensive and difficult, especially if a parent is suspicious and uncooperative. However, social workers and other professionals who have spent sufficient time and energy have become the needed parent-substitute to the abusive parent. He or she thus learns, by experiencing care, how to care for a child.

With greater public awareness of child abuse, more facilities for treatment have been developed. Some of these facilities report excellent results in a majority of cases. For example, Pollock and Steele report improvement in 80 percent of the parents who came to their facility.[5] Kempe and Kempe also feel that four out of five parents can be helped.[6] Help is usually provided by visits, concrete advice, information about what can and cannot be expected of infants and toddlers. The parents receive warm support which gives them an example of how to help their own children.

Given our concern for the family, most of us would feel that some such treatment is a better solution than removing a child. However, it must be carefully weighed, especially in the case of serious child abuse, against the risk of further abuse during the process of treatment, or if the treatment is not successful. Sometimes such treatment needs to be court-mandated, frequent, and intensive in order to be successful.

An Application

Sometimes a doctor or other professional person reports a case of child abuse, which is then investigated. In a typical case, the parent will deny injuring the child. Immediate investigation is then necessary.

If there is evidence of child abuse, it is important to provide immediate help for the family. Sensitive, firm handling by the professional person (usually a social worker) is necessary. Many families will accept help without court orders when they know that they have little choice. Usually, knowing that there is a watchful eye and help available, these families will show some improvement. If, however, the family refuses help, then a choice must be made as to whether the parent should be prosecuted or the case handled as a dependency procedure. If the child becomes a ward of the state, the child welfare agency will be asked to make a placement, either in a foster home or in an institution. If the parent is prosecuted, the child must still be cared for while the case is pending. It is especially important that he not be returned to the home if the parent is still there and the investigation has shown the real possibility of further abuse.

Medical findings and color photographs are essential in such a case, since bruises may heal and a case be compromised while it awaits trial. It is important that the professionals involved be honest with the parents. In criminal procedures they should be advised to obtain a lawyer.

Immediate foster home placement is usually most desirable. If this is not possible, a child may have to stay in an institution until a home is available. In some communities, no care may be available for a child, and it is important that the family be supervised in such situations.

Institutions are an undesirable second choice. In America today most institutions provide such inadequate care that most children who live in them are destined to become unintelligent, unsuccessful, unhealthy, and incapable adults.

In all child abuse cases, whether reported by a doctor or by a neighbor or other concerned individual, it is extremely important that the investigation begin immediately, as children's lives are at stake.

Child Neglect

While it may seem that neglecting and abusing parents are similar, the differences need to be understood.

The neglecting parent pays too little attention to his children;

the abusing parent, too much attention of the wrong kind. The neglecting parent, while immature emotionally like the abusing parent, does not look to his child for love and attention. He may compete with or envy the child: "Those kids all get to go off and play; why shouldn't I do what I want?" But he does not expect children to be parent-substitutes. A husband may be angry and blame his wife—or even the children—for their not being well cared for, but he does not make them responsible for his own feelings of being unloved.

Causes of Child Neglect. There are both social and individual causes of child neglect. As in child abuse, a general breakdown in the family is an underlying social cause. The large, extended family provided security, help, training, and surveillance. There was less likelihood of a mother not caring for her children. She learned what she should do, how she should do it, that she would meet strong disapproval if she didn't do it. In situations of stress other adults were there to help.

General social disorganization has produced and maintained a large number of lower-lower-class families for whom a strong family structure is rare. Parents in these families have never learned how to be mature and therefore cannot teach their children to be mature—the children just "grow."

As a caseworker, I visited one such family, which was by no means an extreme example of neglect. Five small children played, fought, and crawled around the apartment. Grandmother was watching the children and casually mentioned that the two-year-old had taken some medicine. She didn't know what kind or whether it was poisonous. She didn't know quite what to do but evidently had some vague feeling that something should be done. She was more than willing for her visitor to arrange for immediate emergency care.

Complicating the social causes are individual factors. Most neglectful parents have grown up neglected themselves. Looking for something better, they left home at an early age, got married, and produced children. When these adults find that their life is still unsatisfactory, they frequently become depressed and apathetic. They live in squalid surroundings, leading disorganized lives. For example, one such mother insisted that her children were well fed because she gave them potato chips and Coke.

Probably the best way of understanding situations of child neglect is to imagine a five-year-old in charge of a family. While he might make some effort to feed and clothe the family, we would not expect him to do so in any but the most sporadic and ineffective way. Most neglectful parents function in just this way.

A somewhat less obvious type of neglect produces a syndrome called "failure to thrive." Some children, despite apparently adequate care, do not develop. They weaken and may even die. The exact cause is unknown. It seems to be related to the parents' inability to meet the child's emotional needs. For example, it is known that a young child needs a great deal of touching and cuddling, in addition to basic physical care, in order to thrive. He also needs to communicate with and learn from the adults around him.

Mothers of "failure to thrive" children have been found to be chronically depressed. It seems likely that all mothers of neglected children are similarly depressed. These depressed mothers seem to fall into two categories: young girls without the support of husband or family, caring for their babies all alone; and mothers of too many children, who are overburdened and unable to handle the situation.

What Can Be Done?

It is helpful to think of neglectful parents as children themselves. Often the only solution is foster care for the young child. Another alternative is the continued and sensitive support of caseworkers. It is usually wise to make the children wards of the state: Since immature parents are often capricious in their judgments, some legal authority may be necessary.

In the case of mothers of children who simply "fail to thrive," it has been found that financial help, advice, and concern can enable these mothers to take good care of their children. Such help needs to continue until the mother is able to find resources of her own.

Conclusions

Both child abuse and child neglect stem from inadequacies of parents. In the case of child abuse, the parents expect their children to provide the love and care that the parents themselves never received. Many abusive adults were themselves mistreated as children. When the abused child is unable to meet his parents' needs, the rage stored up by the parents since childhood is released.

In the case of child neglect, most of the parents have never been cared for themselves. They leave their parental homes in search of love, only to be burdened with children. They do not abuse these children; they simply do not care for them. The situation is similar to leaving a five-year-old in charge of others.

While child abusers come from all social classes, parents who neglect their children are usually lower lower class and lack the finances that might make it possible to handle difficult situations.

Reporting of child abuse and neglect, especially abuse, has been irregular. Many children are permanently damaged or killed because neighbors, teachers, or doctors are unwilling to report that a child is being abused. Newly enacted laws making it mandatory to report abuse may help. But it does take courage to face an abusing parent, and law enforcement officials may have to take much of the burden.

Prompt action on the part of law enforcement officials is essential for abused children. In more serious situations, where the child has been abused in life-threatening ways, he should not be returned to his parents for even a short time but should be placed in protective custody immediately. Abusive parents can be trusted to care for their children only if treatment and supervision are available. Parents of neglected children also need help; protective custody may be necessary in these situations as well.

Discussion Questions

1. How would you feel about reporting a case of child abuse as a neighbor? How would you feel about intervening as a police officer? Act out a scene involving an officer and an abusive father. Have the actors trade places.
2. What do you feel a community might do to help prevent child abuse and neglect? How can help for parents be provided? How can good foster care be provided?
3. How can an officer deal with parents who have abused their children? Neglected their children?

4. What social welfare agencies are available in your community to help in child abuse cases?

Suggested Reading

Bakan, D. *Slaughter of the Innocents: A Study of the Battered Child Phenomenon.* Boston, Mass.: Beacon Press, 1972.

Besharov, D., Baden, M., et al. *The Abused and Neglected Child: Multidisciplinary Court Practice.* Criminal Law and Urban Problems Course Handbook Series, no. 104. Practicing Law Institute. December-February 1978–79.

Bourne, R., and Newberger, E. H., eds. *Critical Perspectives on Child Abuse.* Lexington, Mass.: Lexington Books, 1979.

Fontana, V. J. *Maltreated Child: The Maltreatment Syndrome in Children.* 2d ed. Springfield, Ill.: C. C. Thomas, 1971.

Gil, D. G. *Violence against Children: Physical Child Abuse in the United States.* Cambridge, Mass.: Harvard University Press, 1970.

Helfer, R. E., and Kemp, C. H., eds. *Battered Child.* Chicago: University of Chicago Press, 1968.

IJA-ABA Joint Commission on Juvenile Justice Standards. *Standards Relating to Abuse and Neglect.* Cambridge, Mass.: Ballinger, 1977.

James, M., and Jongeward, D. *Born to Win.* Reading, Mass.: Addison-Wesley, 1971.

Kempe, R. S., and Kempe, C. *Child Abuse.* Cambridge, Mass.: Harvard University Press, 1978.

Martin, H. P., ed. *The Abused Child.* Cambridge, Mass.: Ballinger, 1976.

The Neglected Battered-Child Syndrome. New York: Child Welfare League of America, 1979.

CHAPTER 17

Youthful Offenders

The problem of working with juveniles is one of the most difficult for criminal justice professionals. Not only do juveniles account for a disproportionate number of crimes, but their activities are the source of innumerable complaints and annoyances.[1] Often they seem to be in the business of making life difficult for adults. It is, therefore, important to understand what this behavior means, how youthful offenders grow up, what makes a person delinquent, and what impact the criminal justice system has on juvenile offenders. With such understanding, we will be in a better position to place the problems of youthful offenders in perspective.

What Is Juvenile Delinquency?

While the term *juvenile delinquency* may conjure up particular images for particular individuals, it covers a wide gamut of behavior, ranging from truancy and stealing candy bars to mugging, breaking and entering, stabbing, and killing.

As in the case of victimless crime, such juvenile behavior as truancy is criminal because it is defined in that way. The extent of delinquency will therefore vary with its definition. Running away from home accounts for a considerable segment of juvenile "crime." So does rebellion against authority. Truancy and traffic offenses are frequent. These crimes are called status offenses because they relate to the status of the offender rather that the act itself. Yet children may end up in detention homes, having committed no crime other than running away. A different handling of status offenses would lead to different dispositions. Some argue that the courts should not be involved with status offenses, others that parents cannot adequately deal with these problems or they would not be in court in the first place.[2] Unfortunately, children charged with such status offenses are sometimes dealt with through the same agencies as children who have committed serious crimes.

Let us begin with a look at more serious crimes. According to the 1979 *Statistical Abstract,*[3] juveniles commit the highest percentage of car thefts (59.5 percent), a high proportion of crimes relating to liquor laws (54.4 percent), 52.3 percent of all breaking and entering, followed by larceny (37.8 percent), forcible rape (35.9 percent), robbery (29.5 percent), aggravated assault (19.5 percent), and murder (6.1 percent). If we could focus on these crimes, rather than the status offenses of defying authority, or the traffic offenses and gambling offenses, we could perhaps be more effective in our work with juveniles (see Figure 17.1).

Do Juvenile Offenses Lead to Adult Crime?

It is sometimes argued that even minor juvenile offenses are serious in that they lead to adult crime. Others feel that such activity is mischievous and normal, in fact developmental, meaning that children usually engage in such acts as a part of growing up.

Research findings are equivocal. Yes, some children who engage in mischievous activity grow up normally. Conversely, some youthful crime does lead to more serious problems.

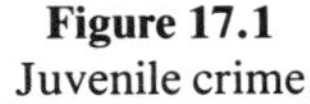

Figure 17.1
Juvenile crime

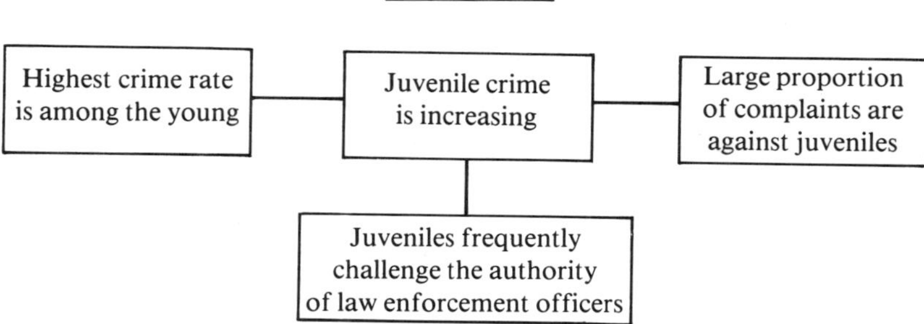

Let us first look at the situation in which juvenile crime is followed by responsible citizenship. Studies in which adults are asked to look back at their youthful behavior, as well as comparisons of delinquent and nondelinquent youth, are striking in their conclusions. Normal adults have committed the same kinds of delinquent acts as juvenile offenders commit. Similarly, normal children commit the same kind of offenses as delinquent children (see Figure 17.2).

What accounts for these findings? Why do some children commit acts of "mischief" and become responsible adults, while others commit the same acts and become criminals?

Figure 17.2
Juvenile offenders

Pranksters?	Criminals?
Juvenile offense may be followed by	Juvenile offense may be followed by
responsible citizenship.	a life of crime.
Middle-class juveniles commit offenses unnoticed.	Lower-class juveniles are more frequently arrested for offenses.
Lack of arrest may lead to not repeating the crime.	Arrest and conviction lead to recidivism.

While nondelinquent and delinquent children do the same sorts of things, those who get caught are more likely to be those who commit offenses frequently. Noncriminal adults have committed offenses with low frequency. One-time offenders are also more similar to nonoffenders than to those who have been defined delinquent.[4]

Children in lower socioeconomic classes are more likely than children in the upper classes to (1) be arrested and (2) continue criminality. They also have less chance for education and employment than do more privileged children. While it is possible to predict future delinquency on the basis of behavior in school, parents' delinquency, etc., some children with a poor prognosis do not become delinquent. It is not clear who these children are who will deal constructively with their problems despite a difficult environment.

Recipe for Juvenile Delinquency

While studies such as those just cited make us skeptical about defining a child as delinquent and a would-be criminal because he has committed certain offenses, other studies give us some ideas of the conditions that frequently lead to defined delinquency.

Living Where Crime Is a Way of Life

Children growing up in ghetto areas are literally taught to become criminals by their frequent association with criminals in the area. Children assume they will steal when they become old enough. Older children who have been arrested become heroes whom the younger ones follow.

This sociological explanation suggests that most causes of juvenile delinquency are related to poor living conditions, particularly conditions found in the cities.

Children in the cities are more likely to be on the streets instead of in spacious homes or on open land. It is easier to get into trouble with not much to do, lots of things to buy, no money to buy them with, many places from which to steal things.

In rural areas things to buy are less available. Children take buses to and from school and have less opportunity to steal.

Children in urban ghettos are rarely encouraged to do well in school, are not able to develop hobbies, and may not have access to organized sports. Their families set a poor example, since they are usually beset by the same problems as the children.

In this setting, children engage in criminal activities as play. Younger juveniles rarely use the things they steal. They may take clothing, only to throw it around exuberantly or destructively. They may steal a basket of apples, eat one or two, and leave the rest to rot. This "play" function of crime, however, soon gives way to a profit motive as children meet "fences" and see other people profiting from stealing. The earlier playful stealing served as training for more professional criminal activity.

In more affluent and less populous areas such encouragement to become a criminal is not readily available. Instead, crime is discouraged and other models of adult behavior are presented.

Disinterested Family. A second factor in delinquent behavior is lack of family concern. In one study, 84 percent of the parents of delinquents were either alcoholic or sociopathic themselves.[5] Most juveniles who have been involved in delinquent acts do not have an interested parent—mother *or* father. It was once thought that it was necessary to have a father in a home, that without a strong father children were likely to become delinquent. Research findings suggest that children may develop normally even without a father to serve as a model and to enforce standards of behavior. A concerned mother can be effective in preventing delinquency. This is not to say that fathers are unimportant, but it does indicate that the essential ingredients for noncriminal development can be provided by either parent.

Another false belief is that children misbehave because they are not physically punished. Although discipline is important,[6] many studies have shown that children who have been punished physically are *more,* not *less,* likely to get into trouble. This does not mean that children do not need discipline. It means instead that children need discipline *other than* physical punishment. If children are loved, the withdrawal of approval proves to be a strong deterrent in regulating their behavior. On the other hand, physical punishment leads children to try to "get away with things." A loving parent has credibility with a child. The child believes him. He listens when the parent tells him something is wrong. The effective parent also gives many rewards for good behavior, which the punishing parent does not do.

A child of a rewarding parent is therefore less likely to be angry and express his feelings in violent, destructive ways.

Many social-class differences also are involved. Lower-class parents are less likely to know methods of discipline that work. They do not explain things; they do not provide rewards for "good" behavior; they are not aware of the many ways in which children are nudged and cajoled into wanting to behave well.

Parental lack of concern combined with harsh physical punishment leads to a poor self-concept: "I am no good." This causes further misbehavior.

School Problems

Besides lack of concern in the family, a major factor in much delinquency is trouble in school. Many children become delinquents because they have reading problems, frequently caused by perceptual difficulties. The way they see and understand letters is different from the way others do. This condition is known as *dyslexia.* Perhaps as many as 25 percent of our children suffer from some degree of dyslexia. It is more common in boys than in girls.

Not being able to read well leads to many other problems. Such children will have difficulty with all subjects that involve reading—English, geography, history, current events, and so forth. These school difficulties mean that children will feel unhappy in school, that teachers will treat them badly, that they will be less likely to be awarded posts in student government or allowed to participate in sports. They will tend to associate with other kids with difficulties, be truant as much as possible, and cause trouble for school authorities whenever they can. These school difficulties alone can lead to "delinquency."

Other school difficulties may occur for students coming from a different culture, such as Latinos, who have little knowledge of the English language. While schools are making efforts to help children of non-English-speaking families, they still have tremendous handicaps. Even ghetto language can cause misunderstanding, as it involves a different vocabulary—slang words like *cat, cool, bread, decent* (as OK)—and different grammar, including double negatives ("He ain't got no bread"), which middle-class teachers label inferior.

Although many students of language have concluded that ghetto language is in some cases richer than standard English and in no way marks its users as inferior intellectually, teachers continue to downgrade those who speak it.

Another problem is that children who come from poor or disadvantaged homes are not provided with proper clothing, are not kept clean, and generally are not sent to school looking and acting like the middle-class children who are accepted and liked by their teachers.

At an extremely early age these children learn that they are no good. Jonathan Kozol has written eloquently about such children in the Boston school system. His book is aptly titled *Death at an Early Age,* for he believes that these children have little hope for a decent life after their experiences in our public schools.[7]

Low Self-Esteem

Since concern, interest, and love make a child feel he is worthwhile, what chance does he have for a positive self-image if he does not receive care at home or at school? If he is also a *failure* at school, he has even less chance for a positive self-image.

The low self-esteem he will probably feel leads the child to try to find other ways to be happy. He cannot find them in school, or at home, so he finds them in the street among kids with similar problems. He does not have sufficient confidence in himself. As a result, he cannot enjoy such activities as raising animals, or making model airplanes, or even becoming good at sports—since these activities require enough self-esteem to suffer the frustrations of long learning processes. Nor does anyone encourage the child in such pursuits.

Characteristics of Delinquent Behavior

Proving Manhood through Violence

Going to the streets for satisfaction leads to associating with other kids with similar problems. How do you get quick self-esteem? One way is to prove your "manhood." How do you prove manhood? By something quick, simple, and violent. Since these children are all angry for the reasons mentioned—lack of love, lack of acceptance—they combine getting rid of anger with proving that they're somebody. Hence, we see senseless beating up of other kids, as well as occasional bizarre killings of older people. We also see kids directly challenging police.

Formation of Gangs

Going to the streets for self-esteem also leads to the organization of gangs, the protection of "turf," elaborate procedures for acceptance that involve violence, and codes of ethics that violate community standards.

Much juvenile crime consists of crime against other juveniles, which is difficult to prove in court. Therefore, many police forces feel it is unproductive to try to protect kids from each other, since the work leads to few convictions. The kids then believe they must protect themselves as best they can, so more of them carry knives and guns, and more crime results.

Violence As a Reaction to Frustration

Violence may also be a way of feeling competent, of being able to effect something in an extremely frustrating world.

To what extent do any of us have a chance to see that we have made an impact on our world? Factory workers may seldom see an end product, just a couple of bolts put into place. Students are not given much of a chance to "do something," but instead are asked to manipulate words and symbols. Law enforcement personnel write tickets, run errands for their community, and keep people from hurting each other when they can. Even though this work has direct effects, it can seem meaningless—a constant round of complaints, demands from superiors, and few accomplishments.

Some people believe that it is therefore characteristic of our kind of complex society to breed senseless violence. This message was presented in a movie of the late 1960s, *A Clockwork Orange,*[8] in which youth roamed a city senselessly raping, beating up older people, and killing.

Why do youth rather than mature persons commit senseless

crimes? Probably because young people have more energy and fewer opportunities for feeling a sense of competence than adults.

Most of us have engaged in small acts of violence as a reaction to daily frustrations. Students queried by the author have done such things as throwing stones, breaking glasses, cursing, as well as shooting slingshots at windows. Young children take pleasure in building up blocks and knocking them over. Carnivals capitalize on this need by letting people pay to smash cups or throw things at other people. Violent crime can represent this same impulse greatly magnified.

Seeking Confrontation with Police

Juvenile offenders frequently seek out police authority. Why? It would seem that to delinquents the police would be hated and avoided. Strangely enough, this is probably not true for most delinquents, even though they pretend it is. Children feel a strong need for control, as they are unable to control themselves, and these children are unwilling or unable to receive control from their families. The police or other criminal justice professionals are the only ones who, even in confrontation, are willing to provide some control. Getting into trouble can, therefore, be a way of finding someone to help you control yourself.

This suggests a very important principle for law enforcement officers. Helping children keep control of themselves when the officer sees potential trouble may avoid a more serious confrontation.

For example, an officer described a complaint of a "corner" situation where some boys were using foul language. The officer stopped his car, got out, and started to talk quietly with the boys in a friendly fashion. He had the situation under control when another officer appeared on the scene, rolled down his car window, and shouted at the boys. Naturally enough, they responded by shouting back, and the first officer's work was destroyed.

It is extremely important that officers *not* incite individuals. If the offender is violent, the officer may have to wait out the situation, perhaps providing physical restraint, but doing it without losing his temper. After the person has calmed down, calm, friendly behavior by the officer will control further outbreaks. The offender will have seen an adult deal with a situation without violence and loss of control. He knows that it can be done.

Juveniles and the Courts

Another serious problem in handling juveniles involves the juvenile court system.

A special set of laws was originally devised to keep children from being thrown into jails with hardened criminals. The assumption was that these children could be treated and rehabilitated more easily than adult criminals. It was a humane and reasonable approach.

Juvenile courts or family courts are quite different from regular criminal courts in the way they deal with juveniles. First, many juveniles never reach court, even though they have been apprehended. The law enforcement officer has initial discretion as to whether or not to proceed with a case. He may bring the offender in while he's deciding what to do and keep him for twenty-four hours, or he may bring him in and turn him over to a probation officer. The probation officer must see him within a few days to decide what to do. Roughly half the juveniles apprehended never see a courtroom; they are given treatment or discharged on the basis of the probation officer's recommendations.

What can the probation officer do? The possibilities vary a great deal with the community. Some areas have a variety of alternative agencies to help the juvenile offender; others have few or none. These alternatives range from "Big Brother" programs, in which the child gets the attention and concern of a reasonable, law-abiding, and caring adult, through therapeutic programs offered by social work agencies or youth service bureaus.

Such so-called "diversionary" programs are designed to help delinquents and relieve the burden on the courts. They may range from minimally effective to maximally helpful. Such programs aid the probation officer in understanding and dealing with the child's underlying problems. He may refer a family for family therapy or marriage counseling. He may secure tutoring for a younger child or vocational guidance for an older one. Work-study or apprentice programs can offer employment to those not ready for the regular job market. Children helped through such diversionary programs neither see the court nor have records.

Other offenders go on for more formal disposition. These children may still be released on probation after a conference with the judge. In this case, they have no record. If they are not released, they may be detained while a social history is developed and while they await court disposition. Court-appointed counsel and private counsel alike may lack time to do more than find out what the offense is. Only occasionally will children have counsel who can make the necessary investigation for an adequate defense. Meanwhile, crowded court calendars often leave children awaiting trial in overcrowded and understaffed facilities.

Following trial, children may be either released or detained. If detained, the alternatives of the courts are usually poor. So-called training facilities, or "study centers," are usually no more than holding facilities. However, this varies throughout the country. In some states, the training schools train for little more than a life of further crime. In other states, facilities may be more adequate. Massachusetts has experimented with the closing down of regular detention facilities and uses halfway houses as rehabilitation centers. While reports of the success of such centers vary, they appear to be a viable alternative to the unsuccessful training schools.

Many correctional officers feel that any programs that tend to equate an institution with a community cannot succeed. These programs teach a person to adjust to the institution but not to the outside world. Many apparently successful behavior modification programs similarly involve reward for learning to conform to the institution, rather than adjust to society. This is because children learn submission and conformity but not the initiative required in the outside world. According to this view, only hard-core juveniles or adults should be detained in institutions. If they are so detained, it should be clear to them and the community that they are not being "helped," but simply prevented from doing harm.

A "rehabilitation" program that is poorly staffed and devised simply makes the community as well as the participants feel that rehabilitation is impossible. Similarly, a rehabilitation program that does not permit separation of those with violent criminal records from those committing minor crimes makes people feel hopeless and frightened of rehabilitation programs. Programs that grant freedom to youths who have repeatedly mugged and killed others are destructive to society. They prevent such programs from being used for juveniles who could be helped and allow other juveniles to continue committing crimes of violence.

Adequate rehabilitation involves not only finding individuals who *can* be helped without doing further violence, but also helping the individual acquire the necessary skills for living and working in society. Programs must also provide a setting in which he can use these skills. Opportunity for employment is most important. Other needs involve such simple necessities as a place to live, money for carfare, and adequate clothing.

What Can Be Done?

What is needed is action on a number of levels—community action, local police action, action on a city or county level, action on a state and even national level. This action needs to be directed toward a variety of targets that together would reduce the causes of delinquency.

Would harsher punishment and stricter law enforcement do the job? Politicians are fond of blaming the police or the courts for crime. "If they did their job, all these criminals wouldn't be on the streets."

Such politicians conveniently forget that recidivism in conventional prisons hovers around 90 percent. This means that nine out of ten criminals who *have* been arrested already will commit more crimes after serving their terms. They also forget that a man who couldn't earn a living in society before he went to jail is most unlikely to be able to do so after. Prisoners are released with perhaps fifty dollars to "get started." After buying a bus ticket home and renting a room to live in, they probably have little or no money left for carfare or food to maintain themselves while job hunting. Even men who get jobs sometimes cannot support themselves legitimately until they get their first paycheck. Society, particularly prison administration or rehabilitation groups, must provide for the simplest financial needs of the returned prisoner.

Most juveniles, however, have no skills with which to obtain jobs when they come out of training schools and need extensive vocational training to be able to hold down jobs. These training programs need to include skills that are often taken for granted, such as learning to get up at a given hour in the morning, learning to budget money, being willing to listen to a boss without feeling it necessary to curse him, and feeling a sense of pride in doing a legitimate, though perhaps poorly paid, job.

Would harsher punishment, perhaps life sentences, be the way to handle crime? Punishment, if sufficiently harsh, is a deterrent. But it is a deterrent primarily to middle-class persons who see going to jail as a disgrace and are horrified at the possibility. Children growing up in the ghettos expect to be arrested. Some authorities suggest that 80 percent of children in ghettos have been arrested by the time they are mature. Others feel the percentage might more realistically be set at 100 percent. Should we then put all minor defendants in jail for life? This is an obvious impossibility. What about more severe offenses? Where do you draw the line here?

Probably some crime could be prevented by spending millions of dollars on life care for those committing serious crimes. However, aside from the expense, this would go against society's idea of giving everyone a fair chance. Further, those criminals who are most destructive would not be deterred by harsher sentencing.

Differential treatment of those likely to commit further crimes would help. Psychological testing could be useful to predict who would be likely to repeat offenses. The Law Enforcement Assistance Administration has been investigating possibilities for more adequate preventive care. Model programs have been initiated and replicated. Promising leads need increased dissemination. Unfortunately, at this writing, the Law Enforcement Assistance Administration has lost most of its funding. A Reagan commission has recommended more prisons instead of preventive programs.

Are more, or more efficient, courts the answer? Certainly this is a pressing need not only for juveniles but for our entire criminal justice system. Without better treatment facilities, however, the courts cannot do their jobs.

What about better law enforcement on the patrol officer level? While adequate staffing of police departments is again important, even quick and efficient enforcement will not help without good follow-up by the courts and the treatment facilities. Before federal funds were cut, the Law Enforcement Assistance Administration actively researched and promoted programs that would enable suspects to be dealt with more effectively.

Is an integrated approach the answer? Obviously the law enforcement aspect of crime prevention does call for an integrated approach—patrol officers, the entire police system, courts, and correctional facilities must all work together to make the job of any one effective.

What can you, as a professional in the system, do to make this happen?

You can do your job as well as possible. Efficient arrest procedures are important. However, prevention of crime is even more important. You can help even if other support systems are not working efficiently. Conscientious, caring correctional work is essential.

Prevention of juvenile-related crimes must be supported by police policies. Many potential trouble spots could be erased if police or probation officers could (1) talk to children who feel resentful about school, (2) meet with children in the community on projects such as sports and helping others, (3) pursue public relations programs that permit kids to identify positively with the police, such as allowing juveniles to ride with police on rounds, encouraging visits to police facilities, and having rap sessions in which young people could be asked to suggest answers to problems caused by delinquents.

Summary

The issue of youthful offenders is complex. Much juvenile crime does not lead to criminal careers, but that which does frequently can be traced to a number of factors: an environment in which crime is accepted, a disinterested family, school problems, low self-esteem, a lower-class family, and a need for authority in an active child.

Dealing with the delinquent when he becomes a suspect is often the responsibility of the probation officer or the arresting officer. Most juveniles are released without court disposition. However, some juveniles go to court, and some go on to detention facilities, which are usually understaffed and overcrowded. Other alternatives are diversionary programs in communities.

Besides helping to promote better facilities for juveniles in the community, the law enforcement officer can be extremely helpful to juveniles by preventive crime work. Most important is spending time with juveniles *before* they are arrested, thus providing them with a chance to view the officer as friend and model. Similarly crucial is the role of probationary and correctional personnel.

Discussion Questions

1. What are the main problems in dealing with delinquents? Role-play a situation in which an officer has to deal with a complaint against juveniles "corner-lounging." Reverse roles during the situation.
   How did the person who was an officer feel? How was the situation handled? What worked? What didn't?
2. What experiences have you had being delinquent? How did they change you as an adult? Why did you do what you did? Could your actions have been prevented? Should they have been prevented, or written off as mischief?
3. What do you think of the preventive measures discussed in the chapter? What "preventive" experiences have you had that kept you out of a delinquent career? Try to write a "recipe for nondelinquency."

Suggested Reading

Bartollas, C. *The Juvenile Offender: Control, Correction and Treatment*. Boston: Holbrook Press, 1978.

Bittner, E., and Krantz, S. *Standards Relating to Police Handling of Juvenile Problems*. Cambridge, Mass.: Ballinger, 1977.

Burkhart, K. W. *The Child and the Law: Helping the Status Offender*. New York: Public Affairs Committee, 1975.

Cloward, R., and Ohlin, L. *Delinquency and Opportunity*. Glencoe, Ill.: Free Press, 1969.

Dodge, C. R. *A World without Prisons: Alternatives to Incarceration throughout the World*. Lexington, Mass.: Lexington Books, 1980.

Edelfonso, E. *Law Enforcement and the Youthful Offender*. 3d ed. New York: John Wiley, 1978.

Federal Bureau of Investigation. *Uniform Crime Reports,* 1978.

Forer, L. G. *"No One Will Listen."* New York: Grosset and Dunlap, 1970.

Griffin, B. S. *Juvenile Delinquency in Perspective.* New York: Harper and Row, 1978.

Kobetz, R. W. *The Police Role and Juvenile Delinquency.* Gaithersburg, Md.: International Association of Chiefs of Police, 1971.

Kornhauser, R. R. *Social Sources of Delinquency.* Chicago: University of Chicago Press, 1978.

Matza, D. *Delinquency and Drift.* New York: John Wiley, 1964.

May, R. *Power and Innocence: A Search for the Sources of Violence.* New York: W. W. Norton, 1972.

Mc Corkel, L.; Elias, A.; and Bixby, F. L. *The Highfield Story.* New York: Holt, 1952.

Neumeyer, M. H. *Juvenile Delinquency in Modern Society.* 3d ed. New York: Van Nostrand, Reinhold, 1961.

Offer, Daniel; Marohn, R. C.; and Ostrov, E. *Psychological World of the Juvenile Delinquent.* New York: Basic Books, 1979.

Rachette, Lisa. *Throwaway Children.* New York: Dell, 1970.

Redl, F., and Wineman, D. *Children Who Hate.* Glencoe, Ill.: Free Press, 1951.

Shickor, D., and Kelly, D. H., eds. *Critical Issues in Juvenile Delinquency.* Lexington, Mass.: Lexington Books, 1980.

West, D. J., and Farrington, D. P. *The Delinquent Way of Life.* New York: Crane Russah, 1977.

Part Five

Our Changing Society

CHAPTER 18

Our Changing Society – What's New, What's Old

One of the most characteristic features of our society is change. Initially our society was founded by people seeking change. The pioneers were dissatisfied with their lives. They were not afraid to face danger in order to change. This has been a major emphasis in our society ever since.

Change or Stability?

Is change good or bad? Stop and think about your own life. You will probably find that you like changes but are glad to have some things remain the same. You like to go to the same bar or restaurant frequently. But once in a while you like to change. This is because neither constant change nor constant sameness is good for people (see Figure 18.1).

Figure 18.1
Change – good or bad

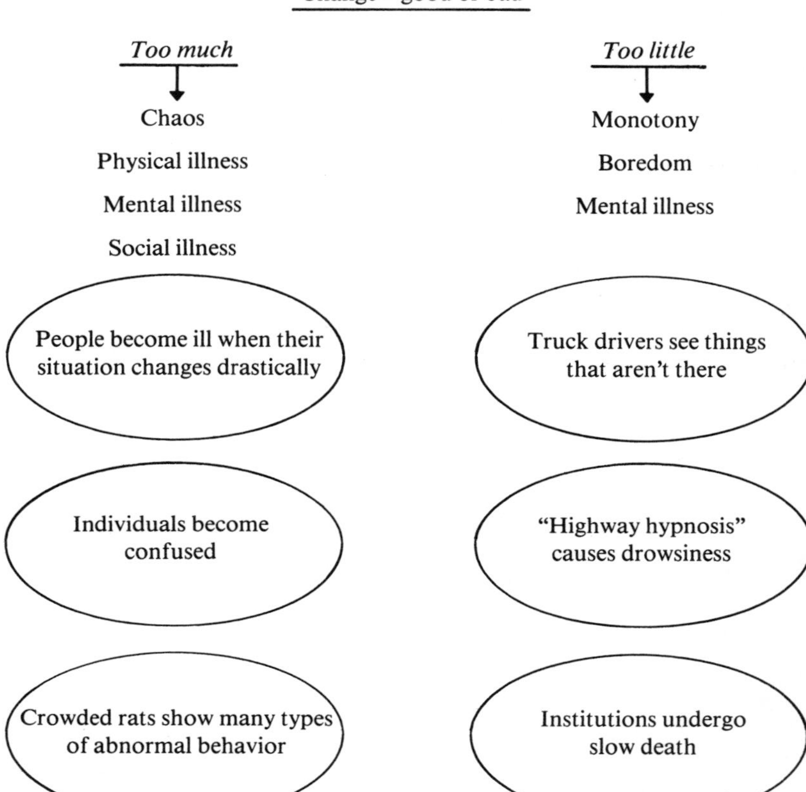

Research findings have shown that too monotonous an environment causes the brain to malfunction. We are no longer alert; we tend to solve problems poorly; and we sometimes misperceive reality.

Truck drivers who have a very monotonous routine are subject to misinterpreting their perceptions – they might see a shadow as a person beginning to cross the road. "Highway hypnosis" is another example. People driving on monotonous roads often become drowsy.

People and even animals work hard to prevent their lives from becoming monotonous. For example, monkeys will work for no reward other than to be permitted to solve a puzzle.

On the other hand, too much change is harmful. Recent studies have shown that even positive changes in life can make a person physically ill. If you lose your job, your marriage breaks up, and your son requires expensive surgery, you know you are in trouble. You are likely to become physically ill. However, if you get a promotion, buy a new house, and marry someone you love, this can also mean trouble. The positive change is just as likely to cause physical illness for some people. Others seem to be able to accept change without illness.

Rats with too much going on in their environment due to crowding develop perversions and cannibalism and have high rates of infant mortality. Too much change in their normal habitat has taken place.

These results suggest that some change and some stability are both important for the mental health of individuals.

Change and Society

How does change affect an entire society like ours? What relevance does it have for criminal justice?

Societies and social institutions are similar to individuals. They need some change, some sameness. For example, if the precinct captain at a police station suddenly changed all the rules, everyone would be confused. We rely on sameness to organize our actions.

Think, for example, of a group of people entering a classroom. If there were no "rules," what would happen? Everyone would mill around. No one would know what to do. Much time and energy would be lost.

Children who are raised without consistent rules sometimes become quite rigid about the way to do things. They need to establish some constancy in their lives. It is only children who can expect *certain things* to happen who feel free to experiment and change *other things.*

On the other hand, what happens if nothing changes in an institution? The institution undergoes a slow death. Everyone is bored. Rules no longer make sense. Protests or even rebellions break out. Researchers repeatedly have found that changes in institutions such as hospitals produce beneficial effects. It doesn't matter exactly what change occurs. It is important simply that there be change. People become interested and hopeful. For example, at one mental institution, walls were painted colorful hues. Staff was told that this would help the patients. Although there was little supporting evidence, the effect of the change was to make everyone happier and more hopeful. In *this* atmosphere people *did* get better.

Conflict As a Result of Differences

Not only is there a problem in a society, institution, or individual in striking the right balance of change and stability; there is also a problem resulting from different rates of change for different segments of society.

Regional Differences

There are, for example, more changes in cities than in rural areas. Cities may tolerate, and even encourage, such actions as cocaine use, while rural areas will be upset at evidence of such goings-on. Abortions may be tolerated in cities while considered unnatural in the country.

Industrialized countries are likely to change quickly for many reasons—the need to compete, new problems arising constantly, and a feeling that newness is desirable.

Similarly, countries that have more contact with other cultures, such as coastal and trading countries, change more than countries that are inland and engage in agriculture.

Age Differences

There are many differences in our society among people of different ages. Most striking are differences in sexual behavior, recreational behavior, and drug use. Older people are sometimes horrified at seeing young people do things they themselves did when they were young.

Some of the differences are due to differences in education of the different generations. People are better educated today than they were at the turn of the century.

Many differences between college youth and the rest of society are simply age differences. Youth may feel there is no basic difference between getting drunk on "booze" and getting high on "pot." For the older person, however, booze is a long-established, well-recognized "friend." Pot holds unknown dangers.

Ours is an "aging" society, with the proportion of older people gradually increasing. The effect is beginning to be apparent, with older people acquiring more influence. Crime rates should become lower as the proportion of young people decreases, although there has been an upswing in the 80s, probably related to problems of unemployment.

Religious and Cultural Differences

Differences are attributable to differing religious or cultural upbringings. One of the most striking religious differences is the attitudes of Catholics and non-Catholics toward abortion. Abortion is criminal to Catholics. Bringing unwanted children into the world seems criminal to many others.

People whose parents emigrated to America probably have been exposed to the ways of "the old country." Their beliefs will be different. For example, those coming from Mediterranean homes are more likely to be expansive. They show their feelings in loud, exuberant ways. People whose families come from Northern European countries do not show emotions freely. They try not to yell and scream or cry or even to be excessively noisy when they are happy.

Social Class Differences

Many differences are also attributable to social class. Ways of dressing, sexual behavior, language behavior, ways of cleaning and furnishing homes, recreation, all differ.

Effect on Criminal Justice System

Because of these differences, the criminal justice system has a hard time regulating such varying behavior. There are bound to be conflicts. For example, pot-smoking youngsters have been considered a menace by alcohol-drinking oldsters. Sexually conservative

Baptists look askance at more liberal Protestants. Effusive Greeks are mistrusted by reserved Scandinavians. Behaviors such as street fights may be accepted in some areas but become grounds for a police call in others.

How does the criminal justice system deal with these many differences? The application of the law varies from place to place and group to group, confusing criminal justice personnel as well as the people they serve. The law is supposed to be an absolute, unswerving, just system of regulation. Yet, *in practice*, enforcement of the law varies to reflect beliefs of local communities.

Because different subgroups have different beliefs, anger results when one group tries to impose its values on another. For example, an issue in the 1970s was the busing of school children. Some people felt very firmly that this busing was right and necessary if our country's aim to give everyone equal educational opportunities was to be realized. Others felt just as firmly that it was wrong to force children to travel to schools which were not as good as the schools nearer them. Much angry debate and violence occurred as a result.

This kind of problem does not arise in traditional societies, where what is right is clear to all and upheld by almost everyone. As soon as things begin to change, however—and this usually happens as societies become industrialized—new problems lead to new and varied definitions of right and wrong (see Figure 18.2).

Figure 18.2
Law enforcement

In traditional societies	In our society
Standards of right and wrong are clear.	Standards of right and wrong are unclear.
Society can band together to enforce its rules.	Society cannot unite to enforce its rules. Factions fight over standards.

Causes of Change in Today's Society

What specifically in today's society produces the changes that cause conflict? Why is it that some perfectly decent people demonstrated in the streets in opposition to the Viet Nam War, which other fine and decent people supported with all their hearts? Why is it that some people accept busing, abortion, "gay rights," while others strongly oppose them?

Inflation

Our society is moving into a new economic phase that requires readjustment. While more people have become affluent, inflation lowers standards of living, causing predictable responses. These angry reactions produce political protests, such as California's "Proposition Thirteen." Citizens there changed the tax structure of the state when they felt that they were being taxed into poverty. The Reagan administration has instituted major changes in federal funding in response to inflation, affecting many social programs adversely.

For those less affluent, though still well off in comparison to the abjectly poor of the world, access to television and its advertising of new cars, beautiful homes, clothes, and innumerable other luxuries causes much dissatisfaction. Expectations rise, and few believe that "the meek shall inherit the earth." However, the increased communication and wide distribution of consumer goods give some credence to those who believe that we have come closer to a classless society.

Ecological Crises

A further aspect of our society's need to change is the ecological crises brought on by the continual attempt to expand industrialism. More particularly, oil supply problems have made it clear that we must change gears. Many people predict catastrophic results from continued economic expansion. The disposal of garbage, sewage, and industrial wastes is a problem of major proportions. A number of areas have had demonstrable and catastrophic chemical or nuclear fallout causing a high incidence of serious illness (e.g. Love Canal). Energy shortage has become a major problem, with political and military as well as economic implications. We must be concerned with further nuclear accidents such as occurred at Three Mile Island as well as not having sufficient energy. We are poisoning our air, our water, and our land. We are using up our natural resources. Ecological needs may make it necessary for us to change patterns of goals, work, and leisure. This will not occur without serious dislocation. High rates of unemployment and inflation have produced serious economic difficulties. Those affected most are those least able to compensate. Young blacks, in particular, were heavily hit by unemployment in the late 1970s.[1]

This is likely to cause further unrest and increased crime.

Higher Educational Standards. As our society has moved to a postindustrial phase, its members have become more educated. Communications have vastly improved. People are more likely to question government, and to believe they can make changes. Both liberal and conservative forces organize to push their interests in what has almost become an era of single-issue politics, whether they be antiabortion, pro-gay rights, antitax, or pro-gun licensing.

Varying Moral Standards. A great change has occurred in standards of right and wrong. Movements to provide equal opportunities to all have expanded to include women as another underprivileged group. Sexual standards are changing. Sex education in the schools has been widely debated and is more generally accepted. Many debate whether marriage, as we have currently defined it, is a viable institution. Divorce has increased, and many single-parent families have resulted. Ways of rearing children have changed. Parents become very uncertain as to what is right and what is wrong; therefore, the children are often left to decide for themselves. Even if parents are certain, their decisions often conflict with peer customs and children argue that their peers are correct.

People wonder how they ought to behave. At less unstable periods in history, right and wrong behavior in every circumstance was perfectly clear. The musical *Fiddler on the Roof*[2] describes a man balancing on top of a roof, playing the fiddle. How does he maintain his balance? By tradition, he tells us. His society is a traditional society, an agricultural society. How a wife behaves, how a daughter behaves, how a son behaves—all this is clear to everyone. The society can unite in condemning anyone who steps out of line.

Today society is completely different. There is no single correct way to behave. Take a recently married young couple as an example. They don't have much money. Should she go to work? If she decides to, who gets the money? Will it be part of the household fund, or will she spend it as she pleases and let her husband take the traditional role of supporting the family?

When a wife stays at home, she is expected to keep the house in order, prepare meals, take care of shopping and laundry. But if both husband and wife arrive home at 6:00 P.M., who shops? Who makes dinner? Who does the dishes? Even more seriously, when children arrive, how are they cared for?

Differing solutions cause conflict in families and societies.

Problems in Criminal Justice: What's New? What's Old?

Let us discuss aspects of change in topics of importance to the criminal justice community: the correctional system, drugs, child abuse, pornography and violence in the mass media, and immorality in high public office (see Figure 18.3).

Figure 18.3
Changes in criminal justice

What's New	What's Old
Correctional system—Some aspects of rehabilitation procedures	Correctional system—Total concept
Particular drugs and society's reaction to them	Drug use
Abuse of children recognized; possibly **more** abuse; more parents seek and receive help	Abuse of children
Controversy over what is good or bad	Pornography
Controversy over reaction to violence and pornography	Violence
Widespread and unabated immorality in government	Immorality in government

The Correctional System

What's New. A number of exciting rehabilitative programs have been initiated in the correctional system. The concept of rehabilitation through living outside of prisons, usually in some type of halfway house, has spread from mental hospitals to the correctional system. Diversionary programs for youth provide help outside of prisons and often without formal arrest. Although some reviews of these programs have been negative, further improvement in the way they are administered may help. Separating those who have committed violent crimes from those whose crimes were minor may improve results considerably.

What's Old. The total concept of punishment by imprisonment is still with us. Despite widespread agreement that it doesn't work, imprisonment is still the principal means of dealing with those who break the law. It satisfies our primitive urge for revenge and will probably always be around.

Drugs

What's New. What's new in the area of drugs? Concern about increasingly younger users of drugs—in high schools, junior highs, and even elementary schools; increasing use of community-based, ex-addict-staffed treatment programs; increased legalization or decreased penalties for the use of marijuana, along with continued warnings of possible ill effects; the growth in popularity of cocaine, particularly among the affluent; the appearance on the scene of "angel dust" (PCP), one of the apparently most dangerous of the mind-altering drugs; the appearance of "T's & blues" as a street substitute for heroin; a change in law enforcement strategies to try to curb the sources of drugs, frequently through international tactics; the widespread use of tranquilizers—although there is less official concern for this problem than for some others.

What's Old. The *use* of drugs is old. Every known society has used drugs to alter states of mind. Attempts to regulate drug usage have also always been with us. Emphasis on pharmaceutical drugs to solve life's problems continues to support the use of nonpharmaceutical drugs among the young.

Child Abuse

A possibly greater degree of child abuse, related to our more isolated families, is present today. Increased awareness has led to legislation requiring reporting and treatment of child abuse victims. The attitude that such tragedies are "none of our business" is decreasing. Whether there is actually more child abuse, or simply more reporting of child abuse, is not clear. Parents Anonymous, a self-help group modeled on Alcoholics Anonymous, is a promising new modality. Other groups are reporting success in treating parents. More parents are seeking help for their problems before they become severe.

What's Old. Child abuse, like drug abuse, has occurred in most Western societies. It has frequently been considered to be an inevitable concomitant of poverty. The acceptance of the right of the parent to be physically violent with his children is also very old. The dividing line between discipline and abuse is a continuing problem.

Pornography and Violence in the Mass Media

What's New. Increased concern over the effect on children of televised sex and adult violence has led to attempts to regulate programming, at least during times when children are likely to be watching TV. Networks have been sued for damage resulting from crimes initially portrayed on television.

Interestingly, there seems to be little concern about violence in children's cartoons, some of which portray a succession of violent incidents.

Recent studies generally show that pornographic materials are not harmful. Studies of violence are mixed, with some showing no effect, others showing that children do imitate adult models of aggressive behavior. Studies from countries that do not prohibit pornography, such as Denmark, have shown a decrease in sex crimes. In general, it appears that violent materials are more dangerous than sexual ones.

A basic flaw in censorship procedures is that they do not distinguish the sex and violence that are natural and part of everyday life—such as animals hunting other animals—from sex and violence that are unnatural. Further, these procedures do not look at the message a TV drama portrays. For example, it has been found that when a TV hero does something wrong and is punished, he is *more* likely to be viewed sympathetically than if he is not punished. When children see violence as a solution to problems, or sex as separate from an important human relationship, they are bound to learn that such behavior is acceptable. Whether such viewing has serious or little effect depends on what else they learn—especially in their own homes.

What's Old. Censorship attempts have been with us as long as pornography and violence have, with the same indifferent results. Historically, periods of rigid censorship are followed by eras of permissiveness, which in turn eventually lead to more repression.

Immorality in High Public Office.

What's New. While power has always bred corruption, the extent of admitted, unabashed immorality in high public office seems to have reached an unprecedented height in the 1970s. The argument advanced by members of the Nixon administration that the powerful may break laws, but the less powerful may not, was bound to make people wonder whether they should be law-abiding themselves. In the wake of Watergate, people became extremely distrustful of politicians. Large numbers of officials who broke the law—frequently accepting money for contracts—were exposed. Tighter campaign contribution laws got other politicians into trouble. The real newness seemed to lie in the public concern, the attempt to control corruption through new laws, disillusionment, and a lack of differentiation between minor infractions that do little harm and infractions that disrupt the democratic process. While some good came from the Watergate era, there was a general lasting conviction that no one is honest, so why try?

What's Old. The use of power for personal gain has always been with us. It is a tendency of human nature, and it is a major reason why the founders of this country set up the system of checks and balances that constitutes our democracy.

Crime As a Result of Changing Definitions

Another major concern cutting across specific areas is how we define crime. If we were to decide that it is a crime to use Anglo-Saxon curse words ("four-letter words"), then our crime rates would be very high.

To the extent that our definition of crime reflects current practices and standards of morality, criminal justice institutions will be respected and laws obeyed. If laws prohibit what is generally accepted as moral and right by large groups, there will be problems. Prohibition was the best example; gambling is another. Much of organized crime flourishes on the basis of laws against gambling, which, in one form or another, is engaged in by the majority of the population. The regulation of sexuality is another example. The prohibition of drug use is still another. Drug distribution appears to be breeding the newest crime syndicates.

This is not to say that excessive drinking, many forms of drug use, and some forms of gambling are good for individuals or society, but we must carefully consider whether it is productive to regulate private conduct.

There are two aspects of private conduct regulation to consider: (1) Is it moral to regulate private conduct if the private conduct does not hurt others? and (2) Is it practical? If we are breeding more crime by prohibiting certain private behaviors, would it not be better to regulate instead of prohibit? The high taxes on cigarettes are an example of such regulation in this country. Frequent health exams for prostitutes would be another example.

Summary

There are reasons for both optimism and concern in the evolution of our society. Changes stemming from developments in our economic system are evolving rapidly at the time of this writing. We must expect many problems as a result. But understanding can help us deal with them reasonably. This can be done, despite the tendency for people with little understanding of social change to blame *something* (like drugs, the young people who use them, or "the politicians") instead of looking at basic social problems.

Laws to *regulate* rather than *prohibit* current practices may be a reasonable solution to many criminal justice problems.

However, questions about what is considered right and wrong will always be hard to resolve. For example, providing opportunity for blacks ultimately has given us "reverse discrimination," which reflects the problem of how we can distribute the good things in life more even-handedly. Attempts to solve social problems will always produce new sources of conflict.

Discussion Questions

1. Can you identify any problems that you, as a group, are having because something is changing too much? Are there some problems caused by too little change? How could you deal with them?
2. Can you identify any times when you, or people you have known, have blamed ills caused by social change on a particular group? Who? Why was that group selected? How could the problem have been worked on?
3. What do you think of the idea advanced in this chapter that changing social practices require changes in the law? Can you think of some examples of laws that should be changed?

Suggesting Reading

Basil, D., and Cook, C. W. *The Management of Change.* New York: McGraw-Hill, 1974.

Bienen, H. *Violence and Social Change.* Chicago: University of Chicago Press, 1969.

Boulding, K. E. *From Abundance to Scarcity: Implications for the American Tradition.* Columbus, Ohio: Ohio University Press, 1978.

Chirot, D. *Social Change in the 20th Century.* New York: Harcourt Brace Jovanovich, 1977.

Cochran, T. C. *Social Change in America: The 20th Century.* New York: Harper and Row, 1972.

Di Renzo, G. J., ed. *We, the People: American Character and Social Change.* Contributions in Sociology, no. 24. Westport, Conn.: Greenwood, 1977.

Dohrenwend, B. S., and Dohrenwen, B. P. *Stressful Life Events: Their Nature and Effects.* New York: John Wiley & Sons, 1974.

Graham, D. T., and Stevenson, I. "Disease as Response to Life Stress." In Lief, H. I.; Lief, V. F.; and Lief, N. R., eds., *The Psychological Basis of Medical Practice.* New York: Harper and Row, pp. 115–36.

Hochman, J. S. *Marijuana and Social Evolution.* Englewood Cliffs, N.J.: Prentice-Hall, 1972.

Janowitz, M. *The Last Half-Century: Societal Change and Politics in America.* Chicago: University of Chicago Press, 1978.

McGrath, J. E., ed. *Social and Psychological Factors in Stress.* New York: Holt, Rinehart, and Winston, 1970.

Rahe, R. H.; McKean, J. D.; and Arthur, R. J. "A Longitudinal Study of Life-Change and Illness Patterns." *Journal of Psychosomatic Research* 10(1967):355–66.

CHAPTER 19

Demonstrations and Riots

Controlling demonstrators and rioters is one of the most demanding of law enforcement jobs. It is an extremely difficult task. Most police training involves instructing officers to work with one person or perhaps two or three. Working with crowds is an entirely different matter. It is frightening, often unpredictable, and demanding. Property and lives may hang in the balance. How police officers handle themselves is of crucial importance.

A crowd is very different from the individuals of which it is composed. Because each member feels less individual responsibility, crowds tend to act impulsively. Although some crowds may be orderly and disciplined, the potential for violence is constant.

It is important for officers to be neither overly confident nor overly fearful of crowds. Planning ahead is important. Such factors as knowing where a crowd may disperse to, using the right amount of force, knowing the mood of the crowd, and controlling information that the crowd may be receiving (rumor centers) are all important.

When and Why Do Demonstrations and Riots Occur?

Demonstrations and riots occur as a result of anger and frustration. A demonstration is a way of communicating—of making a statement about something that the crowd feels is intolerable. Demonstrators are saying, "We don't know how else to get this message across." While this does not excuse their behavior, it is important to understand that people who demonstrate and riot usually feel that there is no other way to right what they consider to be crucial wrongs or frustrations. A demonstration can become a riot if something touches off the crowd's feelings of anger, frustration, and helplessness. This is why officers must be in complete control of their own behavior. They cannot allow themselves to respond to taunts with counteraggression. Such counteraggression can turn a peaceful demonstration into a real riot (see Figure 19.1).

Figure 19.1
Demonstrations and riots

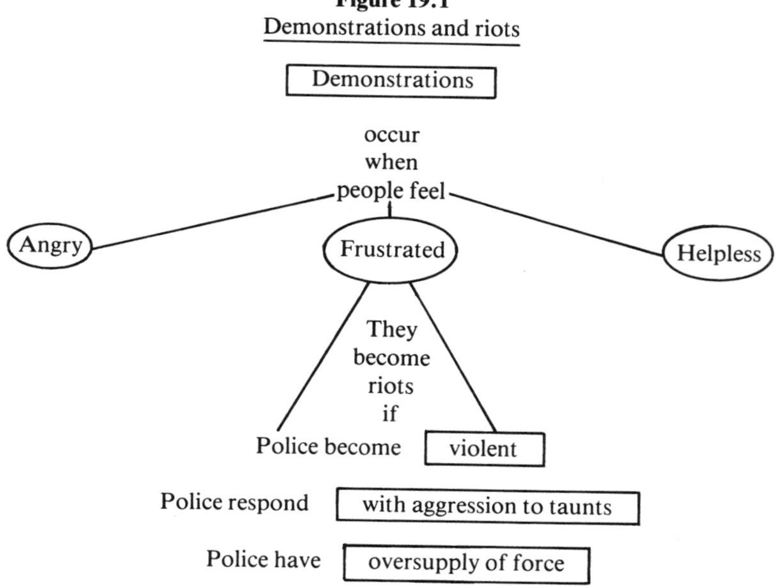

Two major groups of demonstrations have been extensively studied in recent times: (1) the ghetto riots that spread through inner cities in the late 1960s, and (2) riots throughout the country during the same decade, usually in protest to the Viet Nam War, frequently on college campuses. These groups of riots represent the two major types of protest: (1) against property and (2) against government actions.

Ghetto Riots

Most students of the ghetto riots in the late 1960s and early 1970s agree that the basic cause was the mistreatment of ghetto residents. This was true even though many of the cities with major riots had had human relations councils, programs for minorities, blacks on police forces, and other nondiscriminatory programs.

The problem with all these attempts to give inner-city residents equal opportunities was that they did not go far enough. They raised hopes, only to frustrate them.

Special job and training programs in major cities might have reached between 5 and 50 percent of the population who needed them. This left from 50 to 95 percent of the people who had hoped for relief through such programs disappointed and bitter. Such raising and dashing of hopes causes more resentment and frustration than if the programs had not been offered in the first place.

What *was* the major frustration of the people who rioted in these cities? People in inner-city ghetto areas have less in every respect than people in affluent suburbs. For example, many rioters had, prior to the riots, complained unsuccessfully that city garbage collection was inadequate, leading to filth and rats in their neighborhoods. Bad treatment of tenants by slum landlords was another continuous problem. Police patrol was insufficient, comparing unfavorably to areas where congestion and crime were lower. Schools were inadequate and overcrowded. Stores overcharged for inferior merchandise.

At the root of all these problems was the major concern: unemployment. Ghetto unemployment, even in periods of relatively full national employment, is extremely high. For example, in 1975, when unemployment rates overall climbed above 8 percent, ghetto areas had unemployment rates of 45 percent.

There are several reasons. One is that the population of ghetto areas is young. Young people without special training have a hard time in the job market. They are last to be hired, first to be fired.

A second reason is that ghetto areas house a large percentage of nonwhite Americans. Unemployment figures for blacks and other nonwhites are much higher than similar figures for whites. This is due partly to discrimination, partly to ghetto conditions. These conditions make it difficult for youths to learn skills required for employment. Such skills as being able to get up in the morning, accept criticism, or wait for promotions are not commonly learned in the ghetto.

A third reason is the lack of formal education among ghetto youths, most of whom have not completed high school.

When ghetto residents are employed, they are usually in menial and unrewarding jobs. Not only are these jobs unrewarding financially, but they do not offer security, status, or interest. They are jobs that nobody else wants—dull, with no guarantee of steady employment. They are jobs that other people look down upon.

The problem of unequal justice is also a factor in ghetto discontent. It has become clear that everyone is not equal before the law. Blacks, the poor, and other minorities are overrepresented as clients in the criminal justice system. There are more arrests, more people held for trial, and more people serving prison sentences from these groups. This occurs for two reasons: (1) more crime occurs in poor and ghetto areas, and (2) wealthier persons, whites, and those with more education are less likely to be arrested even though they may have committed serious crimes. If arrested, they are less likely to be held, and this inequality continues throughout the process.

Do Ghetto Residents Have Justification for Rioting?

An interesting point is that ghetto residents riot precisely because they are not utterly poor and without resources. They are likely to riot, instead, because they have a little something and feel keenly the desire for more. They are not poor by international standards, but they are constantly bombarded with evidence (TV, radio, billboards) that other people have much more than they do.

Sociologists have discussed this problem as one of visibility of wealth. If individuals see nothing around them except what is accessible, they will not feel dissatisfied. If everyone is eating rice with a few bits of fish, no one may feel very *good,* but no one feels cheated. On the other hand, people eating hamburgers, knowing that others can afford steaks, are likely to be dissatisfied.

A society that shows people luxuries must provide people the means to obtain them. Middle-class blacks did not riot in the 1960s. They already had, or expected to have, the good things that other parts of the population enjoyed.

This is a crucial point. It is not necessary to *have* what others have, only to *know* there is a legitimate way of getting these things. The lack of a legitimate means of obtaining the goods and services people see in store windows, on television, and in other parts of the city is what is so troublesome. For example, a ghetto man interviewed on television stated that he had no hope at all of ever getting employment, that the current wave of unemployment (1975) was nothing different from what his neighbors in the ghetto had experienced all their lives.

Attempts to get more lead nowhere. Buying furniture on time without steady employment invites repossession. Borrowing money from loan sharks invites greater financial problems and sometimes threats of physical attack. Stealing leads to arrest.

The most eroding aspect of poverty in America is the lack of self-respect felt by the poor. Welfare is administered in degrading ways. Employment is unavailable to many, or is defeating because it is undesirable employment. This situation is set against the background of an America that prides itself on providing equal opportunity for all, an America that is prosperous and proud of it, and an America that bombards its citizens with advertising about all the material things necessary for the "good life."

It is not surprising that, in such a setting, people with no way of getting these good things feel frustrated. I remember living in New York City with a modest income; I felt poor. There were too many attractive things that I could only dream of buying. In rural areas I have also been poor, but it has not bothered me. Rich and poor alike lived similarly. Their bank accounts were not visible. I had no reason to feel envious.

In ghetto areas the reality of poverty set against the wealth of America makes people feel left out. It isn't too bad if you believe that you can earn these things sometime in the future; and you do believe this if you are middle class. It's worse when you know you'll never improve your lot. This is the experience of the urban poor.

Another factor is at work as well—*crowding*. As noted earlier, studies of crowding in animals have shown that crowded animals display disturbed behavior. While things may be different among humans, many people believe that crowding has serious negative effects. People need space of their own, and space is not available in most poor areas.

At the very least, we can indict crowding as *one* of the preconditions of violence—and riots.

Who Were the Ghetto Rioters?

The National Advisory Commission on Civil Disorders (the Kerner Commission) identified rioters in major cities in the late 1960s as primarily young, better educated than nonrioters, mostly male, and well informed politically. They were not different in employment from nonrioters.

This adds to our picture of the causes of riots. Riots seem to occur among those with (1) some awareness that social conditions can be changed, and (2) little to lose by rioting. While not educated enough to be employable in the modern job market, rioters studied by the Kerner Commission tended to have had *some* high school education. (The average educational level in their areas was no high school education.) They were therefore more likely to be aware of the need for change. Rioters were young and energetic and more likely to be single than married. Most were jobless. They therefore had little to lose if they were arrested. They were primarily nonwhite and extremely angry at whites. They were also angry at the black middle class, whom they saw as having betrayed them.

Counterrioters (area residents who supported the police), in contrast, were more frequently the black middle-class residents of the area. They were propertied, with more to lose. They tended to be even better educated, with some college training, than the rioters.

College Demonstrations and Riots

While ghetto riots may be easy to understand (the poor are frustrated, with little to lose), how can we explain college riots? College students may or may not come from wealthy families, but they rarely are ghetto-poor. Their parents are employed. Their homes range from modest to opulent. They may come from the lower-middle or even upper-lower class, from the upper-middle class, or from the upper class. However, they rarely come from the lower-lower class with its unemployment, low-status jobs, and ghetto housing.

Furthermore, it is hard for another reason to believe that poverty caused student frustration; demonstrations and riots during the 1960s and early 1970s were more common on expensive private campuses than at state-supported public colleges. However, the same general psychological principles apply.

Student Attitudes

The students felt frustrated and impotent, just as did the ghetto residents. They too wanted something they did not have. Students traditionally have been concerned with social issues. (Once a person has what he needs, he becomes frustrated over the problems of others.) They may see social issues as the way to deal with their own needs for satisfaction. *The* social issue of the 1960s was the Viet Nam War.

The war was frustrating because citizens knew it was there, while official sources pretended it wasn't. It was frustrating because young people were sent to fight and die, but they did not believe it was a necessary war. To many young people, the war must have represented all that they hated about the adult world around them: hypocrisy (doing things for one reason and saying you're doing them for another); concern with strategic gains but not with people; citizen helplessness to influence their government. Many people—adults and students alike—felt it was an unlawful war. Similar to the ghetto people, the students felt they could see injustice all around them but could do nothing about it. Similarly, they felt their lives directly threatened because they might be drafted to fight in Viet Nam.

Police Attitudes

Police attitudes toward these young people tended to be extremely negative. The study of student riots showed that police saw the students as their archenemies. Just as students called officers "pigs"—among other insults—the officers had insults for the students. This was natural. Officers saw the students as privileged, as having opportunities they themselves often had not had. They saw students as violating the "rules" that they had learned, often painfully, to respect. Many of these rules governed dress and grooming. Students notoriously have been quick to pick up faddish, strange-looking styles. Blue jeans and long hair seemed to many officers to violate the standards they had learned. Here were young people enjoying all the things adults had learned to give up—and still the young people were not satisfied.

Many observers of the college riots could see the anger of the police officers in their insults and manhandling of the students. Students reciprocated with insults and sometimes with bottle- and rock-throwing. However, there is little evidence to suggest that student rioters *planned* to be violent. The exceptions were a few leftist groups such as the Weathermen, who claimed responsibility for the violent acts (such as bombings) that occurred.

The result, however, of some officers' expressing their anger against students was to "radicalize" many students, who might otherwise have been politically inert or have used quieter means of expressing themselves.

Possible Solutions

One solution to this kind of antagonism is planning for student groups and police to get acquainted, to review their common problems, and to discuss ways of solving them together. Such groups decrease the fear of the unknown, the anger and distaste that can characterize relationships with strangers.

Police should be better paid so that students would not appear more privileged in comparison. Police too should be given a chance to be educated, and to profit from an education—as the students do. Most officers in 1975 had no such opportunity. This was unfair and caused as much resentment on their part as that felt by ghetto residents or by students who suffered from other types of unfair treatment.

The Conspiracy Theory—Communism or Complaints?

The conspiracy theory has been advanced by many people in the law enforcement area because they feel that demonstrations and riots cannot be explained in any other way. Ignoring social causes, this theory holds that it is not the people in the ghetto who are angry and frustrated, or students and young people who are angry and frustrated, but Communists who are "stirring things up." Believers in the conspiracy theory cite the fact that radical leaders and sometimes known Communists appear at rallies and riots. These leaders claim credit for the demonstrations. The argument seems a good one until it is examined. What is the reasoning behind it? Aren't police at all such functions, too? Members of the FBI? Members of the press? Yet no one would blame a riot on any of these groups. Being somewhere suggests an interest, not a cause.

What evidence would we need to prove that a conspiracy of Communism was causing these problems?

If the conspiracy theory were true, we would be able to see Communists in positions of power in the organizations supporting rallies. Yet every commission investigating riots or rallies has decided that no significant Communist influence and no conspiracy were involved. These commissions included such prestigious ones as the Kerner Commission and the Walker Commission, both comprised of people conservative in their outlook.

Are conspirators still lurking behind doorways? This seems unlikely, especially since the groups who have been responsible for violent actions have been totally open, even bragging about their violence.

It would be comforting to believe that rallies and riots are the work of only a few. If we could only find these few, we would be able to eliminate them. It seems hard to believe, however, that the FBI could not have found these few people in all these years. On the other hand, belief in the conspiracy theory has led to tragic consequences. Police have underestimated the number of people who would turn out for an issue. They thought that only a few conspirators were involved. Instead, crowds of demonstrators showed up, leading the police to overreact with violence. In other cases, police have been overarmed, as though to fight a Communist-armed uprising. No such uprising has ever taken place, but the excessive force did escalate the demonstrations.

In fact, even though riots have caused considerable property damage, some loss of life, and much uneasiness, they have been largely ineffective in their goals. Not until 1974 was the war in Viet

Nam ended, although our involvement had been considerably reduced earlier. Unemployment skyrocketed for blacks and other minority groups in the 1960s. Ghetto conditions were getting worse and not better. Further, by believing the conspiracy theory, we lose the opportunity to change factors underlying social unrest. If social problems are ignored, riots will continue, and the police, as well as the average citizen, will suffer.

The Officer's Role—Protector or "Pig"?

What is the officer's role in relation to riots? Can he do anything at all when so many factors lead to rioting, factors that are obviously beyond his control? Social conditions that no one at all seems able to change, economic conditions that keep large groups of people poor, historic conditions that have dictated that some people will be treated badly while others are honored—none can be changed by a single individual. The police in such situations are victims of society, just like the ghetto residents who explode into violence.

Society, while not able to correct the wrongs that cause people to riot, must nevertheless preserve law and order. The officer on the beat is supposed to step in and prevent people from doing something about the many wrongs they suffer. The legislator who decreed that the job training programs should take care of only 5 percent of the people is *not* out on the streets, nor is the city councilman who has been unwilling to appropriate money for swimming pools in ghetto areas (even though not having a place to cool off has often caused hydrant opening and other incidents that sparked riots).

Police Feelings and Behavior

Meanwhile, the officer on the beat has a few beefs of his own. His salary is low, and the status once given to policemen frequently is not evident. His job seems dangerous (although it is less dangerous than farming); it involves a lot of hassles and not too many benefits. He is in a perfect spot to turn his anger against the people he is supposed to serve.

Although many officers serve their areas with courtesy and concern, there are some, probably a minority, who do not. One of the problems here is personnel assignment. Often the newest or most insensitive officers are assigned to the hardest, most sensitive jobs, those in the ghettos. They do not have the experience and skill to manage a job that is sometimes impossible, at best extremely difficult. Instead, they express their own frustrations and cause more resentment among the people in their care. Such police sometimes feel that verbal abuse is acceptable, even though physical abuse is not. Verbal abuse, however, can cause as much or more resentment than physical abuse.

However, many *good* officers lose their cool in riot or demonstration situations. How can we account for this?

Police are called upon to control themselves in very difficult circumstances. The fact that they usually do this very well is attested to by the low rates of physical abuse recorded.

However, sometimes policemen's *feelings* are different from their *behavior*. When attitudes of officers are tapped, they are often found to have negative feelings about minority groups, including blacks and college students. In the normal routine, police do not treat minority groups badly. In fact, the rate of mistreatment of blacks appears to be lower than that of whites, even with a predominantly white police force. However, resentment is likely to accumulate in many officers who keep their feelings under control. This stored resentment is triggered by the riots. A riot then becomes a free-for-all in which both police and residents or students try to "get" the other group.

How Can the Situation Be Changed?

It is here that "psychology" could work. It would be of great benefit for police to have a chance to express their hidden resentment in groups under the direction of a leader who could help them understand and deal with frustrations. Another help is to have meetings between police and leaders of the groups with whom they come into conflict. The latter type of meeting has often been successful in easing tensions and making life less difficult for criminal justice personnel.

Demonstrations and Riots—How Similar Are They?

Is a demonstration a prelude to a riot? Or is it composed of people who are not ready for violence, but merely protesting peacefully?

Many authorities believe that most demonstrations are peacefully planned. Demonstrations turn into riots when acts of violence on the part of a few people cause resentment to flare into anger.

Many people feel that much of the violence stemming from demonstrations comes from improper police preparation. This argument suggests that police are mobilized to expect violence. They overreact, and violence occurs. The Kerner Commission suggested that this was true in some of the student riots, when police were mobilized with gear heavy enough to resist an invasion. This made the police extremely nervous. Without adequate planning and supervision, they overreacted. Strict supervision of individual patrolmen is necessary to prevent such nervous overreaction. Police-community relations training is also helpful.

Riot Prevention

We have discussed reasons *why* riots get started, but not how they begin. *How* is important for riot *prevention,* which is the only really successful way to handle a riot.

Riots usually start when a group of people is "around"; when people are uncomfortable, as in the hot months of summer; when there is some provocation; and when rumors circulate and a large number of people is willing to believe them.

Examples of incidents that have started riots include shutting off fire hydrants used to keep cool in the summer, routine arrests for traffic offenses, stopping boys who are "corner-lounging" and asking them to leave, and large displays of force during demonstrations that might otherwise have remained peaceful.

Police departments and other urban groups can do a number of things to prevent riots (see Figure 19.2).

Confidence that a demonstration will not turn into a riot can be extremely important in police handling of a riot. Keeping cool in the face of name-calling and even bottle- or rock-throwing can be

Figure 19.2
Avoiding violence

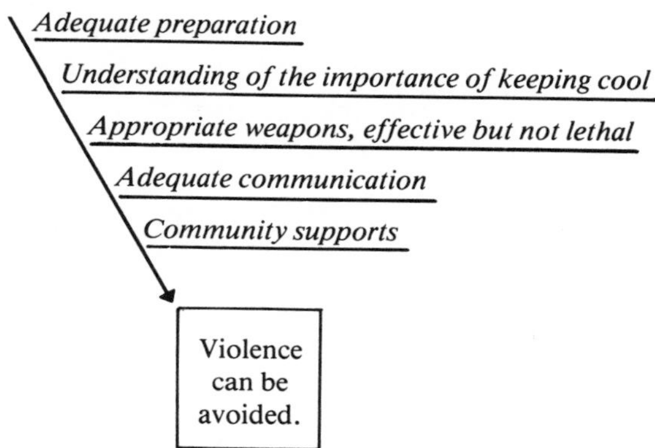

vitally important. An understanding of the group involved, such as that gained through police-community relations training, is important.

Most college demonstrations are initially nonviolent. If police understand this, they will be less fearful. A small part of any crowd may become violent. This smaller group should be quickly removed from the main part of the demonstration. Adequate communication among small groups of police is essential. Weapons of more deterrent power than a nightstick, but of less lethal ability than a gun, should be available. Continued communication with leaders of demonstrators and antidemonstration groups is essential.

What about riots that start without an initial demonstration? Perhaps the major immediate cause of such riots is rumors that quickly spread in overcrowded areas. Such rumors need to be rapidly scotched. Some cities, such as Chicago, have developed rumor centers where individuals who hear rumors can call to find out what is actually happening. These centers have proved to be highly effective.

In riot-prone areas, extreme care in the handling of routine arrests should be taken. Rough handling of suspects should be eliminated if possible. If a suspect requires firm handling, it is essential to communicate immediately with individuals who can pass on the information that firmness was necessary and why. Allowing a few key individuals in the community to know how a case proceeds can stop inflammatory rumors about police beatings. Sufficient police reserve must be available to replace officers who have been pushed to the limit of their endurance. Suspects should be removed from an area quickly before a crowd can gather and take sides.

In many instances, courtesy can be a potent weapon. It is extremely difficult to escalate hostility with someone who, although firm, is polite and respectful of your concerns. Promises to look into grievances can be helpful. However, promises will only make matters worse if the responsible administrative bodies ignore grievances. Police communication with other governmental groups could be a potent force in emphasizing that grievances *must* be dealt with, that the police cannot do a job if government bodies do not uphold the law. Police in these situations could become natural allies of their constituents, making the officer's job a much easier one. Again, police-community relations are of extreme importance!

Riot Control

It might appear that little can be done once a riot starts. However, police action can make a tremendous difference in the outcome of a riot. Restrained police action can allow a riot to simmer down quickly without loss of lives. Or police action can cause a riot to become a slaughter.

In investigating ghetto riots of the 1960s, the Kerner Commission found that unrestrained action by forces whose job was to contain riots instead caused frequent loss of life. For example, green troops would hear a loud noise. There would then be a report of a sniper. The troops would then fire volleys into a house. Women and children would be killed, as well as unarmed males. In one case, a man lit a match for a cigarette. A nervous "protector," seeing the light in the window, interpreted it as gunfire and started shooting. Once the shooting started, others joined in, shooting out lights in houses where they mistakenly thought snipers were ready to shoot at them.

In contrast, a more experienced commander of a National Guard unit walked down the *middle* of a street to investigate a shot. He found that a guardsman had fired the shot. He reprimanded him, telling him that he could have caused loss of lives. He prevented his other troops from shooting. The result: no snipers, no deaths.

Police officers need to remember that guns cause death. Experienced commanders tell their men not to shoot unless they can actually see a sniper. Most of the reports of snipers in the riots investigated by the Kerner Commission were unfounded. Many lives were lost, however, because people *believed* there were snipers.

Darkness is the enemy of order. Lights should never be shot out.

Further, while looting can cause serious property loss, it is not a crime punishable by death. Looters should be arrested, not shot. Property loss must be expected. Though regrettable, it is not as serious as loss of lives.

While there are many techniques of crowd control, several important psychological factors underlie them. Being careful not to incite a crowd is the most important. It is also important that a crowd have somewhere to move to. A crowd cannot be penned in without serious consequences. Parade or demonstration permits should be given with an eye to where a crowd can move. Many people will not fight unless their "backs are to the wall." This can easily happen if a crowd is pinned down in a small area. On the other hand, if an escape route is available, a crowd will be likely to disperse. For example, during the New Haven riots, police provided areas for crowds to move to, which they did. Removing more aggressive members of a crowd is also important.

Race Relations

It is clear that many, though not all, of our problems stem from difficulties in race relations. What we know about prejudice can help us understand why we have so many of these problems.

There are two key points in understanding prejudice. One point involves the causes of riots discussed in this chapter. Injustices, promises that are not fulfilled, having a little when other people have a lot, believing that you are being lied to, insecurity in jobs — all these can cause problems in race relations.

But why problems in *race* relations rather than *people* relations? There must be another element. There is. This is the element of *visibility*. You can *see* that a person is black or white or, to some degree, Chicano. This is a vital element in prejudice, which is an underlying problem in race relations.

It is very difficult to be prejudiced against someone you cannot find. This is why, for example, Hitler made Jews wear armbands; if the victims were not identified, they could not be the object of prejudice. Racial groups are easy to identify. So prejudice maintains itself.

Further, prejudice is usually exercised against people with whom we are in contact. This is why the absentee slum landlord, or the politician who legislates against free lunch programs, or against pay raises for police, can feel safe. Nobody sees much of him: we save our anger for someone we can see. This is *scapegoating*, the familiar "kick the dog" complex.

It is not only blacks, or Chicanos, or Puerto Rican Americans who have a hard time. Many white Americans also have troubles. Americans of whatever race or color or creed can get pretty angry if they don't have what seems to be their fair share.

Americans get particularly angry when their jobs are made insecure by others coming into an area. Instead of being angry at people who make it impossible for *everyone* to get a job, they get angry at the people applying for *their* jobs. Many unions, for example, have excluded blacks for this reason.

Americans get mad at poor people who receive welfare payments, forgetting that there is evidence of more welfare given at the millionaire level in the form of tax loopholes and other business advantages than poor people collectively receive. Such evidence was discussed by President Carter in relation to the oil companies in 1977. President Reagan has mandated many such inequities.

In 1975, when the economy was abruptly starting to turn down, welfare cuts were suggested for the poor while profits of 300 percent and more went to oil and sugar companies.

How does prejudice affect the police in particular?

The police are one of those groups who are disadvantaged. They are not as dramatically disadvantaged as the ghetto residents, but nevertheless they do not get a fair share of the good things of society. It is not surprising that they are angry, and frequently angry in the same way as other groups. They become prejudiced against groups who cause them difficulty, including blacks, students, liberals, and others. While no comprehensive data are available, small studies have suggested that policemen tend to feel prejudiced against blacks. They also tend to feel angry about advantages, such as welfare, given to the poor. This anger makes for a potentially explosive situation, since most police in black areas are white.

What can be done? It seems almost impossible for the police to do what others have not been able to do, to turn their anger toward real causes instead of against those who are nearby and easy targets. The answer lies in further professionalizing criminal justice personnel. Better education, more respect, careful recruitment and training, and higher salaries would produce personnel able to feel they are doing an important job and being rewarded for it.

While we're waiting, criminal justice personnel and society alike will have to settle for something much less than perfection. The more understanding officer will realize that his job will be easier and safer if he appreciates that he and the people he serves share the same problems. His work will also become more satisfying. The violence, insults, and degrading living conditions that the police and others involved in criminal justice experience when they work with the poor can make them miserable and frustrated. The only possible reward to offset this is to see miracles of human reaction; small miracles *can* occur when officers offer understanding and help to those who expect only contempt and insults.

Summary

Demonstrations and riots occur when people feel helpless to do anything about conditions that cause them frustration and rage. Two major types of civil disorder in the late 1960s were extensively studied—ghetto riots and riots protesting government policies, particularly the Viet Nam War.

Ghetto riots occurred in response to conditions of poverty and hopelessness. In areas where people were crowded together, rumors were quick to spread, and police and National Guard were frequently untrained and unprepared. Also, the frustrations of police probably provoked more violence than necessary. The police found it difficult to restrain themselves when others were violent.

The riots protesting the Viet Nam War also started in response to feelings of frustration and rage in a situation where hypocrisy, threatened danger to lives, and concern for others led many students and other middle-class persons to the streets. Again, lack of preparation and resentment by law enforcers produced more violence than necessary.

Crowd control methods include rumor control centers, adequate but not excessive availability of force, restrained and courteous law enforcement, removing the source of potential trouble, places for crowds to go, preplanning preparation of a realistic nature, and constant communication with demonstration leaders.

Discussion Questions

1. What are the similarities between antipoverty and antigovernment rioters?
2. What can the police do to keep casualties to a minimum during a riot?
3. Think of examples of times when you have "kept your cool." Think of times when you haven't. What makes the difference?

Suggested Reading

Griffin, G. R. *A Study of Relationships between Level of College Education and Police Patrolmen's Performance.* Saratoga, Calif.: Century Twenty-one Publishing, 1980.

Henderson, B. *Ghetto Cops.* Canoga Park, Calif.: Major Books, 1975.

Knopf, T. A. *Rumors, Race and Riots.* New Brunswick, N.J.: Transaction Books, 1975.

Lipsky, M. *Law and Order: Police Encounters.* Chicago: Aldine, 1970.

Minuchin, S.; Montalvo, B.; Guerney, B.; Rosman, B.; and Schumer, F. *Families of the Slums.* New York: Basic Books, 1967.

Report of the National Advisory Commission on Civil Disorders. Washington, D.C.: U.S. Government Printing Office, 1968.

Rights in Conflict: The Walker Report of the National Commission on the Causes and Prevention of Violence. New York: Bantam Books, 1965.

Rossi, P. H., ed. *Ghetto Riots.* Chicago: Aldine, 1970.
Smith, R., and Kobetz, R. *Guidelines for Civil Disorder and Mobilization Planning.* Gaithersburg, Md.: International Association of Chiefs of Police, 1975.
Wright, S. *Crowds and Riots: a Study in Social Organization.* Beverly Hills, Calif.: Sage Publications, 1978.

CHAPTER 20

Conclusions

Criminal justice professionals deliver human services. Their jobs involve understanding other people. If one can understand what people are like, it is possible to predict their behavior. If one can predict behavior, one can handle a variety of problems.

The Importance of Understanding

Understanding is necessary before we can predict. Prediction is important for those who wish to *use* psychology. This is so because those of us who work in applied fields usually cannot spend time *thinking* about what we are going to do. We must make quick predictions and translate them into action.

The more we have studied possible situations—why they occur and how they can be handled—the better our quick reactions will be.

A knowledge of psychology means that, if we encounter someone standing on a bridge threatening to jump off, we'll know how to talk to him. It means that if someone reports a neighborhood disturbance, we can deal with it in such a way as to leave the neighbors less angry and less likely to call us in the future. This means that, if we see someone acting peculiarly on the street, we'll have some idea whether to arrest him, send him to a mental hospital, haul him off to an emergency room, or just ignore him.

Understanding promotes efficient and safe action. The riot control officer who knows what to say to calm a crowd will be safer and will protect the safety of others. The officer trying to control a knife-wielding, jealous husband will be able to protect himself and the man's family—if he understands what to do.

Understanding others, however, is not enough. One also must understand oneself. What drives me up the wall? If someone insults me, will I react? When I get anxious, do I overreact or underreact? Knowing about myself means that I can make automatic adjustments when necessary. "Counting to ten" to control my temper may seem like a foolish, home-grown remedy, but it could be just the thing to prevent me from starting a riot when someone has thrown a bottle at me.

Understanding oneself and others also is not enough. It is important to understand how society works, what's happening to people in different social classes, how a person's behavior can change in a crowd, and how changing social conditions can affect individuals. This knowledge may not change the mechanics of dealing with a specific situation, but it can greatly increase one's ability to handle these mechanics with authority and tact.

For example, if I feel that a sex offender is an animal, I won't be able to talk with him effectively. I won't be able to handle myself or the offender in a calm and authoritative fashion.

Working with murderers has been a learning experience for me. Without an understanding of what has caused them to murder, I could not possibly have made recommendations or treated any of them.

One must also develop tolerance. Start with yourself: be tolerant of your own shortcomings. Learn to recognize your feelings. Realize that anyone who says he doesn't get angry or frustrated or feel mean, lazy, and a lot of other things is simply lying. We are all human, composed of both good and bad. This is *all right*. We may need to change our *behavior* some, but our *feelings*, good or bad, are always based on something that has happened to us and must be accepted.

Review of Important Topics

In this book we have covered general principles of psychology, what the jobs of psychologists and other mental health professionals are, what the psychologist might be able to do in a police force, and some of the tests he uses.

We have talked about human relations in police forces, particularly how criminal justice personnel can use authority effectively. Unfortunately, many of us have lived too long under authority that does not respect our needs—authoritarianism. This must be remedied.

We have discussed special problems in criminal justice—interviewing and traffic control.

Reward and punishment are basic considerations in a criminal justice system that is primarily a criminal *punishment* system. Punishment is much less effective than reward. Reward teaches correct behavior; unlike punishment, it does not motivate the individual to do worse things because he's angry. Rewards do not make people muddled and anxious, and rewards can work even if they are only occasional. Current alternatives to prison must be made more effective, so that the police officer's work in a community can be supported by successful rehabilitative work.

We have considered some of the problems of perception and memory. We can't rely either on ourselves or on witnesses to give us a totally accurate story. Reports must be carefully pieced together for the just and effective detection, understanding, and prosecution of criminal acts. Principles of perception may also help us understand highway accident problems.

Social class differences are too frequently ignored. These differences are important, since much behavior is predictable on the basis of understanding groups to which people belong. These groups might be as small as corner gangs in a ghetto, but the major groups in society are socioeconomic classes. People in the different classes aren't better or worse because they belong to a lower or upper class, but they have different life-styles. The officer must know that the rough-and-ready approach with an upper-class person will produce as many problems as trying to wait politely for a lower-class family to listen to abstract arguments about why they shouldn't fight. Dealing with others politely and firmly is essential, no matter what their social class. What is considered polite, firm behavior may vary from class to class.

Understanding mental illness is an obvious must for those working in criminal justice. Not only is there a fine line dividing the sane, the insane, and the criminal; but important practical decisions must often be made on the street.

The chapter on mental illness illustrates that "kooks" are people, too. Knowing that they are frightened people whose symptoms serve to keep them from total panic can be extremely useful. I have known individuals accosted by a mentally ill criminal who later murdered others. Those who did not become victims were those who could help the mentally ill person control himself by being calm and steering him into a different kind of behavior. The officer must communicate such calm control; in this way he can save himself and others in those rare but dramatic cases where mental illness means danger. In other cases, his understanding will enable him to deal with a mentally ill person humanely and without the need for physical force.

Part 2 of this book dealt with criminals who have no victims, and who may indeed be victims themselves, such as prostitutes. A large percentage of our criminal justice resources are devoted to such crimes, and many people believe that a redefinition of what is a crime is in order. This would mean that certain victimless sex crimes, drug crimes, and so on could be redefined as noncriminal, and criminal justice resources could be diverted to violent crime, organized crime, and white-collar crime.

The discussion of some of those we define as criminals, but who hurt only themselves and their families, was intended to make dealing with such criminals easier. When studied, most such criminals have been found to have serious personality difficulties: prostitutes have been found to be depressed, gamblers usually very immature, would-be suicides both angry and depressed. Drug addicts may not be as destructive as we have thought, but most need intensive psychological help. Homosexuals may be the only group without serious personality problems; recent work suggests that their adjustment may be no better or worse than that of heterosexual people.

Part 3 dealt with crimes that do have victims. Sex crimes were singled out because they produce such horror in our society. It seemed important that persons in criminal justice know that only a small percentage of sex crimes are serious; that only when a sex criminal's acts show a progression toward increasing violence should he be considered dangerous; that defining some acts as victimless sex crimes constitutes an invasion by society on an individual's private means of achieving sexual satisfaction. If society at large were more tolerant of sexual needs, much of the sex crime, or sex-related crime such as pyromania, would not occur. If, however, a person's sexual crimes are progressively more serious, he should not be released to society.

White-collar crime—"respectable," nonviolent crime—was discussed because it is probably at least as prevalent as visible crime. It is important that white-collar crime be identified and dealt with if the law is to regain the respect it needs and deserves. Further, the fact that "respectable," well-salaried individuals also engage in crime is important in understanding other types of criminals. Perceived need, inability to share problems with others, and ready opportunity seem to be reasons for some types of white-collar crime (as embezzlement). The need to outdo others, find excitement, and prove oneself to be powerful and successful may be important in other types of white-collar crime (executive crime, shoplifting).

Part 4 dealt with problems involving children, families, and neighborhoods. Such problems are frequent in the day-to-day work of the police. Domestic and neighborhood disturbances can be dangerous as well as time-consuming. It is important that criminal justice personnel, and especially the police officer, know how to deal with them.

Reported child abuse or neglect is on the upturn. For example, it has become the most frequent crime in the state of Florida. Police officers are often the only ones with the ability to save a child who might otherwise be killed. It is essential to understand what is going on in these situations, how to identify abuse or neglect, and what action to take.

Youthful offenders make up a large part of the work of a policeman on the beat. They account for much of the street crime as well as much of the panic about street crime. We discussed how to define a delinquent, how he gets that way, and how he can be handled.

The final section of the book dealt with problems related to our changing society. Since social unrest can lead to increased criminal problems, it is important to understand the social changes that can produce unrest.

Concluding Psychological Guidelines

Reviewing these areas suggests some further principles that apply to the job of the criminal justice professional.

An important factor necessary for any worker in human services is the belief that he or she will be able to improve a situation. As suggested in Chapter 2, your self-concept and your prediction about what you can do in a situation can make all the difference in the outcome. In practicing, observing, and reading about psychology for the past twenty years, I have come to what I consider to be an important though simple discovery. If you approach people with the idea that bad situations can be changed, if you care enough to work hard, you will get results.

It does not matter what kind of situation we are dealing with – a "bug" in the TV, an attitude of hatred and contempt in a juvenile, or an addict who is ready to OD – whether or not the situation can be improved is based in large part on how much of a commitment someone, or some group of people, is willing to make.

Results may not come overnight, or even dramatically, but they will come. You must learn to be aware of small changes in attitude, such as the way kids say hello to you if you're a patrolman on a beat. In doing psychotherapy, I have found that, while patients make a dramatic initial improvement due to lessened anxiety, later improvement must sometimes be measured in micrometers.

Another important guideline is that people are people. They will respond to your own sense of honesty and concern. They want to be liked but are frequently angry and closed. By setting an example of a person who is open and honest and likes himself, you can show others how to deal better with life. Many problems come from inability to develop competence step by step in dealing with both tasks and emotions. If I can learn to take apart a car engine gradually, the engine as a whole will not discourage me. If I can learn to deal with small frustrations or blows to my self-esteem, helpless rage will not immobilize me.

You can see that this involves a two-fold approach: (1) dealing with situations competently so that we have a high level of satisfaction and (2) learning to deal with negative emotions when things do not work out.

The Problem of Negative Environments

Another guideline worth thinking about is that, in an oppressive environment, one must take strong action to deal with life competently. Many institutions are oppressive; mental hospitals, prisons, and sometimes police stations can be hard places in which to work. Long-term staff frequently lose hope.

Yet we use these institutions to try to change people. It is true that hospitals and prisons, by providing a different environment, may produce change. However, since they are oppressive, they are not very successful. Halfway houses provide a different environment that can be more successful.

Changing the situation of the poor, who present many police problems, is more difficult and requires social reform. As long as there are people in situations that produce smoldering anger, there will be police problems. As long as some people have too much, while others have nothing much, there will be problems. Sometimes it is possible to create a "pocket" of something better in a bad situation. Programs like PAL, Big Brothers, or neighborhood houses can provide such pockets in ghettos. They are helpful because they are based on the real concern of one or more persons. In areas where neighborhood residents have been able to band together to deal with problems, a much different, more hopeful attitude develops.

Preventive work on the part of professionals in all the human relations fields is necessary. Particularly for the police, changing the police image in ghetto areas can produce many improvements. If kids could begin to look up to police instead of making them scapegoats, a good part of the police job would be done.

You may be asking yourself a further question at this time. Since many governmental institutions are corrupt, what happens if you are part of a situation that you cannot support?

There are two possible lines of action. One is to leave; the other is to stay and make it work as well as you possibly can. This involves working within the rules and regulations, but in a human way. Those of you who are police probably are well aware that even in a traffic arrest, your own good will can make the difference between a real hassle and a situation accepted reluctantly but politely. Some child psychologists suggest that you say to a child, "I'm sorry I cannot give you all the toys in the store. I wish I could." A statement that carries the message, "I'm on your side, but I must enforce the law," or "I know this seems like a bum rap, but I have to do it," can make a difference.

This will be easy or hard for you to do, depending on how you deal with your own emotions. If you have allowed yourself to get uptight, whether with a kid or a criminal, you won't be able to be on anybody's side but your own. Results will be much worse.

It is best to do the following: (1) Try to avoid situations where you are not in control. This can often be done by thinking ahead and planning for unexpected contingencies. (2) Learn to be aware of your own reactions. If you know you can't stand certain kinds of things, try to get someone else to handle them, or try to minimize what you do until the situation improves. (3) Try to make your life and work as satisfying as possible. You will then find that feelings of frustration can be handled more easily.

If It Works for Others, It Will Work for You

You have probably noticed something in the discussions in this book. What works for other people works for all of us! What works for you works for others! If you feel uptight, finding yourself a quiet, safe refuge will help you calm down. If someone you are arresting feels panicky, quiet firmness will help him behave in a controlled and controllable way. Being in a situation where people feel hopeful will help you as well as those you work with. If you can respect yourself, you will feel better, too. If your clients feel respected, they will feel better. If you feel people are on your side, you will feel good. If a suspect feels you are on his side—even though you must arrest him—he will feel better. If others put time and energy into working with you, you will learn what they have to offer. If you put time and energy into the people you work with, they will respond also.

Summary

In general, principles to remember are: (1) *understand,* (2) *accept yourself,* (3) *use your understanding to increase your competence,* (4) *don't give up!*

To do this, you need to (1) like yourself, (2) find outlets for your needs, (3) arrange your life so that it is more satisfying than frustrating, (4) deal with others in a firm but understanding fashion.

I hope learning some of these principles will increase your competence and pleasure in your work. I hope you will continue to learn about people. Some people learn best by observing, some by interacting with others, some by reading. I hope you will do a little of each and a lot of what helps you most. Good luck!

APPENDIX A

Applications: Suicide

Dealing with a suicide emergency requires showing both concern and control. Often decisions must be made very quickly. To illustrate the principles discussed in Chapter 11, here are examples of specific situations an officer might encounter.

Example 1: A Solitary Person

You receive a call. A young woman has threatened to kill herself. She is alone in her apartment. You are given the address. When you arrive on the scene, the young woman tells you she does not want help, and she refuses to open the door.

The Alternatives

What do you do? What alternatives are possible?

You have two basic alternatives, with variations. Either you take her at her word and leave, or you try to intervene in some way.

The first alternative, *A*, is simply to leave. The second alternative, *B*, is noncoercive intervention. You persuade the young woman to open the door, put your foot in the door, engage her in conversation, and try to find out what she has done. Has she taken pills? Slashed her wrist? Is it serious? If possible, you talk her into going to a hospital. If not, you leave.

A third alternative, *C*, is to engage her in conversation and, if you are unable to persuade her to come to the hospital of her own volition, to force her to do so.

The Decision-Making Process

How do you decide what to do? Let us go back to our decision-making model (Chapter 2). The first question is, "How would I feel in this situation?" If you were suicidal, would you want to be left alone to complete your act of self-destruction? Have you ever felt this way? If you have, you probably felt that to be left alone was to be abandoned. You probably felt more angry and more likely to try to complete the attempt if no one intervened.

If you selected action *B*, you *would* be showing concern. You might well be able to persuade her to get some help. However, if this didn't work, only forceful intervention could let her know that you cared enough to do something about it, even without her cooperation. She might act angry, but underneath she would feel that someone had answered her call for help.

The second question is, "What are the realities?"

What is the physical situation? You do not yet know whether she is still threatening, or has made an actual attempt. If she has, has she taken pills? What kind? How many? Has she slashed her wrist? Wrist slashing is often dramatic but ineffective. Taking pills can be lethal, or just provide someone with a long sleep. Some suicidal actions are medical emergencies; some are not. If you aren't sure whether the situation is a medical emergency, a quick phone call to the emergency room of your local hospital might help. However, it is usually best to assume an attempt is a medical emergency rather than err in the other direction. Allow a physician to take the responsibility for deciding. However, your own information will help you know how long you may spend talking to someone without endangering a life.

Let us now look at the consequences of the alternative actions.

The consequence of *A,* simply leaving, would be difficult to predict. There are two possibilities: (1) she will survive; or (2) she will die. You might be leaving without knowing which is more likely. A patient once called me in the middle of the night. She had taken pills. I called the police, who came, were refused entry, and left. Fortunately, she had taken too few pills to kill herself. I saw her the next day. But a return phone call from the police could have enabled me to go to see her and exert my influence in getting her help.

If you took action *B,* you would have gotten a better idea of what was going on. You would have had a chance to find out how dangerous her situation was. If it was not dangerous, she would recover till the next time. You could leave her the name of an agency or suicide center to help. You could also call the referral source, if there was an identifiable one.

The third alternative, *C,* taking her to the hospital whether she was willing or unwilling, would be the safest. You could then be sure that she would receive appropriate medical attention. In many states, a suicide attempt also ensures that the would-be suicide receives mental health care as well.

What about your professional responsibilities? How would the three alternatives mesh with laws and obligations?

First, what state and local laws apply to this situation? When you know the law for your locality, you will know what actions will fulfill your obligations. You will also know what you cannot do; for example, in some jurisdictions an officer does not have the right to enter a would-be suicide's home against her will. If you have discretion according to the law, what alternative would best fulfill such discretion?

In answering these questions, consider the following general principles:

1. It is best to give a person a chance to make up his own mind—within limits. If you set such limits, "I will take you forcibly, or you may come on your own," a person feels a greater sense of self-respect. As a criminal justice professional, you cannot,

however, simply allow a person to do what he wishes. He and you must act within the law.

2. Did you select an alternative that is likely to discourage further attempts in the future?

Allowing a person to discuss his situation with you, giving him a feeling of being understood, is always more helpful than acting forcibly without such understanding.

However, you must remember that you cannot always do the things that would be most effective. Sometimes you can only behave in a way that averts immediate danger, or that is in accordance with local practices. You must not feel that you have done something wrong if your activities are constrained. We are talking about what you would do under optimal conditions.

Example 2: A Family Situation

A hysterical mother calls the police. She reports that her teenage son Jimmy is locked in the bathroom and is threatening to kill himself. Nothing helps. You answer the call and are admitted into a neatly furnished apartment. Mother is frantically talking to her husband, her son, and you all at once. You have the strong impression that the situation is beyond her ability to cope with. Similarly, her husband is sitting in a chair looking agitated and helpless. Mother scolds and directs her husband. It is obvious that you must deal with a disturbed family as well as with a potential suicide.

The Alternatives

What are your alternatives?

A. Go immediately to the bathroom. Knock down the door and remove the son. Take him to the nearest police station. Or:

B. Do the above, but take the son to the emergency room at the closest hospital. Or:

C. If you have ascertained that there is no immediate danger, politely take your leave. Or:

D. Attempt to deal with the situation noncoercively. If you are with another officer, go to the bathroom door while your partner speaks to the parents. Your partner should calm the mother. He can tell her that you will do what is necessary to save her son. This officer can also find out what is happening. What is she afraid of?

Has he done this before? What happened? When your partner returns, act on the basis of the information provided.

If it appears that there is an immediate danger, tell the boy he should immediately unlock the door or you will have to remove him forcibly. This judgment is made on the basis of your first aid training or a call to an emergency room or physician. Perhaps he will be doing something that is not immediately dangerous—such as slashing his wrists, which is often harmless. Aspirin must also be taken in large quantity to be lethal. Guns, however, pose an immediate threat.

The Decision-Making Process

Going back to the decision-making model, your first question is "How would I feel?" Consider your options in the light of how the individuals involved would feel. Remember that you are dealing with a disturbed group, not just the suicidal son. In all probability, the entire family has serious problems communicating with one another.

In option *A*, how would the parents as well as the son feel?

First, all parties concerned would be reassured that something was being done. Whether or not the boy was in immediate danger, you would have acted in a direct and clear-cut fashion. The family would be relieved that you had taken over. They might also be angry at your having assumed control. Being taken to a police station would label the son as bad. This might make him angry, the parents relieved.

In option *B*, the same factors would operate, except that the son would be labeled as ill rather than bad.

If you followed option *C*, everyone would be angry. Their anxiety would remain, and they would feel that they had not been taken seriously.

Option *D* is obviously the most difficult, time-consuming alternative. However, the family would feel that you were considering their feelings as well as being helpful. This could produce a strongly positive feeling about your intervention, a feeling that they might or might not express. The son would have a sense that you were concerned about his well-being as an individual and would be more likely to behave maturely.

What would be the immediate consequences of *A*, *B*, *C*, and *D*?

Option *A* would remedy the immediate situation. It might, however, leave a residue of bad feeling in the family, solidifying the family illness by making the son the bad person. The son would continue to be made a scapegoat, and he might make further attempts at suicide.

Option *B* would produce a similar result, except that the son's role would be that of a sick person. He might get some treatment that could help him. The family, however, might continue to see him as *the* problem rather than facing up to their collective problems. You would have averted the danger to his life, though there would probably be continuing problems of a similar nature.

Option *C* would allow the family to continue to squabble. The son would have a better chance of "winning" the current battle, since the parents would not have successfully enlisted your aid. However, this kind of "winning" is rarely decisive; it keeps the pot boiling instead.

The consequences of alternative *D* could well be more positive than those of *A, B,* or *C.* There would be some possibility of the family as a whole getting help. They would see you as concerned and might take your suggestion to contact a local crisis center or mental health agency. There would, therefore, be a greater chance of diminishing the problems in the future.

What are your professional responsibilities and how would they mesh with each of these options?

First of all, you would want to save this boy's life, if it were indeed in danger, in any way you could. *A, B,* or *D* would probably fulfill this function. However, you must also apply the law. How does the law of your locality apply to the situation?

D would fulfill the discretionary function of helping a family beyond the immediate dictates of the law. You might not have time to do all of what is suggested in *D,* but even minimal fact-finding and reassurance can be helpful.

Understanding the Behavior

As discussed previously, there are four ways of understanding behavior.

1. The Past. What has happened in the past to make Jimmy

and his family behave as they do? To understand this, you need to consider particular patterns of family interaction. Families behave as units and resort to particular kinds of interactions time and time again. These patterns may be either helpful or destructive, depending on the amount of real communication involved.

For Jimmy's family, at least some of these habitual interactions must have been of a negative nature. Perhaps when people in Jimmy's family didn't get what they wanted, they tried to make someone else feel guilty. Such exchanges may be common: "Jimmy, you're driving your mother to an early grave. If you don't pick up those clothes this minute. . . ." or "Jimmy, I spent the afternoon baking for you, and now you won't even talk to me." These comments produce guilt, not communication.

Jimmy has acquired this same pattern of trying to make others feel guilty. He has learned that by suffering—even by threatening to kill himself—he can excite the whole family.

2. The Present. What has happened in the present to precipitate this crisis? Perhaps a particular frustration has caused Jimmy to feel very angry. He has learned to express anger, not directly, but by trying to make others feel guilty. His suicide attempt is a way of making his family feel sorry for him.

The direct cause of Jimmy's frustration and anger is not dealt with at all.

3. Influence of Others. How have others contributed to Jimmy's situation? Jimmy and his family seem bound together in a close, almost suffocating, relationship. The entire family needs help to break the pattern of assigning guilt and learn to deal with problems directly. If *Jimmy alone* is treated, the family's problems will not be solved.

4. Group Pressures. Have social groups contributed to Jimmy's problems? While family pressures seem to be Jimmy's major difficulty, peer groups are usually extremely important to teenagers. It is likely that further frustration comes from something unrelated to his family—difficulties in school, with teachers or schoolmates. This added frustration, which Jimmy doesn't know how to face directly, could have sparked his suicidal behavior.

In this example, it is apparent that the professional person must deal not only with the immediate emergency but also with the overall family problems. He must try to see that the entire family obtains help. If they do not, such emergencies probably will occur again in the future.

However, it is also important to remember that one can only do one's best, that some suicidal crises will end in death despite your best efforts.

APPENDIX **B**

Applications: Family and Neighborhood Crises

Because domestic and neighborhood disturbances are such an important, complex, and dangerous part of criminal justice work, this appendix will provide examples to help a practitioner to understand and act effectively in family and neighborhood crises.

We will look at three examples—a lower-lower-class family crisis, a middle-class family crisis, and an upper-lower-class family crisis. We do so because, while the emotional problems are very similar, the framework of the problems, hence the interventions, will differ somewhat from class to class.

Example 1: A Lower-Lower-Class Family Crisis

You respond to a call in a poor neighborhood. Mrs. X, a neighbor of the Y family, states that she is concerned because Mr. Y is beating up his wife. You arrive at the Y's in the midst of a heated argument. Mr. Y opens the door a crack, and you have a view of what must be the living room. Clothes, beer cans, and dirty dishes are strewn about. A rancid smell seeps out to the hall. A pale, thin woman, dressed in a ripped cotton housedress and bedroom slippers, continues to shout from one corner of the room. You assume, but are not told, that this is Mrs. Y. Three children peer at you with blank expressions. The youngest is dressed in a filthy pair of underpants and a shirt. The older two wear street clothing. The little girl's dress is much too long. The little boy has a shirt hanging over trousers that drag on the floor. The children look pale and drawn.

While you have been observing, Mr. Y has been letting go with a stream of curses, the gist of which is "Stay the ____ out of here. We don't need none of your ____ butting in."

The Alternatives

What do you do?

A. Exercise your authority. Subdue Mr. Y forcibly since the chances are that he won't listen to reason. Tell him you will get the neighbor to swear out a complaint and you will arrest him if he doesn't stop. Or:

B. Since it does not appear that anyone's life is in danger, Mrs. Y has not complained, and the situation is not directly affecting the neighbor, leave, with or without apology. There is no point in getting involved. Or:

C. Ask Mr. Y to step into the hall or another room or to talk to you in the car. Tell him you are aware that he has not asked for your help, but that you would appreciate it if he and his wife could tell you what the problem is. Tell him you'd like to check with his wife as well so that you can all discuss the problem. It may be necessary to wait until his burst of profanity has subsided to be heard at all. Allow him to "get it out."

If he and Mrs. Y are unwilling to talk to you, tell him that what they are doing is just going to lead to further trouble. Be graphic. The neighbor will call again. There will be further embarrassing interference. If they talk about it now, maybe you can help them avoid that. Why does the neighbor complain? How could they work out their differences so that she wouldn't? Be firm about the need to do something different, but sympathetic with the problem. If they still do not cooperate, tell them you will expect them to do so in the future. Leave them the name of a family service agency or other agency you think might be appropriate.

The Decision-Making Process

You don't have very much time to decide what to do in such a situation. If you have thought through the possibilities earlier, however, you will be able to make sound decisions more quickly. Although they will not always be right, they are more likely to be effective than if you had not done your thinking in advance.

Using the decision-making model, ask, "How would I feel?" If you ask yourself this question, you are more likely to understand Mr. and Mrs. Y and be able to calm them.

Everyone has had some family quarrels. Ask yourself how you would feel if you had been fighting with your spouse and a neighbor came in. Pretty angry? Maybe you would feel like cursing just as Mr. Y has done. You might, however, argue that you would not be beating your wife. If you were, you would probably want someone to stop you.

Even though you would want to be stopped, you would turn your anger against any intruder. You would probably also feel picked on, persecuted by interfering neighbors. Your self-respect would be seriously threatened and you would want a chance to save face.

Here are possible reactions to the alternatives:

It is likely that, if you chose *A,* Mr. Y would feel extremely resentful, as we all would. He would feel helpless and cornered. He would be unlikely to change his behavior.

If you chose *B,* Mr. Y would feel less angry and resentful. His self-esteem might rise. However, he might also feel confused. Is it really all right to beat your wife? Do authorities think it is?

If you chose *C,* Mr. and Mrs. Y might both feel angry at you for interfering. But if you remained calm, they would react in a way leading to change. Do authorities really see me as someone who wants to be an OK guy? The couple would probably initially reject the idea that you might be helpful, but they might have a lingering thought: "Maybe there are solutions. Maybe this isn't the way it has to be."

Next ask yourself, "What are the realities?" First, what is the situation? How immediate is the physical danger to you and the family members? Are knives or guns in use? Or are the people fighting with words and handy objects?

What has caused the disturbance? Are drugs or alcohol involved? Is sexual jealousy a factor? Do the children need protection?

Second, what would be the consequences of *A, B,* and *C*?

If you chose *A* and forcibly restrained Mr. Y, you would have stopped the disturbance of the moment. You would feel more comfortable yourself. You would have *done* something. We feel better when we take decisive action. You would have satisfied the neighbor and have some positive action to report. No one likes to be cursed at, and it is natural to use counterforce. The man was obviously uncooperative and causing a disturbance. Why be so careful of his feelings?

Is *A* the best course of action? What are the negative consequences?

1. You have taken sides. You have assumed that Mr. Y is wrong and Mrs. Y right. This may be incorrect: you don't know the situation.

2. You have made Mr. Y lose status in Mrs. Y's eyes (and in the eyes of everyone else who saw the fracas or heard about it later). Mr. Y has also lost status in his own eyes—and, in a lower-class culture, this may mean he will beat up Mrs. Y more severely. He may also turn more anger against the police.

3. You have dealt decisively with a symptom, but not with a cause. You don't really know what has been happening. The fighting will continue, as well as, perhaps, any alcoholism that may be involved, or the young children's neglect, or an older daughter's promiscuity. Not that you could solve these problems. But you might be able to open the door to a later solution. You don't know whether Mr. Y is really dangerous, or uses cuffing people around as a way to let off steam. Is Mr. Y on hard drugs? Is he working? Knowledge of either situation could be valuable in dealing with the family again.

If you chose *B,* and left, you would have similarly gone away without knowing what the situation was. Mr. Y may see this as permission to continue to be violent. Mrs. Y and the children could be in danger. However, Mr. Y would be less likely to feel further threatened and would not escalate his hostility. Neither would your action decrease the chance that he would continue to attack.

If you chose *C,* you would know better what to expect from the family. You would know how serious the situation was. You would have presented yourself as a fair, concerned, but authoritative figure. You would have taken the role of a person who was interested in helping but not afraid to take a stand—someone strong enough to resist name-calling. You would have made a first step in putting the argument on another level where solutions could be achieved. You also would have demonstrated your belief that problems can have solutions other than violence. You would have helped by providing referral information as well as by opening new avenues of thought through your questions.

However, pressures of time may make it difficult to follow through in a way similar to alternative *C.* Remember, too, that you can take only a small step in correcting such situations. Multiplied by the number of times you deal with family crises, this small step could make a big difference. These accomplishments could include changing the image of authority, helping at least some families to change, and making your work less dangerous.

Understanding the Behavior

The behavior of Mr. and Mrs. Y can be understood by looking at it in four different ways.

See if you can fill in the following model with the information from Chapter 2.

1. The Past. What kinds of problems antedate such crises? Mr. Y is likely to have grown up in a neighborhood similar to that in which he now lives. He probably received little care from his parents. From the time he was young, he may have been left to roam the streets. Not knowing any ways to accomplish goals by working and trying harder, having had other kids abuse him, he has learned to do the same to others. His whole life is likely to have been one of repeated frustrations, with some pleasures seized momentarily. He

Figure A.1

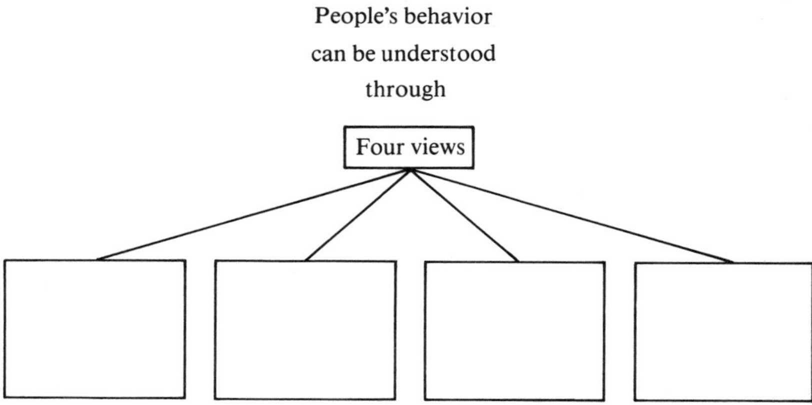
People's behavior
can be understood
through
Four views

may have had little purpose in life. He has learned to believe that when you're frustrated, you fight.

2. The Present. What has happened in the present that may have raised Mr. Y's temper to the boiling point? Is he tired? Hung over? Sick? Hungry? What psychological factors are involved? Is he disgusted with not having enough money and enough things? Laid off from his job? Unhappy? With little hope?

These factors decrease a person's ability to control himself (see Figure A.2).

Figure A.2

Factors in the present relating to control

Physical factors

Hungry

Tired

Sick

Hung over

Loss of control

Psychological factors

Lowered self-esteem

Lack of pleasure

Loss of hope

Many factors may have contributed to his loss of self-esteem. Mr. Y cannot pull out a roll of bills when he wants something. He surely isn't a success, and he may be a downright failure. Physical factors work together to produce loss of control (see Figure A.3). They also amplify the psychological feelings—his self-image as a person who cannot really cope with life.

Figure A.3
Indicators of loss of control

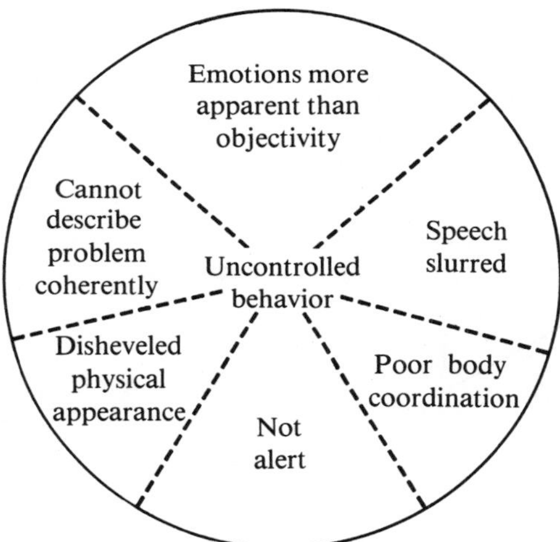

What happens when a person feels he cannot cope with life? Some get depressed. Some become ill. For the most part, the people the police deal with don't suffer quietly. They look for someone to go after! Verbally, sometimes physically, they look for a way to increase their feeling of being able to cope. They abuse their wives and feel strong again. Or they attack someone else. They don't want to blame themselves because deep down they feel they're "no damn good"—and are helpless to do anything about it.

It might be helpful to look further at the kind of life Mr. Y is likely to lead. What kind of job does he have? What kind of hope for the future? How is it different from your life?

First of all, he may not have a job—or it may be a dead-end job. People thrive on hope. You are reading this book because you have the hope of getting a good job, improving your skills, doing a more effective job, or getting promoted. You have overriding goals. If you didn't, what would happen to you? When one doesn't have something important to live and work for, what happens? You live for the pleasure of the moment. Do you remember when you were small and couldn't have the money to go to a movie all your friends were attending? That was the end of the world. Your disappointment was great.

Look at the infant—when he is disappointed he believes it is the end of the world. He loudly lets everybody know about it. He will learn, gradually, to wait for "later" or "tomorrow"—providing promises are kept, providing there is some hope for the "tomorrow."

To summarize, it is likely that there have been recent frustrations for Mr. Y. It is likely that there is little hope in his perception of his situation. Therefore the frustrations we have learned to bear because we know they don't last forever may seem intolerable to the man who is still, in many ways, a child. He doesn't believe that things will be better tomorrow—and maybe they won't.

3. The Influence of Other People. We have considered a number of factors—and many factors are responsible for a single action. However, we have left out the area of how other people have been treating Mr. Y most recently. For example, a likely possibility in this case is that relatives, friends, coworkers, or neighbors have been contributing to his frustration.

Perhaps his wife has been attacking him, and he's getting back at her. What are some of the possibilities? The most striking ones are simple, though there may be more complex issues as well. Mr. Y may have come into the house hungry, and there wasn't anything to eat. Not on the table—there might rarely be anything on the table—but not even in the refrigerator. Or it might be something a little less direct—say he heard some remarks about Mrs. Y being friendly with another guy. This violates every code of manhood he knows, and he can't let her get away with it.

His violent feelings might also be indirect. This leads us to psychological defense mechanisms. One of these, called *displacement,* is the familiar reaction of kicking the dog instead of your boss. This might well be Mr. Y's problem. If his boss made some nasty remark to him, he might have felt he couldn't fight back. When he came home he was really ready to let somebody have it. His wife was a handy target.

It could be that Mr. Y is using another defense mechanism—*projection.* In projection, when we don't like something in ourselves, we say that somebody else is the one who really has that bad characteristic.

For example, suppose Mr. Y was given a bad time by his boss for being careless. He comes home and accuses his wife of being careless. He expresses his irritation with her. He could also blame society (see Figure A.4).

PEANUTS ® **By Charles M. Schulz**

Figure A-4

Source: Charles M. Schulz, *You're a Winner, Charlie Brown!* (Greenwich, Conn.: Fawcett, 1969). ©1959 United Feature Syndicate, Inc.

4. Group Pressures. In the situation of Mr. and Mrs. Y, group pressures might not be too important, except indirectly. For example, Mr. Y's notion of what the boys at the bar would be thinking if they saw Mrs. Y with another man might make him feel that he had to make an issue of a slight bit of gossip. Without that pressure, he might have ignored the gossip.

Example 2: A Middle-Class Family Crisis

You have a call in a middle-class suburb – neat houses, well-kept lawns, good cars. As you pull up to the house, a tidy yellow and white Cape Cod with flowering shrubs in the front, you wonder what could be wrong enough to have caused a disturbance here. Yet the situation was described in much the same way as the Y situation: a neighbor has complained that Mrs. J's husband is abusing her, and you hear sounds of a noisy argument.

Again you are told by Mr. J. that there is no problem and no reason for you to stay. He does, however, open the door wide enough for you to see signs of a violent fracas – chairs and lamps in disarray. Mrs. J looks frightened. When Mr. J says, "There's no reason for the police to be here, is there, dear?" she just shakes her head.

The Alternatives

What are your alternatives?

Exercise your authority (*A*). Tell Mr. J that it appears that there has been more than just a family disagreement. If the neighbor is willing to file a complaint, take Mr. J to the station house. Mrs. J obviously is frightened and subdued, and there is a good chance that Mr. J will injure her if you don't book him. Or:

Since there is no one complaining at the moment, and Mrs. J looks as though she is safe, although frightened, believe Mr. J's statement that it is a family matter and leave politely (*B*). If the neighbor contacts you again, tell her it is simply a family matter and a complaint would complicate matters. Or:

Tell Mr. and Mrs. J that it is evident that there has been some serious trouble; you need to know more about it; perhaps there is a problem with which you could help (*C*). Would they like a few minutes to pull themselves together? You will be back and discuss it. Stop at the neighbor's to find out more about the situation. When you return, listen to Mr. and Mrs. J and make an appropriate suggestion for referral.

How do you decide?

The Decision-Making Process

First ask yourself, "How would I feel?" Before answering this question, consider whether there is any difference in the Y and J situations. Would Mr. J feel any different from Mr. Y? The answer is probably not. If you do not see him as similar to Mr. Y, it is because of the way we feel about different social classes. We find it much easier to empathize with people of similar social class. We usually feel deferential to those of a higher social class and less respectful toward people of a lower social class. Therefore, you might feel like leaving the J family alone because you would be hesitant to take an authoritative role toward a family with social position. The opposite would be true of the Y family. It would be hard to see them as capable of taking responsibility for themselves.

Let us now look at how Mr. J might feel if you chose *A, B,* or *C.*

If you chose *A,* Mr. J would probably feel just as resentful as Mr. Y. He might not show it openly. He might feel more shame than Mr. Y, since being arrested is less common in a middle-class area. The person arrested may feel he cannot face his employers, neighbors, and friends. There also is less acceptance of someone who has been arrested in a middle-class neighborhood.

If you chose *B,* Mr. J, like Mr. Y, would feel much less anger and resentment. He might feel a strong sense of relief that he was not going to be bothered. However, he might also be frightened by his own destructive impulses. If you chose *C,* the J family—like the Y family—would probably feel angry and resentful at your interference. However, having had better experiences with both parents and society, Mr. and Mrs. J might be more willing to see you as wanting to help. Mr. J might feel relieved to be offered help.

Next ask yourself, "What are the realities?" First, what is the situation? Appropriate answers regarding the consequences of your actions and your professional responsibilities come from accurate assessment of the situation.

If there is no immediate danger from guns or knives, a stop at the neighbor's could tell you a lot about the severity of the problem. Does she report drug or alcohol addiction? If she reports any increase in frequency or intensity of fighting, this might indicate a serious problem. Does she report strange behavior—things like disheveled appearance, inability to carry on a simple conversation (not simply unfriendliness)? Does she report bizarre behavior? This would include such actions as walking around unclothed, making peculiar motions, or talking to unseen persons. Bizarre behavior, if it is correctly reported, is a sure sign of mental illness. In many communities, a mentally ill person may be brought to a reception center or mental hospital for evaluation and possible help. If this is the case, Mr. J could probably be held at a mental hospital for a brief period without formal commitment or arrest. He could also be held on a charge of disturbing the peace.

What if you don't have the time to talk to the neighbor, or if the complaint was anonymous? How would you assess the situation? It is likely that this situation is more dangerous than the Y situation. This is so because the behavior is less usual in a middle-class neighborhood. If Mr. J is an alcoholic, his prior behavior would provide a good clue to the likelihood of serious harm to Mrs. J. If, however, Mr. J is described by others as a quiet respectable person, such behavior might indicate mental illness. Many homicides in families are committed by quiet, respectable persons who are seriously mentally ill. If anything about the situation makes you feel peculiar, it would be wise to have Mr. J evaluated at a mental health reception center. Or perhaps you could persuade the couple to see a mental health professional on their own. Family service centers also make appropriate referrals.

It is also possible that the family's usual behavior is somewhat different from their neighbors', and that there really is nothing wrong. What would be the indications of "normal" fighting?

You may be able to tell whether the person complaining is a "crank." Such persons usually become well known to police by the frequency and triviality of their calls.

What if you have to go by your perceptions alone? There are several clues to look for:

1. How defensive are Mr. and Mrs. J? If fighting for them is a normal way of clearing the air, they will be relatively open about it—even if resentful at your intrusion. "Well, what's wrong with

fighting? Don't you and your wife ever have a fight?" Responses like, "No, we haven't been fighting," or "There is nothing whatever wrong," are indications of defensive behavior.

2. Does the situation seem imbalanced? If neither spouse looks frightened of the other, this is good evidence that it is a private matter. A scared expression on one of their faces, or even one person doing all the talking, suggests an imbalance. If there is such an imbalance, it is unlikely that the fight fits into the "normal fight" or "letting off steam" category. While many psychologists recommend fighting to get rid of tensions, imbalanced situations, where one person is afraid of the other, do not help.

What would be the consequences of *A, B,* and *C*? We have already discussed the consequences in terms of Mr. J's feelings. We have also discussed possible meanings of this particular situation. The consequences of *A, B,* and *C* depend on what the situation really is. Let us explore the various possibilities.

If you chose *A,* and Mr. and Mrs. J were having a normal fight, you would have caused yourself and them unnecessary trouble. If, however, one or both were mentally ill or had a drug problem or some other serious disturbance, forceful action could be the only means of getting them urgently needed help. Courts have the authority to insist on treatment. While many mental health professionals prefer to treat voluntary patients, it is altogether possible to help persons who have been forced to seek treatment. Many such persons would receive no help unless forced into the treatment situation.

If you chose *B,* and the situation was a normal fight, you would have chosen the appropriate alternative. However, if the situation was serious, you would have opened the door to further difficulties for the family and further trouble for the police. While it may seem wasteful to spend time finding out about such a situation, the information could help prevent more serious crimes in the future.

If you chose *C,* the consequences would again depend on the actual situation. If Mr. and Mrs. J were having a problem, but one of only moderate severity, you may have provided enough direction for them to get help. Or, by giving the partner who might be likely to get hurt some practical words of advice—to call before the spouse lost control, to contact a crisis center, to leave the house at that point, or to see a mental health professional—you could have helped avoid serious difficulty.

However, it is also possible, in a severe situation, that such intervention would not be enough, and that *A* would have been the better course of action.

Finally, what professional responsibilities do you have? What laws apply? What does your role as a professional person require? Since procedures vary, you will have to consult local laws for specific information. However, it is likely that your role as a professional person will include discretionary functions. You must assess whether you want to do such things as investigate fully a situation which is frequently only noted. You must decide whether you can and/or wish to do preventive work rather than crisis work. Often you simply will have to respond to immediate pressures. You will not have time to do more. However, sometimes you will be able to decide on your own priorities. At these times you may be able to give priority to situations such as domestic difficulties. If this is possible, your actions may prevent more serious problems, or even prevent having to respond repeatedly to the same situation. You may also want to consult with some of the mental health professionals in your community. These people can give you valuable information about methods of referral and resources available. Their cooperation can give you the sure knowledge that taking the time to get a family to an agency will pay off, that the family will be treated.

Understanding the Behavior

Let us now return to our four ways of understanding behavior—through looking at the past, the present, the influence of others, and group pressures. This will help us understand the J family situation more fully.

1. The Past. We will discuss two possible reasons for a domestic crisis—addiction and mental illness.

First, addiction—drug or alcohol. The addict who is middle-class and not part of the youth culture has usually had a history of passivity. He (or she) has never been taught to solve problems actively. He turns to a "magic solution"—drinking. He is usually a pleasant person who, in this case, would be turning nasty under the influence of alcohol. This means that in the past he has been rewarded, or reinforced, for being pleasant and unaggressive. Therefore, his anger gets buried (*suppressed*) and only comes out when controls are gone—when he has been drinking. He may also have been treated cruelly or with excessive severity as a child. This would make him unable to express anger under normal circumstances. Drugs and alcohol reduce the fear of expressing anger.

The spouse of an addict has been described (in the case of alcohol addiction) as commonly having had an alcoholic father or mother. She (or he) seems to need to have a partner who behaves as the parent did. The spouse is usually efficient and effective. However, she seems to need to play the part of a martyr. While she may be willing to help change the situation, she is usually psychologically unready to see her partner change.

Second, mental illness. If one of the partners is more actively assaultive than the other, he may or may not be the person who is mentally ill. Practical considerations are most important here. If one partner is assaultive to the point of being likely to cause serious injury or death to the other, it is unimportant who is most seriously ill. A wife who submits to such treatment may be mentally ill but is not in immediate need of restraint.

The history of the mentally ill person will have included the reward of behaviors that are no longer appropriate—like generally being meek and mild but letting a burst of anger take over and completely control him. Murders within families are frequently committed by persons who are described as having been "model children" or "fine upstanding citizens."

2. The Present. Something in the present has happened to reduce the controls for either Mr. or Mrs. J—or possibly both. From our previous discussion of Mr. and Mrs. Y, can you think of what some of the factors might be?

It is important to consider that, while the J's have much more in life than the Y's, this doesn't mean that they can't feel frustrated, helpless, and hopeless. For some middle-class people, success itself is depressing, since it does not bring the happiness expected. An even stronger possibility is that the family has real economic pressures. Many middle-class people overspend. Parkinson's Law states that expenditures rise to meet and exceed income. Pressures of paying the mortgage, installments on the new car, the rising taxes, may turn the dreamhouse into a nightmare.

If Mr. or Mrs. J is an alcoholic, any frustration at all can send him or her into a state of panic.

3. Influence of Others. The influence of one marriage partner on the other can be exceedingly important in domestic troubles. Often one partner will tease and aggravate the other to a point at which he or she loses control.

Often a partner will put up with aggravating behavior without a murmur and then suddenly let loose. The important thing to remember is that people are *interdependent*. They will often try to maintain behavior that others would think was "crazy" because it serves a purpose for them psychologically. An example would be the man with an alcoholic or mentally ill wife. Having such a weak partner makes a husband or wife feel stronger.

The other person gives the spouse a chance to get rid of anger that can't be directed elsewhere. Or it may keep a person from directing anger at himself—if he sees himself as a failure.

Group Pressures. Again, the J family's fight is a private situation, and groups do not determine the behavior directly. They do determine behavior to the extent that an individual thinks, "What would my friends think of me if. . . ?" Or they may contribute to frustrations and thus indirectly to fights: "My friends would certainly think I'm a failure if they knew how I had to scrounge to get the mortgage paid."

Example 3: An Upper-Lower-Class Family Crisis

You are called to a home in a poor neighborhood, with homes that are neat and reasonably well maintained. You find a woman living alone who has complained that her estranged husband has been threatening her. She is afraid that he will break into the house and assault her, as he has done before. You come to the house and, after looking around the area, find no sign of the husband. Mrs. C, however, is hysterical, crying that he has threatened to kill her.

The Alternatives

What are your alternatives?

Tell her that her husband is nowhere near and there is therefore nothing for you to do (*A*). Leave promptly.

Tell her that you can understand her concern (*B*). Find out what makes her believe that her husband will kill her. Make whatever concrete suggestions you can (for example, changing locks), and indicate her alternatives in terms of arrest. Suggest that there may be other ways for her to find out how to deal with her husband. For example, she could talk to a social worker in a family service agency if she wanted to explore other possibilities.

The Decision-Making Process. If you can put yourself in the place of such a woman, you will probably realize that she would feel most frightened and helpless if you simply chose *A*. If you chose *B*, she would have avenues of problem-solving to follow, and would feel less helpless. She might feel resentful that you did not provide more help. Or she might feel that you were doing as much as you could and appreciate, perhaps later if not now, what you had done. Again, appropriate action depends on your realistic assessment of the situation. Is Mrs. C. in actual danger? Does her husband carry a weapon? Has he had a history of any serious assaultive behavior? Psychologically, it is obvious that Mrs. C. is very upset and not able to think clearly. What you do not know is how much she provokes her husband's violence and in what way; nor do you know how violent her husband is. Simply asking her the question, "Can you think of anything you do that contributes to this?" could help. If her husband is very violent, a center for abused wives might be the most appropriate referral. What would be the consequence of *A* and *B*? Have you thought of the consequences of not taking the situation seriously if it were indeed serious? At the least, *A* would lead to further calls when Mrs. C. was again upset. The consequences of *B* might mean avoiding further trouble for yourself. Mrs. C would have a start in thinking of ways to solve the problem, or a referral to turn to protect herself.

What are your professional responsibilities? What laws apply? In terms of your role as a professional person, if you chose *A*, you would have fulfilled minimal requirements in the least possible amount of time. You would, however, have left a frightened woman without knowing whether she would or would not be in real danger. You would have followed the letter, but not the spirit, of your professional obligations.

However, what about the fact that, if you chose *B*, you would be spending a good deal of time counseling and not enough time responding to calls? Sometimes you may have to curtail your questions and comments. However, sticking to the basic principles of trying to find out what is going on, to reassure the person, and to provide him with some alternatives will help you even if you are under time pressure. You must also consider that time demands in the future will be greater if you do not resolve a present situation satisfactorily.

Understanding the Behavior

Let us now return to our four ways of understanding behavior.

1. The Past. This kind of situation is more typical of a certain type of poverty, or lower-class culture, than it is of a particular background on Mr. C's part. This type of culture, however, rewards impulsive, spur-of-the-moment behavior, which causes women and men to become troublesome partners. It does not permit the kind of cautious waiting and evaluating that middle-class persons learn.

What about Mr. C's past? If he is seriously threatening his wife's life, we know that he too has come from a culture in which direct expression of impulses is normal. If he's mad at someone, he slugs him. If Mr. C had come from a culture where this was not normal, we would consider the strong possibility that he was mentally ill. This behavior would not be normal in middle-class culture.

The Present. Again, frustrations of the moment may well be contributing to Mr. C's desire to seek revenge. Leaving Mrs. C may have been very disturbing to him—he will no longer be cared for in the most basic kinds of ways—food, shelter, sexual satisfaction. If Mr. C is unable to meet these needs without Mrs. C, he is likely to return to her to express his anger. Perhaps he has been unable to eat decently. He may be living in a furnished room without cooking facilities. His meals may consist of beer and potato chips, or peanut butter sandwiches. Such basic frustrations can be small, but still lead to uncontrollable anger.

If Mr. C does not have goals to pursue, these frustrations become even more important. Having no other goals can make seeking revenge a way of life. Mr. C may hope that somehow he can coerce the other person into giving him some kind of satisfaction. Almost never does he realize consciously that he has this hope.

3. Influence of Others. Here the influence of one family member on another is extremely important. Mrs. C may have provoked Mr. C directly. She may have been insulting to him rather than calmly telling him she did not wish to be with him.

Why do family members have such a great influence on one another, even if the family is broken? Family members are interdependent. They rely on one another for physical, social, and emotional needs. Having someone to fight with or insult often means that a person has an outlet he would not otherwise have. This is why he may "look for trouble." He is not really looking for trouble but for a way of keeping himself from having to deal directly with his problems and frustrations.

4. Group Pressures. It is quite likely that, in such a situation, friends of both Mr. and Mrs. C may be adding fuel to the fire. Friends of Mrs. C, themselves frightened of violence around them, may dwell on the dangers Mr. C poses. Mr. C's friends may make him feel degraded because his wife did not wish to live with him. Mr. C may then develop the feeling, "If I can't have her, no one else should either."

The more concern you can give to the underlying causes of such crises, the more likely you are to solve present problems and prevent future ones.

Glossary

ADDICTION: may be physical or psychological. Physical addiction means that the body depends on the drug for normal functionings, psychological addiction means a person strongly feels the need for a drug.

ALCOHOL: a depressive drug which, though legal, causes the major drug problem in America.

ALCOHOLICS ANONYMOUS: an organization of alcoholics and ex-alcoholics helping people to stay away from alcohol.

ALIENATION: a feeling of being isolated from one's community, or one's own feelings.

AMBIVALENCE: a person is said to be ambivalent when he has mixed and opposing feelings about someone or something.

AMNESIA: an infrequent emotional problem in which a person under stress forgets who he is, his address, and his personal past.

AMPHETAMINES: pharmaceutical drugs which stimulate, cause restlessness, and reduce appetite. Include Methedrine (speed), Dexedrine, Benzadrine, and cocaine.

ANGEL DUST: also known as PCP; perhaps *the* most dangerous of the illicit drugs.

ANNALINGUS: sexual contact using mouth and anus.

ANOMIE: a feeling of alienation or isolation from one's group and society.

ANTIDEPRESSANTS: pharmaceutical drugs used to relieve depressions. Include Ritalin, Elavil, Tofranil, Nardil, and Parnate.

ANTITRUST LAWS: laws that prevent businesses from combining or cooperating to keep normal market conditions from operating (for example, price-fixing).

ANXIETY: a feeling of discomfort frequently not attached to any conscious concern.

ANXIETY NEUROSIS: a condition in which a person feels fearful and upset without knowing why.

ASSOCIATION: a way of learning. When two things happen together, they are associated or learned, as "two plus two" and "equals four."

AUTHORITY: legitimate responsibility to see that certain procedures are followed.

AUTHORITARIAN BEHAVIOR: when a person uses authority to dominate others instead of fulfilling responsibilities.

AUTHORITATIVE BEHAVIOR: when a person uses authority carefully so as to fulfill responsibilities without misusing others.

BEHAVIOR MODIFICATION: a way of changing behavior using learning principles. Appropriate behavior is rewarded, inappropriate behavior is ignored or punished.

BESTIALITY: sexual interest in animals, frequently when other means of sexual arousal are not available.

BIG BROTHER PROGRAMS: volunteer programs in which adults act as friends to boys without fathers to care for them.

BIZARRE BEHAVIOR: behavior which is very peculiar. Usually a sign of psychosis.

BODY LANGUAGE: changes in a person's posture or expression in movement which indicate his feelings.

CALL GIRL: a prostitute who meets clients by appointment.
CANNABIS: plant producing marijuana and hashish.
CHILD WELFARE AGENCIES: agencies which provide care for dependent and neglected children. Often may be used for information and referral in any situation involving children.
CHLORAL HYDRATE: see sedatives.
COGNITIVE DISSONANCE: when ideas, behavior, and attitudes are in conflict, a state of discomfort occurs leading a person to try to achieve consistency.
COMPAZINE: see tranquilizers.
COMPULSIVE GAMBLERS: people who gamble to such a degree that it becomes the most important thing in their lives.
CONFIDENCE MAN: an individual who defrauds others through gaining their confidence.
CONSCIOUS AWARENESS: things that we are aware of make up the conscious part of our personality.
CONSPIRACY: an illegal act performed secretly by a small group of people.
CONVERSION NEUROSIS: a type of neurosis in which individuals express problems through bodily symptoms.
COPROLALIA: using profanity as a means of achieving sexual satisfaction.
CORRUPTION: dishonest practices by public officials, such as taking bribes or using an office for other illegal means.
COUNTER-RIOTERS: residents of a community who try to stop a riot started by other members of the community.
CULTURAL SUICIDE: when a culture traditionally demands a person kill himself (same as traditional suicide).
CUNNILINGUS: mouth-genital contact, the male making contact with female genitals.

DMT: a synthetic drug similar to peyote.
DELUSIONS: thinking that something we see is something else, as perceiving a shadow of a tree as a figure.
DEMEROL: a narcotic used frequently as a pain-killer.
DEMONSTRATION: an assembly of persons gathered together to communicate a need to the larger community; for example, demonstrations against busing seek to revoke busing legislation. Usually peaceful but can become violent if mishandled.

DEPRESSION: feelings of lack of energy and pessimism—the world is not much good.

DEPRESSIVE NEUROSIS: a neurosis in which people are not able to function well and are tired and listless most of the time.

DEPRESSIVE PSYCHOSIS: psychosis in which an individual is apathetic and self-blaming.

DISCRETIONARY AREAS: areas where one has the freedom to make a choice.

DISPLACEMENT: expressing feeling meant for one person to another—e.g., kicking the dog when a person really wants to kick the boss.

DISSOCIATIVE NEUROSIS: a neurosis in which a person's upset causes him to develop distinct personalities—"multiple personalities."

DORIDEN: see sedatives.

EMBEZZLEMENT: stealing money through falsifying records.

EMPATHIC: the state of having empathy, seeing a situation through another person's eyes.

ENERGIZERS: any of a variety of drugs which give a person more pep, or energy; also known as "uppers."

ENTRAPMENT: setting up a situation so that a person is encouraged to do something against the law.

EQUANIL: see sedatives.

EUPHORIA: a feeling that all is well—a "high."

EXHIBITIONISM: displaying the genitals as a way of discharging sexual needs.

EXTENDED FAMILY: large kinship groups including aunts, uncles, grandparents, etc.

EXTRINSIC REWARD: reward which is not part of an activity, but comes from outside, such as being paid for a job.

FAMILY SERVICE AGENCIES: nonprofit agencies usually staffed by social workers. They serve as referral and information agents as well as providing direct treatment.

FANTASY: daydream—something we wish to have happen or think will happen.

FELLATIO: mouth-genital contact, where female makes oral contact with male genitals.

FETISHISM: attaching sexual interest to particular items of clothing or other objects associated with past sexual arousal.
FIGURE-GROUND: that part of something which is most clearly seen is the figure; the rest of the perception (the background) is the ground. This concept comes from Gestalt psychological principles.
FORNICATION: having sexual intercourse outside of marriage.
FROTTEURISM: achieving sexual satisfaction through rubbing.
FRUSTRATION: when we do not get something we want and expect, we feel upset or frustrated. Frustration frequently leads to aggression.
FUNCTIONAL PSYCHOSIS: psychosis caused by emotional problems.

GAMBLERS ANONYMOUS: a self-help organization of gamblers and ex-gamblers which has been said to have a good record of helping gamblers.
GAY: homosexual, as the "gay world," "he's gay."

HALFWAY HOUSE: a home where individuals who are readjusting to the community can live until they are fully able to deal with community living.
HALLUCINATION: also hallucinate (verb) and hallucinogens (a drug which produces hallucinations)—to perceive (see, hear, smell, or touch) something which is not present. Frequent in psychosis.
HARD-CORE: used to describe offenders or others for whom change does not seem possible.
HARD DRUGS: see narcotics.
HELPING PROCESSES: a term used to include all the ways in which individuals and groups help one another.
HEROIN: a "hard," addictive, illegal drug.
HETEROSEXUALITY: preferring the opposite sex.
HOMOSEXUALITY: sexual interest in persons of the same sex (more specifically called lesbianism in women).

IMITATION: a major way in which children learn how to live—by doing things the way their parents do.
IMPULSIVITY: doing whatever occurs to you at the moment—

following one's desires without thinking about the consequences.

INCEST: sexual intercourse between blood-related members of a family.

INTRINSIC REWARD: reward which comes from pleasure in an activity.

JUDGMENTAL: telling someone he is right or wrong—passing judgment.

JUVENILE DELINQUENCY: a wide range of crimes including nonserious offenses, like petty theft or running away from home, and serious offenses. Any offense of a minor.

KERNER COMMISSION (National advisory commission on civil disorders): studied disorders of the 1960s and made recommendations.

KLEPTOMANIAC: sexual arousal through stealing articles associated with previous unconscious sexual arousal.

LSD: (lysergic acid diethylamidel) known popularly as "acid." A hallucinogenic, illegal, nonaddictive drug. Said to have a "repeater" effect.

LIBRIUM: see tranquilizers.

LIE DETECTOR TEST: see polygraph.

LOAN SHARKS: individuals making loans at exorbitant rates of interest, usually collected by force if not paid.

MDA: a synthetic drug similar to peyote.

MHMR: agencies which deal with a variety of community mental health and mental retardation programs.

MANIC-DEPRESSIVE PSYCHOSIS: psychosis in which people have extreme ups and downs.

MARIJUANA: a nonaddictive drug used for a "high" which also goes by the names of pot, grass, hash (for hashish—a stronger version), mary jane.

MARK: the victim or intended victim of a confidence game. Also known as the "vic," presumably for victim.

MASOCHISM: seeking punishment or pain as a means toward sexual satisfaction.

MESCALINE: a hallucinogenic drug.
METHADONE: a narcotic used to cure heroin addicts of their addiction.
MILTOWN: see sedatives.
MOTIVATION: people's behavior is based on their desires or motives.

NARCOTICS: hard drugs including opium, opium derivatives, heroin, Demerol, and methadone. Produce feelings of euphoria (highs) and deadened sensitivity.
NECROPHILIA: sexual interest in the dead (quite rare).
NEMBUTAL: see sedatives.
NEUROSIS: a mild form of mental illness in which some goals are not conscious, but people appear relatively "normal."
NUCLEAR FAMILY: small family groups consisting of parents and their children – typical of modern urban societies.

OD: overdose of drugs. Often used to say a person has died from an overdose: "He ODed."
OBJECTIVE PSYCHOLOGICAL TESTS: psychological tests that ask you to answer specific questions about yourself (what you know, what you like). These include intelligence tests, aptitude tests, and certain personality tests.
OBSESSIVE-COMPULSIVE NEUROSIS: a neurosis in which a person feels forced to follow rituals, such as Lady Macbeth's handwashing.
ORGANIC PSYCHOSIS: psychosis caused by physical problems.

PEDOPHILIA: the preference for children as sexual partners.
PERCEPTION: the filter through which our minds interpret what comes to us through our senses.
PEYOTE: a hallucinogenic drug used by American Indians.
PHARMACEUTICALS: any drug which can be obtained legally through a druggist – sometimes with a prescription, sometimes without.
PHENOBARBITOL: see sedatives.
PHOBIC NEUROSIS: a neurosis in which a person's upset and fear are tied symbolically to specific situations (fear of heights, outdoors, etc.).

PIMP: the person who finds customers for a prostitute, lives off her earnings, and often provides care and protection for her.

PIQUERISM: sexual arousal through stabbing.

POLICE-COMMUNITY RELATIONS: how police and the community communicate each other's needs and problems.

POLYGRAPH: lie-detector test. Through detecting physical changes associated with anxiety, lies may be detected.

PROHIBITION: refers to the period when the Volstead Act made alcohol an illegal drug.

PROJECTION: seeing in others what one cannot tolerate in oneself.

PROJECTIVE TESTS: these include personality tests which require a person to interpret unclear material. This interpretation shows how a person views himself and others. Major projective tests include the inkblot or Rorschach and Thematic Apperception Test.

PSYCHOANALYSIS: a particular form of psychotherapy using the ideas of Sigmund Freud. It emphasizes the reevaluation of an individual's past experiences so that he does not need to repeat them.

PSYCHOPATH: see sociopath.

PSYCHOSIS: the most severe form of mental illness in which people become unaware of what is reality and in which the personality is severely disorganized.

PSYCHOTHERAPY: the treatment of emotional problems through psychological means, frequently discussion of problems.

PYROMANIA: sexual arousal through fire setting.

RATIONAL SUICIDE: suicide when life is realistically worse than death – as a prisoner who may be tortured.

RECIDIVISM: repeating an offense so as to return to a treatment or correctional facility; as "the recidivism rate in our prison system is high."

RECOVERY, INC.: a self-help organization of ex-mental hospital patients who meet to help each other live satisfying lives in the community.

REINFORCEMENT-REWARD: children learn to behave in certain ways because they are "reinforced" or rewarded.

RESERPINE: see tranquilizers.
RIOT: a disorder on the part of a group of people who use violent means to redress what they consider to be wrongs.
ROLE-PLAYING: a technique to try out a situation by taking roles appropriate to a situation (for example, acting the part of a rioter attacking a policeman).
RORSCHACH TEST: the inkblot test. See projective tests.

SPCC: Society for Prevention of Cruelty to Children. An agency which seeks to protect children from neglect and abuse.
STP (DOM): a synthetic drug similar to peyote.
SADISM: using violence as a means of sexual satisfaction.
SCAPEGOATING: using one or more individuals as a target for general feelings of frustration.
SCHIZOPHRENIC: the most common psychosis involving severe disorganization of the personality.
SCOPTOPHILIA: peeking as a way of expressing sexual needs.
SCORE: gambling jargon for a big win.
SECONAL: see sedatives.
SEDATIVES: drugs that induce sleep and decrease anxiety. They include barbiturates and the meprobamates.
SELF-CONCEPT: all the ideas an individual has about who he or she is.
SIBLING: brother or sister.
SOCIAL CLASS OR SOCIOECONOMIC CLASS: the status of an individual or family in the eyes of the community.
SOCIAL ISOLATION: not being part of a network of family and friends.
SOCIALIZATION: teaching children how to behave to become acceptable members of society.
SOCIOECONOMIC CLASS: see social class.
SOCIOPATHY: the mental illness in which individuals do not believe in the usual moral standards of the society. Same as psychopathy—the new term sociopath recognizes society's role in this type of behavior.
SOFT DRUGS: nonaddictive drugs. They include the drugs producing "highs" and frequently hallucinations—peyote, mescal, mescaline, psilocybin, DMT, STP (DOM), MDA, marijuana, and LSD.

SPOUSE: wife or husband.

STATUTORY RAPE: rape when the female may have consented but is underage.

STELAZINE: see tranquilizers.

SUICIDE-PREVENTION CENTERS: agencies which provide for immediate help—usually primarily by phone—for potential suicides.

SWINDLES: transactions with the intent to take advantage of a customer.

SYNANON: a group meeting in which people frankly confront one another with their problems. Also, an organization which helps drug addicts to readjust to society.

THEMATIC APPERCEPTION TEST: see projective tests.

THORAZINE: see tranquilizers.

TRADITION: ways of doing things which a society passes on from generation to generation.

TRADITIONAL SUICIDE: suicide when custom demands it—as a wife killing herself when a husband dies, or a person killing himself when he is disgraced.

TRANQUILIZERS: pharmaceutical drugs which decrease anxiety. Occasionally have physical side effects. Include Librium, Thorazine, Compazine, Stelazine, and reserpine (rauwolfia).

TURF: an area which gangs of juveniles consider to be theirs and which they will fight to protect.

UNCONSCIOUS: a collection of motives, ideas, and memories of which a person is not aware even though these motives can be made evident through behavior, dreams, etc.

VENEREAL DISEASE: Diseases spread through genital contact—syphilis and gonorrhea.

"VIC": see mark.

WHITE-COLLAR CRIME: "respectable," nonviolent crime—usually committed by business and professional persons.

WOLFENDEN COMMITTEE: an English group that recommended that consenting acts of homosexuality be legalized.

Notes

CHAPTER 3

1. See R. R. Carkhuff and C. B. Truax, "Lay Mental Health Counseling: The Effects of Lay Group Counseling," *Journal of Consulting Psychology* 29 (1965) 426–31.

2. Reviews of these and similar tests may be found in Oscar K. Buros, ed., *Mental Measurements Yearbook* (Highland Park, N.J.: Gryphon Press, 1965).

CHAPTER 4

1. See, for example, A. Campbell and H. Schuman, "Police in the Ghetto," in A. Cohn and E. Viano, eds., *Police-Community Relations, Images, Roles, Realities* (Philadelphia: J. B. Lippincott, 1976).

CHAPTER 5

1. This issue is addressed by John Monahan, ed., in *Who Is the Client? The Ethics of Psychological Intervention in the Criminal Justice System* (Washington, D.C.: American Psychological Association, 1980).

2. According to R. J. Lundman, traffic law violations comprise the single most frequent reason for contacts between police patrol officers and citizens. See R. J. Lundman, "Police Work with Traffic Law Violators, in R. J. Lundman, ed., *Police Behavior: A Sociological Perspective* (New York: Oxford University Press, 1980), pp. 212-24.

CHAPTER 6

1. A. D. Yarmey in *Psychology of Eyewitness Testimony* cites the cases of Adolph Beck and of Alfred Dreyfus.

CHAPTER 7

1. For example, excessive drinking, along with chronic unemployment, desertion, and nonsupport appeared to cause delinquency in children who had not been antisocial. In L. N. Robins, *Deviant Children Grown Up* (Baltimore: Williams and Wilkins, 1966), p. 161.

2. See, for example, Jonathan Kozol, *Death at an Early Age: The Destruction of the Hearts and Minds of Negro Children in the Boston Public Schools* (Boston: Houghton, Mifflin, 1967).

CHAPTER 8

1. New York: Liveright, 1972. While this was written some years ago, current statistics continue to emphasize the wide disparity in income and wealth between the rich and the poor.

2. See R. P. Coleman and B. Neugarten, *Social Status in the City* (Chicago: Jossey-Bass, 1971).

3. See J. H. Reiman, *The Rich Get Richer and the Poor Get Poorer: Ideology, Class and Criminal Justice* (New York: John Wiley, 1975).

4. See William Labov, "The Logic of Nonstandard English," in William Labov, ed., *Language in the Inner City* (Philadelphia: University of Pennsylvania Press, 1942), pp. 201–40.

5. Robert Coles, *The Privileged Ones,* Children of Crisis Series, vol. 5 (Boston: Little, Brown, 1978).

6. Slang expressions courtesy of Lisa Revere.

7. See M. Gregory and S. Carroll, *Language and Situation: Language Varieties and Their Social Contexts.* (London: Routledge & Kegan Paul, 1978).

CHAPTER 9

1. C. Thigpen and H. M. Cleckley (Los Angeles: Regent House, 1974).

2. J. Breuer and S. Freud, *Studies on Hysteria,* standard ed., vol. 2 (London: Hogarth Press, 1953), pp. 1–105.

3. See "Songs My Mother Taught Me," in R. M. Lindner, *The Fifty-Minute Hour* (New York: Bantam, 1976) for an in-depth description of a sociopath.

4. See, for example, R. M. Restak, "Complex Legal Issue Raised by Sam Case," *New York Times,* Sept. 4, 1977, p. 12E, in which Restak argues that the foremost issue is whether the accused has committed a crime or is innocent.

CHAPTER 10

1. At the time of this writing, the exclusionary rule is being reexamined by a presidential commission on violent crime and may well be made less rigid.
2. Jay Livingston, *Compulsive Gamblers* (New York: Harper Torch Books, 1974).

CHAPTER 11

1. U.S. Bureau of the Census, 100th ed. (Washington, D.C.: U.S. Government Printing Office, 1979).

2. Ibid.

3. Ibid.

4. This approach is described more fully by B. P. Karon in his paper "Suicidal Tendency as the Wish to Hurt Someone Else and Resulting Treatment Techniques," *Journal of Individual Psychology* 20 (1964):206–12.

CHAPTER 12

1. *Adamha News,* 6, no. 2, Jan. 25, 1980.

2. Lewis Carroll, *Alice's Adventures in Wonderland* (New York: Viking Press, 1975).

3. However, at the time of this writing, marijuana use for certain medical conditions was in process of being legalized.

4. Ruth Benedict, *Patterns of Culture* (Boston: Houghton-Mifflin, 1959), p. 86.

5. For example, Carlos Castaneda claims new realms of being. See *A Separate Reality* (New York: Simon & Schuster, Touchstone Books, 1972).

6. W. J. Coggins, E. W. Swenson, W. W. Dawson, A. Fernandez-Salas, J. Hernandez-Bolanos, C. F. Jiminez-Antillon, J. R. Solano, R. Vinocour and F. Faerrow-Valdez, "Health Status of Chronic Heavy Cannabis Users," in R. G. Dornbush, A. M. Freedman, and M. Fink, *Chronic Cannabis Use* (New York: New York Academy of Sciences, 1976), pp. 146–61.

CHAPTER 13

1. Harold Greenwald, *The Elegant Prostitute: A Social and Psychoanalytic Study* (New York: Ballantine, 1973).

2. Alan P. Bell and Martin Weinberg, *Homosexualities: A Study of Human Diversity* (New York: Simon & Schuster, 1977).

3. Ibid.

4. See, for example, J. H. Gagnon, *Sexual Encounters between Adults and Children,* Sex Information and Education Council of the U.S. 1970, p. 8. The author states that "for most children, in most situations, the victim situation is of short duration and of minimal effect."

5. C. M. Kelley, *Crime in the United States, 1972,* U.S. Department of Justice, FBI Uniform Crime Reports, U.S. Department of Justice, 1972.

6. U.S. Bureau of the Census, *Statistical Abstract of the United States, 1979,* 100th ed. (Washington, D.C.: U.S. Government Printing Office, 1979).

7. In *Violent Crime: Homicide, Assault, Rape, Robbery,* U.S. National Commission on Causes and Prevention of Violence (New York: George Braziller, 1969).

8. *The Report of the Commission on Obscenity and Pornography* (Washington, D.C.: U.S. Government Printing Office, 1970).

CHAPTER 14

1. Edwin M. Schur, *Our Criminal Society* (Englewood Cliffs, N.J.: Prentice-Hall, 1969).

2. Edwin H. Sutherland, *White-Collar Crime* (New York: Dryden Press, 1949).

3. See, for example, an article in *Time,* Jan. 21, 1980, p. 61, on Pintos, agent orange, and asbestos entitled "Who Pays for the Damage?"

4. For example, "CU Wins 'Consumer Voice' in Important New Area" (overcharging oil companies), *Consumer Reports* 42 (May 1977), p. 253.

5. Much has recently been written in this important area. See, for example, S. W. Leibholtz, *Users' Guide to Computer Crime: Its Commission, Detection, and Prevention* (Radnor, Pa.: Chilton Book Co., 1974).

6. R. H. Blum, *Deceivers and Deceived* (Springfield, Ill.: C. C. Thomas, 1972).

7. Blum, *Deceivers and Deceived,* p. 55.

8. Frank Gibney, *The Operators* (New York: Harper and Row, 1960), p. 201.

9. See M. Lipman, in *Stealing: How America's Employees Are Stealing Their Companies Blind* (New York: Harper's Magazine Press, 1973).

10. Ruth Benedict, *Patterns of Culture* (Boston: Houghton Mifflin, 1959).

CHAPTER 15

1. Campbell and Schuman quote a study in which 94 percent of police said they were frequently called upon to intervene in domestic quarrels. See A. Campbell and H. Schuman, "Police in the Ghetto," in A. W. Cohn and E. C. Viano, eds., *Police Community Relations: Images, Roles, Realities* (Philadelphia: J. B. Lippincott, 1976), p. 199.

2. U.S. Bureau of the Census, 99th ed. (Washington, D.C.: U.S. Government Printing Office, 1978).

3. Stanley Milgrim, *Obedience,* a film distributed by New York University Film Library. Also, "Some Conditions of Obedience and Disobedience to Authority," *Human Relations,* 18 (1965), pp. 57-76.

4. See George Bach and Peter Wyden, *The Intimate Enemy* (New York: Avon, 1968).

5. See Ross V. Speck and Carolyn L. Attneave, *Family Networks* (New York: Pantheon Books, 1973).

6. Freedman, *Crowding and Behavior* (New York: Viking, 1975).

CHAPTER 16

1. As reported in D. Besharov, "Child Abuse Rate Called 'Epidemic,' " *New York Times,* Nov. 30, 1975.

2. See Ruth Benedict, *Patterns of Culture* (Boston: Houghton Mifflin, 1959).

3. Thiry-six percent of black families had a female head, according to the U.S. Bureau of the Census, *Statistical Abstract of the United States, 1979* (Washington, D.C.: U.S. Government Printing Office, 1979).

4. Muriel James and Dorothy Jongeward, *Born to Win* (Reading, Mass.: Addison-Wesley, 1971), p. 54.

5. As quoted by A. H. Green, "Child Abuse," in D. H. Schetky and E. P. Benedek, *Child Psychiatry and the Law* (New York: Brunner/Mazel, 1980).

6. Ibid., p. 8.

CHAPTER 17

1. Quoting a study of how police spend their time, G. P. McManus noted that 16 percent of all police calls were for gang disturbances. If other youth-related crimes were added, the rate would be even higher. See "What Does a Policeman Do?" in A. W. Cohn and E. C. Viano, eds., *Police-Community Relations, Images, Roles, Realities* (Philadelphia: J. P. Lippincott, 1976), p. 144.

2. H. S. Sacks and H. L. Sacks, "Status Offenders: Emerging Issues and New Approaches," in D. H. Schetky and E. P. Benedek, *Child Psychiatry and the Law* (New York: Brunner/Mazel, 1980), pp. 156–93.

3. U.S. Bureau of the Census, *Statistical Abstract of the United States, 1979,* 100th ed. (Washington, D.C.: U.S. Government Printing Office, 1979).

4. See, for example, D. J. West and O. P. Farrington, *The Delinquent Way of Life* (New York: Crane Russak, 1977), p. 150.

5. L. N. Robins, *Deviant Children Grown Up* (Baltimore, Md.: Williams and Wilkins, 1966), p. 164.

6. Ibid. Robins found strong discipline to be a deterrent to development of sociopathy.

7. Jonathan Kozol, *Death at an Early Age: The Destruction of the Hearts and Minds of Negro Children in the Boston Public Schools* (Boston: Houghton Mifflin, 1967).

8. From the book by Anthony Burgess, *Clockwork Orange* (New York: Norton, 1963).

CHAPTER 18

1. For example, blacks and other minority workers had an unemployment rate of 34.4 percent in 1978 according to the U.S. Bureau of the Census, *Statistical Abstract of the United States, 1979,* 100th ed. (Washington, D.C.: U.S. Government Printing Office, 1979).

2. *Fiddler on the Roof* (1964), a musical play, with book by Joseph Stein, based on stories by Sholom Aleichem. Lyrics by Sheldon Harnick. Music by Jerry Beck.

Index